JEFF LEMIRE
DAVID RUBÍN
SHERLOCK FRANKENSTEIN™
AND THE LEGION OF EVIL

JEFF LEMIRE
DAVID RUBÍN

SHERLOCK
FRANKENSTEIN
AND THE LEGION OF EVIL

WRITTEN BY JEFF LEMIRE

ART, LETTERS, AND COLORS BY DAVID RUBÍN

FLATS KIKE J. DÍAZ   COVER BY DAVID RUBÍN

CHAPTER BREAKS BY DAVID RUBÍN, MIKE MIGNOLA,
DEAN ORMSTON, DUNCAN FEGREDO, JEFF LEMIRE, AND DAVE STEWART

METAL MINOTAUR CO-CREATED BY GUS LEMIRE

BLACK HAMMER CREATED BY JEFF LEMIRE AND DEAN ORMSTON

DARK HORSE BOOKS

PRESIDENT & PUBLISHER **MIKE RICHARDSON**

EDITOR **DANIEL CHABON**

ASSOCIATE EDITOR **CARDNER CLARK**

ASSISTANT EDITOR **BRETT ISRAEL**

DESIGNER **ETHAN KIMBERLING**

DIGITAL ART TECHNICIAN **CHRISTINA McKENZIE**

SPECIAL THANKS TO **BRETT BUTT** FOR THE NAME CONCRETESTADOR.

SHERLOCK FRANKENSTEIN AND THE LEGION OF EVIL
Sherlock Frankenstein™ © 2017, 2018 171 Studios, Inc., and Dean Ormston. Sherlock Frankenstein and all characters prominently featured herein are trademarks of 171 Studios, Inc., and Dean Ormston. Dark Horse Books® and the Dark Horse logo are registered trademarks of Dark Horse Comics, Inc. All rights reserved. No portion of this publication may be reproduced or transmitted, in any form or by any means, without the express written permission of Dark Horse Comics, Inc. Names, characters, places, and incidents featured in this publication either are the product of the author's imagination or are used fictitiously. Any resemblance to actual persons (living or dead), events, institutions, or locales, without satiric intent, is coincidental.

Collects issues #1–#4 of the Dark Horse Comics series *Sherlock Frankenstein and the Legion of Evil* and collects *Black Hammer* #12.

Published by
Dark Horse Books
A division of Dark Horse Comics, Inc.
10956 SE Main Street
Milwaukie, OR 97222

DarkHorse.com

To find a comics shop in your area, visit comicshoplocator.com
International Licensing: (503) 905-2377

First edition: May 2018
ISBN 978-1-50670-526-2

10 9 8 7 6 5 4 3 2 1
Printed in China

Neil Hankerson, Executive Vice President ▪ Tom Weddle, Chief Financial Officer ▪ Randy Stradley, Vice President of Publishing ▪ Nick McWhorter, Chief Business Development Officer ▪ Matt Parkinson, Vice President of Marketing ▪ Dale LaFountain, Vice President of Information Technology ▪ Cara Niece, Vice President of Production and Scheduling ▪ Mark Bernardi, Vice President of Book Trade and Digital Sales Ken Lizzi, General Counsel ▪ Dave Marshall, Editor in Chief ▪ Davey Estrada, Editorial Director ▪ Chris Warner, Senior Books Editor ▪ Cary Grazzini, Director of Specialty Projects ▪ Lia Ribacchi, Art Director Vanessa Todd-Holmes, Director of Print Purchasing ▪ Matt Dryer, Director of Digital Art and Prepress ▪ Michael Gombos, Director of International Publishing and Licensing ▪ Kari Yadro, Director of Custom Programs

Library of Congress Cataloging-in-Publication Data

Names: Lemire, Jeff, author. | Rubín, David, 1977- artist. | Díaz, Kike J., artist.
Title: Sherlock Frankenstein / script by Jeff Lemire ; art, letters, and colors by David Rubín ; flats, Kike J. Díaz.
Description: First Dark Horse edition. | Milwaukie, OR : Dark Horse Books, 2018- | "Metal Minotaur co-created by Gus Lemire" | v. 1. "Collects issues #1-#4 of the Dark Horse Comics series Sherlock Frankenstein and the Legion of Evil."
Identifiers: LCCN 2017052677 | ISBN 9781506705262 (v. 1 : paperback)
Subjects: LCSH: Comic books, strips, etc. | BISAC: COMICS & GRAPHIC NOVELS / Superheroes. | COMICS & GRAPHIC NOVELS / Science Fiction. | COMICS & GRAPHIC NOVELS / Literary.
Classification: LCC PN6728.S4665 L46 2018 | DDC 741.5/973--dc23
LC record available at https://lccn.loc.gov/2017052677

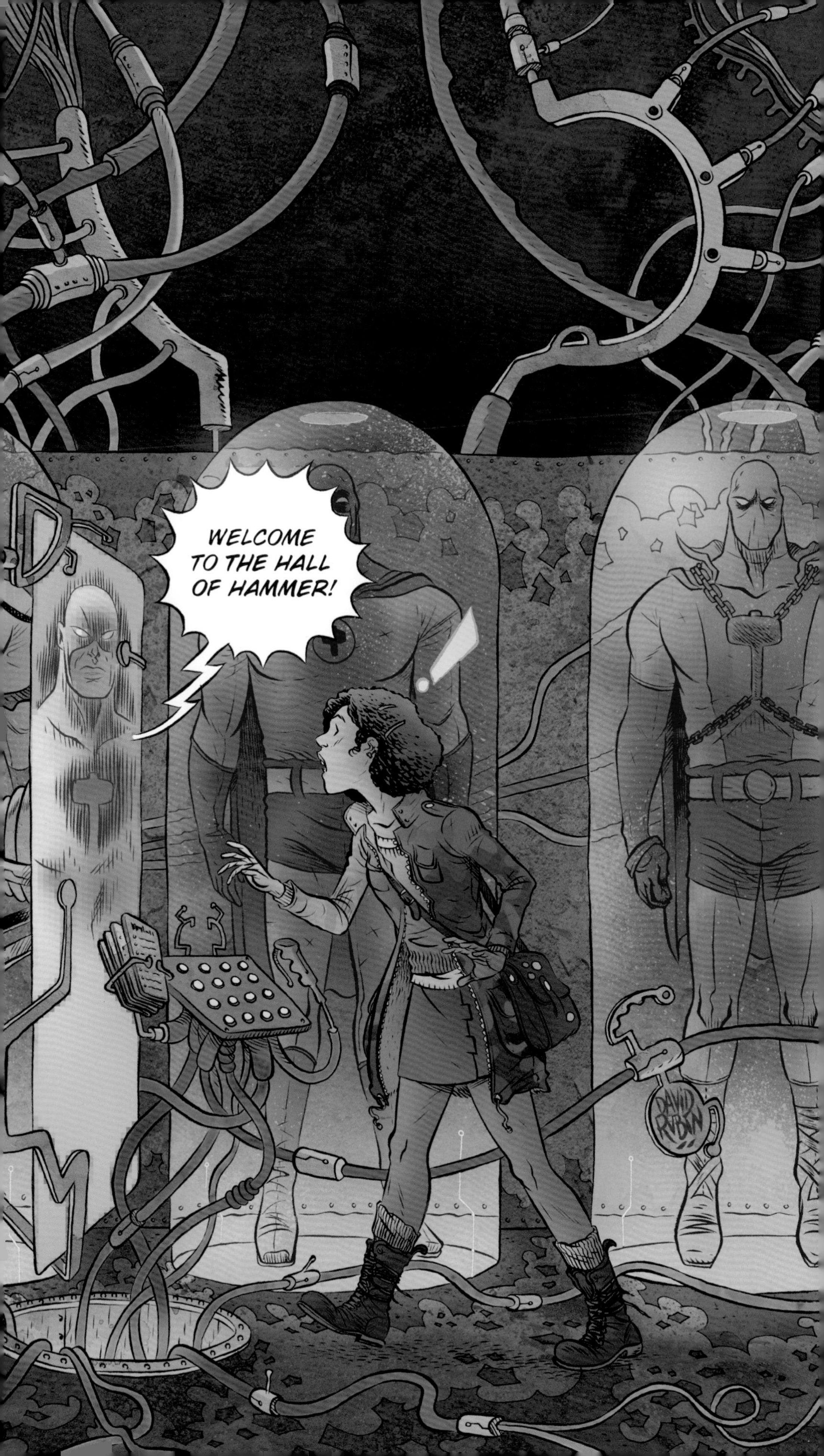
WELCOME TO THE HALL OF HAMMER!
!
DAVID RUBIN

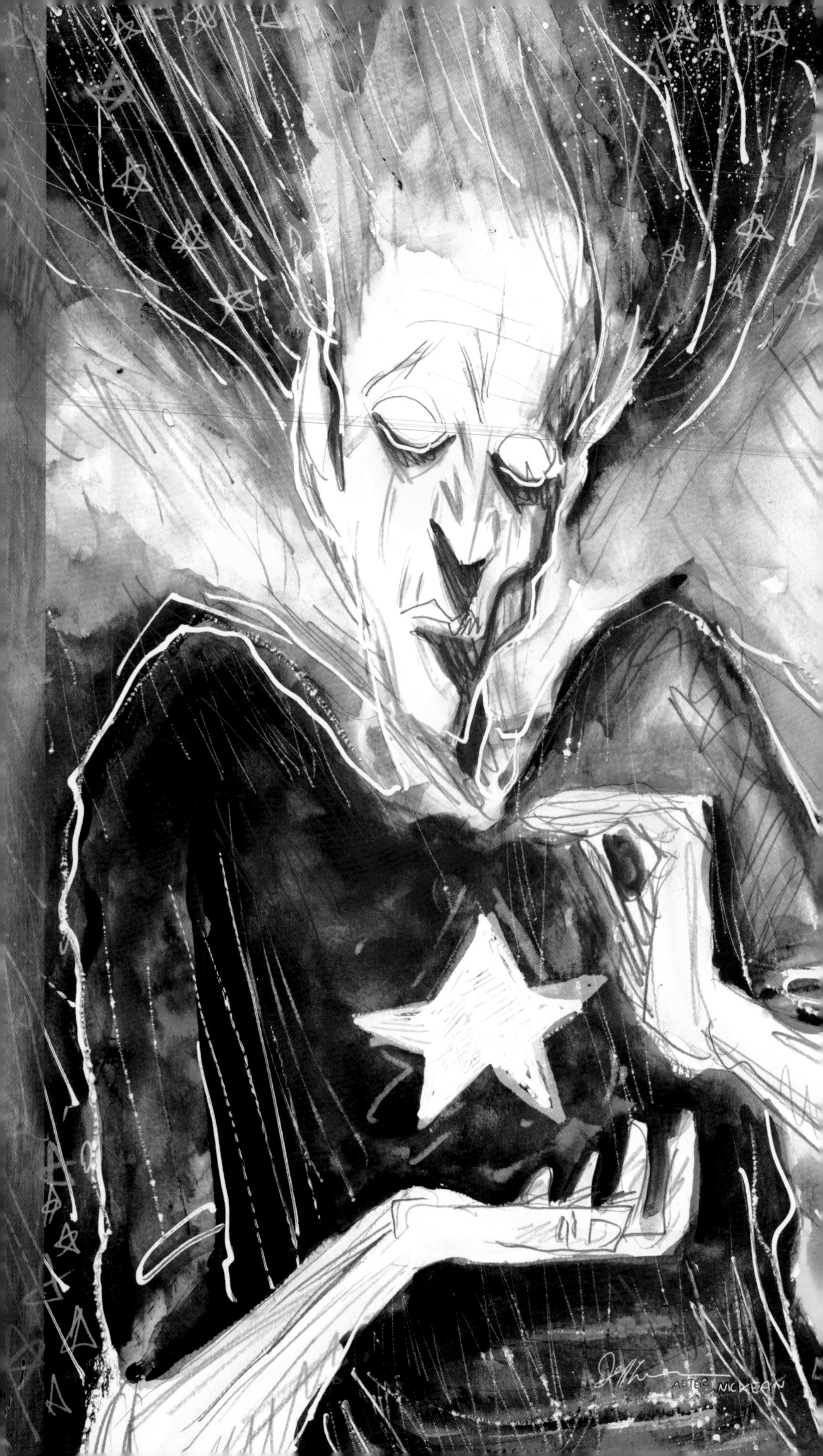
AFTER MCKEAN

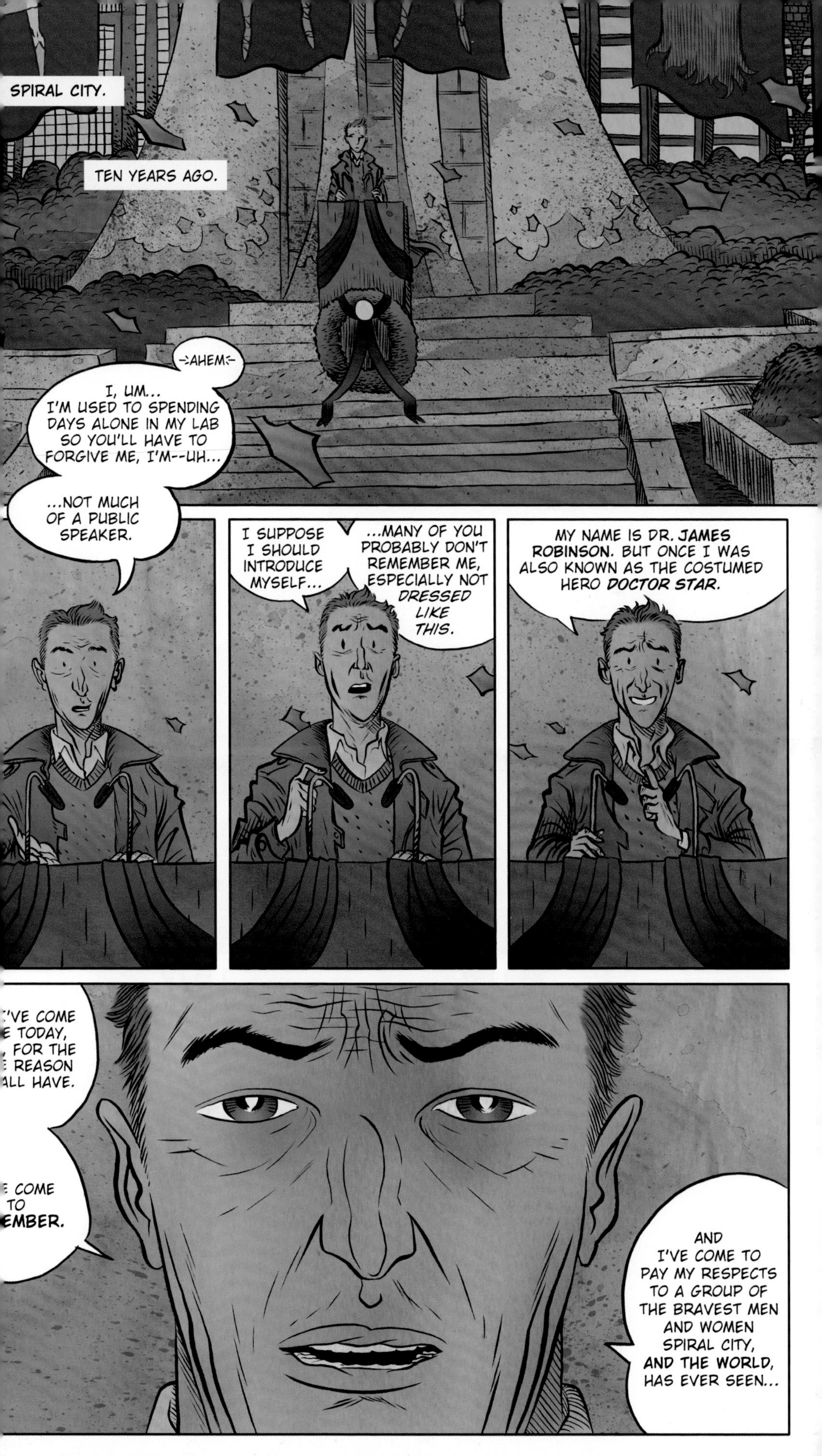

SPIRAL CITY.
TEN YEARS AGO.
AHEM
I, UM... I'M USED TO SPENDING DAYS ALONE IN MY LAB SO YOU'LL HAVE TO FORGIVE ME, I'M--UH...
...NOT MUCH OF A PUBLIC SPEAKER.
I SUPPOSE I SHOULD INTRODUCE MYSELF...
...MANY OF YOU PROBABLY DON'T REMEMBER ME, ESPECIALLY NOT DRESSED LIKE THIS.
MY NAME IS DR. JAMES ROBINSON. BUT ONCE I WAS ALSO KNOWN AS THE COSTUMED HERO DOCTOR STAR.
'VE COME TODAY, FOR THE REASON ALL HAVE.
COME TO EMBER.
AND I'VE COME TO PAY MY RESPECTS TO A GROUP OF THE BRAVEST MEN AND WOMEN SPIRAL CITY, AND THE WORLD, HAS EVER SEEN...

ABRAHAM SLAM...

...GOLDEN GAIL...

...BARBALIEN...

...COLONEL WEIRD...

...MADAME DRAGONFLY...

...AND BLACK HAMMER.

WE STILL DON'T FULLY UNDERSTAND WHO THIS "ANTI-GOD" WAS.

AND WE DON'T KNOW WHAT **REALLY** HAPPENED TO ABE AND GAIL AND THE OTHERS.

ALL WE KNOW FOR SURE IS THAT THEY ARE GONE.

AND IT WO[ULD] SEEM TH[AT] THEY SOME[HOW] GAVE TH[EIR] LIVES TO THE CATACLY[SM]

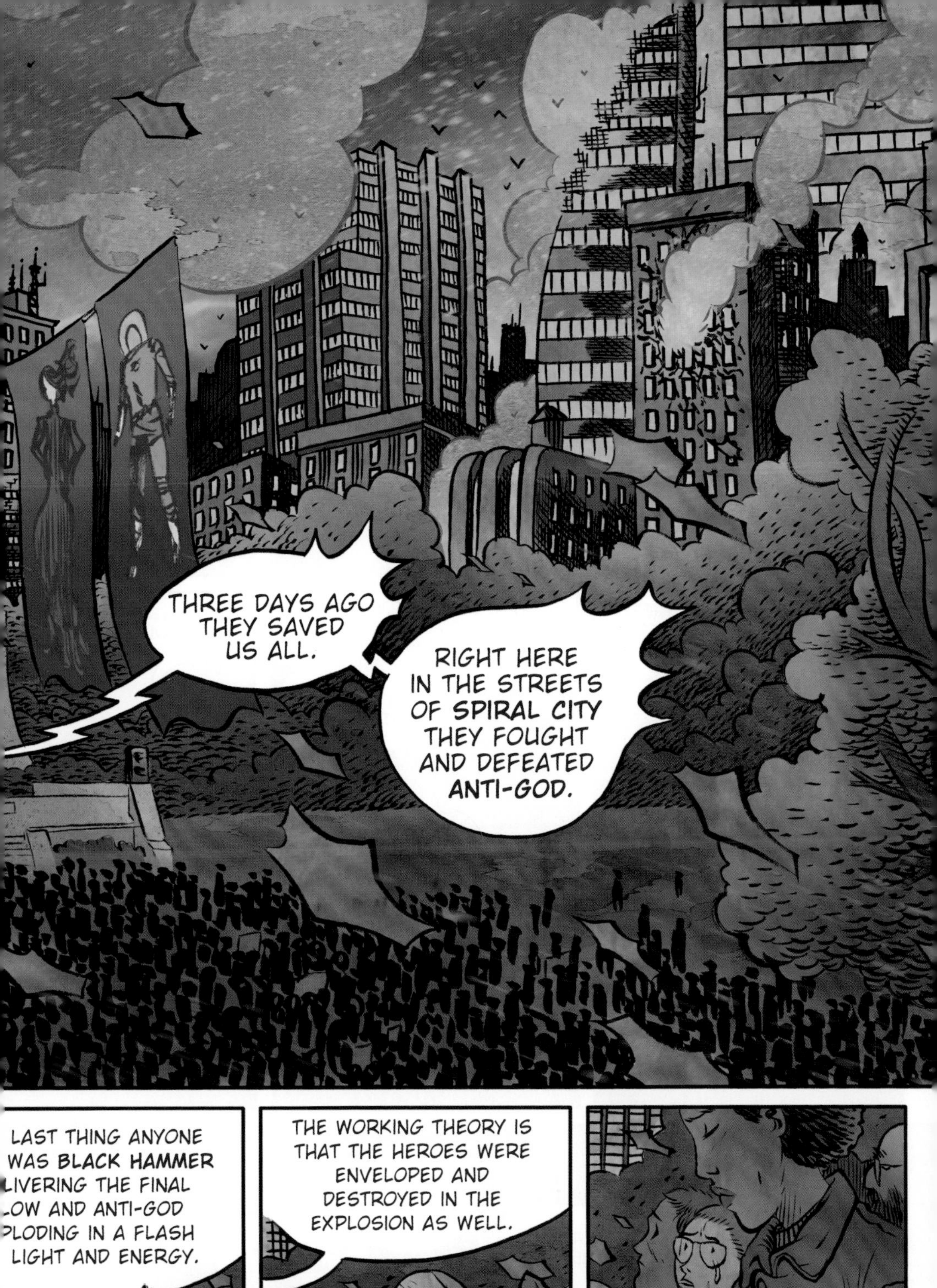
THREE DAYS AGO THEY SAVED US ALL.
RIGHT HERE IN THE STREETS OF SPIRAL CITY THEY FOUGHT AND DEFEATED ANTI-GOD.
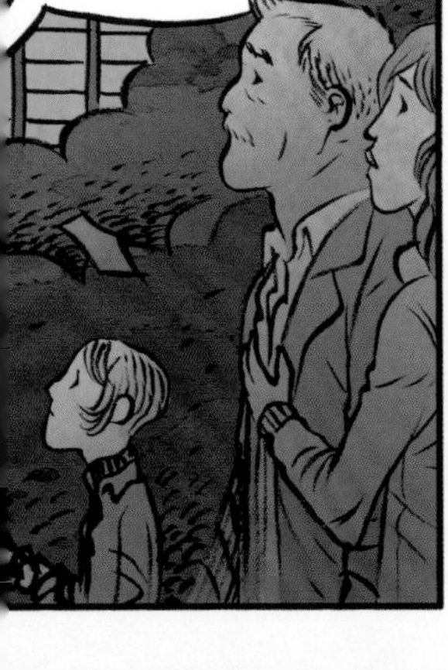
LAST THING ANYONE WAS BLACK HAMMER LIVERING THE FINAL OW AND ANTI-GOD PLODING IN A FLASH LIGHT AND ENERGY.
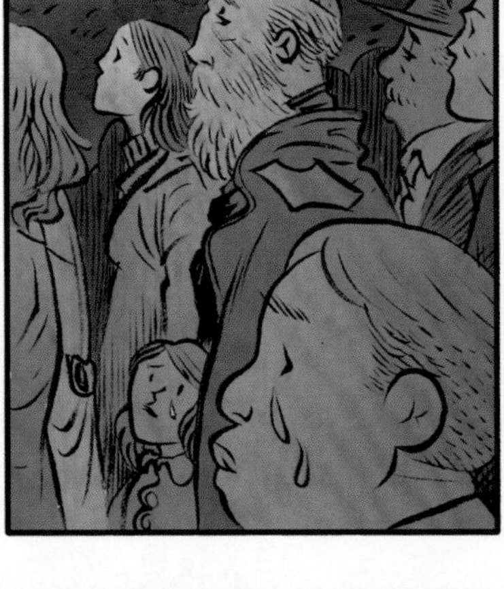
THE WORKING THEORY IS THAT THE HEROES WERE ENVELOPED AND DESTROYED IN THE EXPLOSION AS WELL.
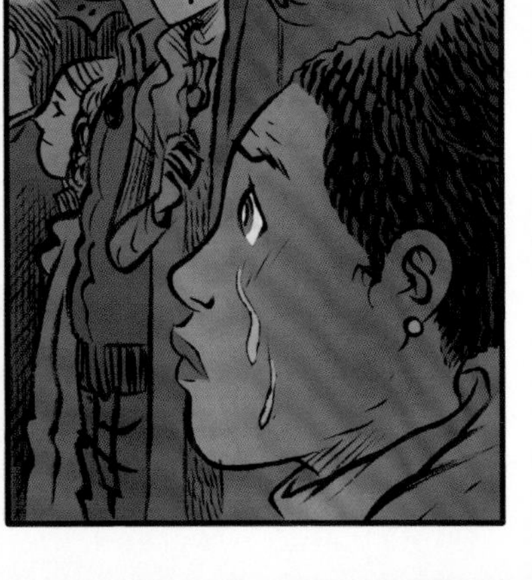

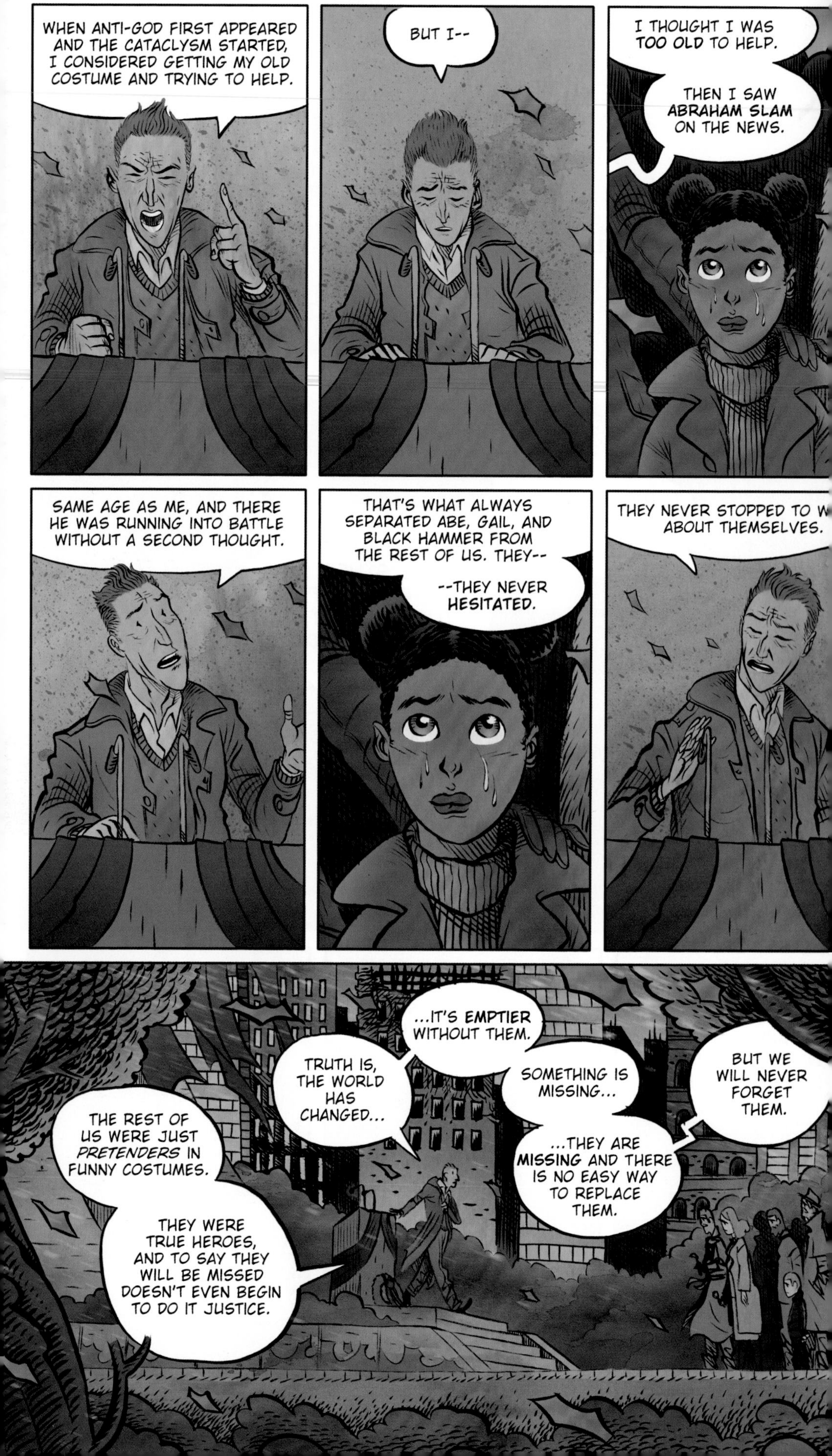
WHEN ANTI-GOD FIRST APPEARED AND THE CATACLYSM STARTED, I CONSIDERED GETTING MY OLD COSTUME AND TRYING TO HELP.
BUT I--
I THOUGHT I WAS TOO OLD TO HELP.
THEN I SAW ABRAHAM SLAM ON THE NEWS.
SAME AGE AS ME, AND THERE HE WAS RUNNING INTO BATTLE WITHOUT A SECOND THOUGHT.
THAT'S WHAT ALWAYS SEPARATED ABE, GAIL, AND BLACK HAMMER FROM THE REST OF US. THEY--
--THEY NEVER HESITATED.
THEY NEVER STOPPED TO W
ABOUT THEMSELVES.
THE REST OF US WERE JUST *PRETENDERS* IN FUNNY COSTUMES.
THEY WERE TRUE HEROES, AND TO SAY THEY WILL BE MISSED DOESN'T EVEN BEGIN TO DO IT JUSTICE.
TRUTH IS, THE WORLD HAS CHANGED...
...IT'S **EMPTIER** WITHOUT THEM.
SOMETHING IS MISSING...
...THEY ARE **MISSING** AND THERE IS NO EASY WAY TO REPLACE THEM.
BUT WE WILL NEVER FORGET THEM.

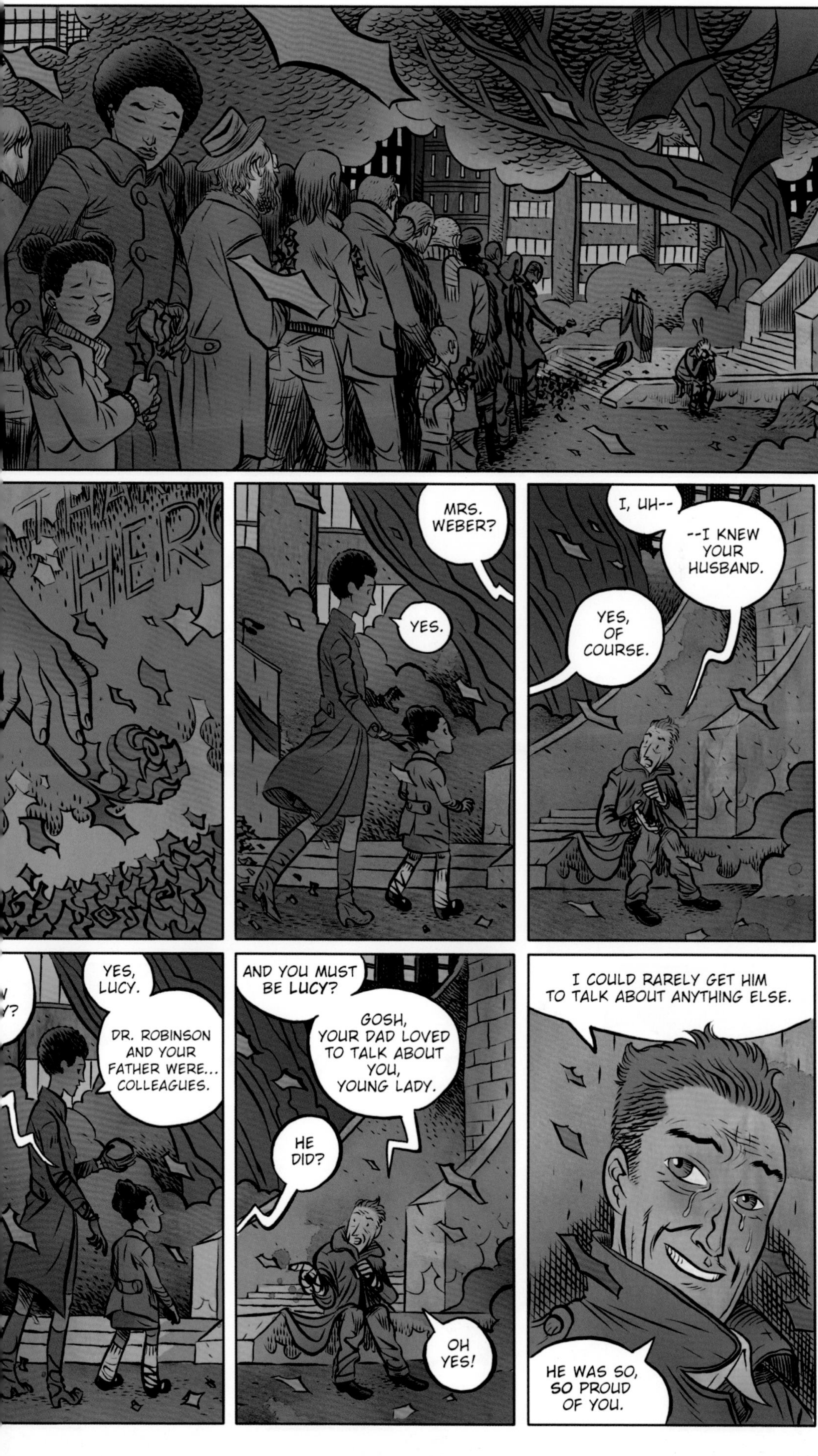
MRS. WEBER?
YES.
I, UH--
--I KNEW YOUR HUSBAND.
YES, OF COURSE.
YES, LUCY.
DR. ROBINSON AND YOUR FATHER WERE... COLLEAGUES.
AND YOU MUST BE LUCY?
GOSH, YOUR DAD LOVED TO TALK ABOUT YOU, YOUNG LADY.
HE DID?
OH YES!
I COULD RARELY GET HIM TO TALK ABOUT ANYTHING ELSE.
HE WAS SO, SO PROUD OF YOU.

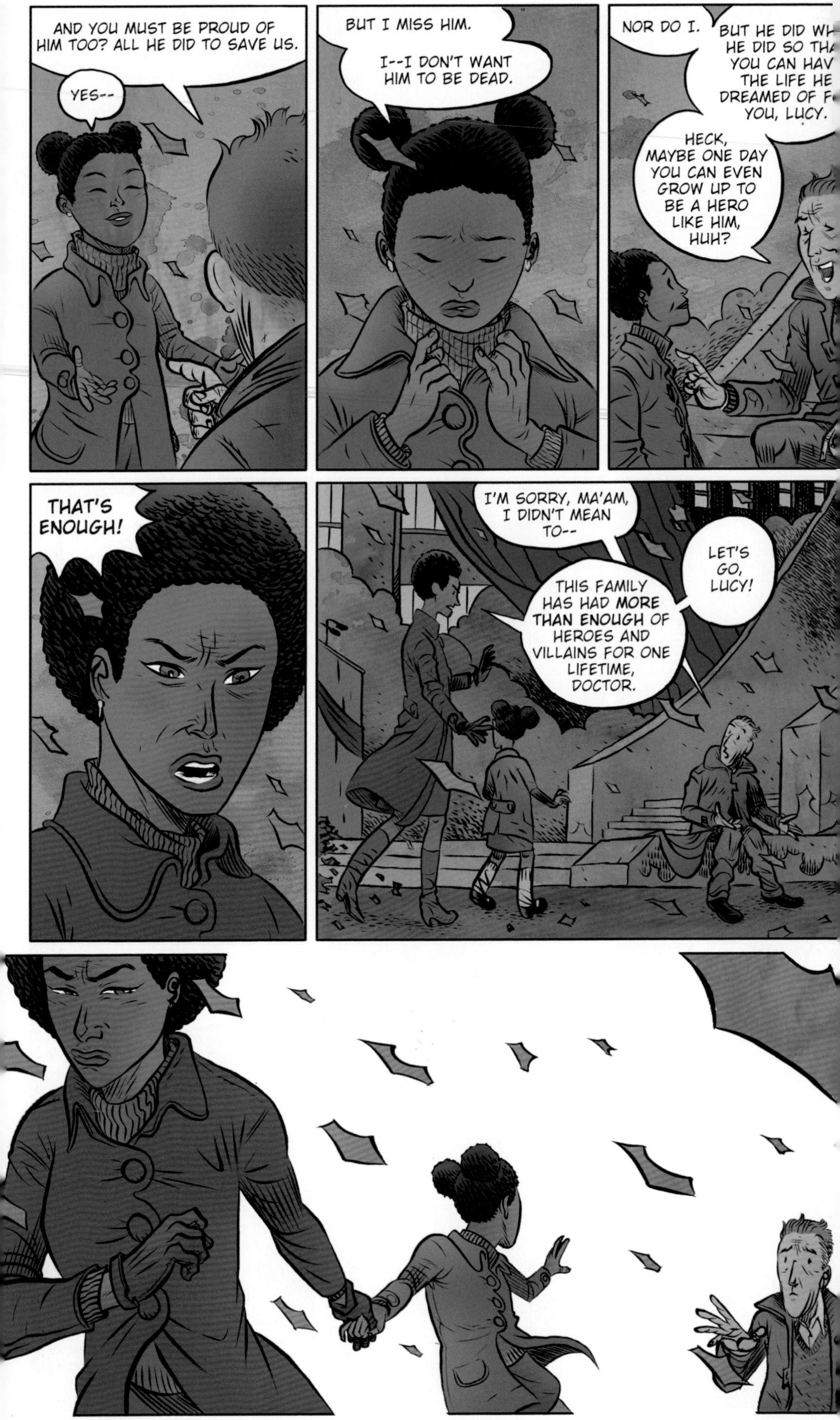

AND YOU MUST BE PROUD OF HIM TOO? ALL HE DID TO SAVE US.
YES--
BUT I MISS HIM.
I--I DON'T WANT HIM TO BE DEAD.
NOR DO I.
BUT HE DID WH HE DID SO THA YOU CAN HAV THE LIFE HE DREAMED OF F YOU, LUCY.
HECK, MAYBE ONE DAY YOU CAN EVEN GROW UP TO BE A HERO LIKE HIM, HUH?
THAT'S ENOUGH!
I'M SORRY, MA'AM, I DIDN'T MEAN TO--
LET'S GO, LUCY!
THIS FAMILY HAS HAD MORE THAN ENOUGH OF HEROES AND VILLAINS FOR ONE LIFETIME, DOCTOR.

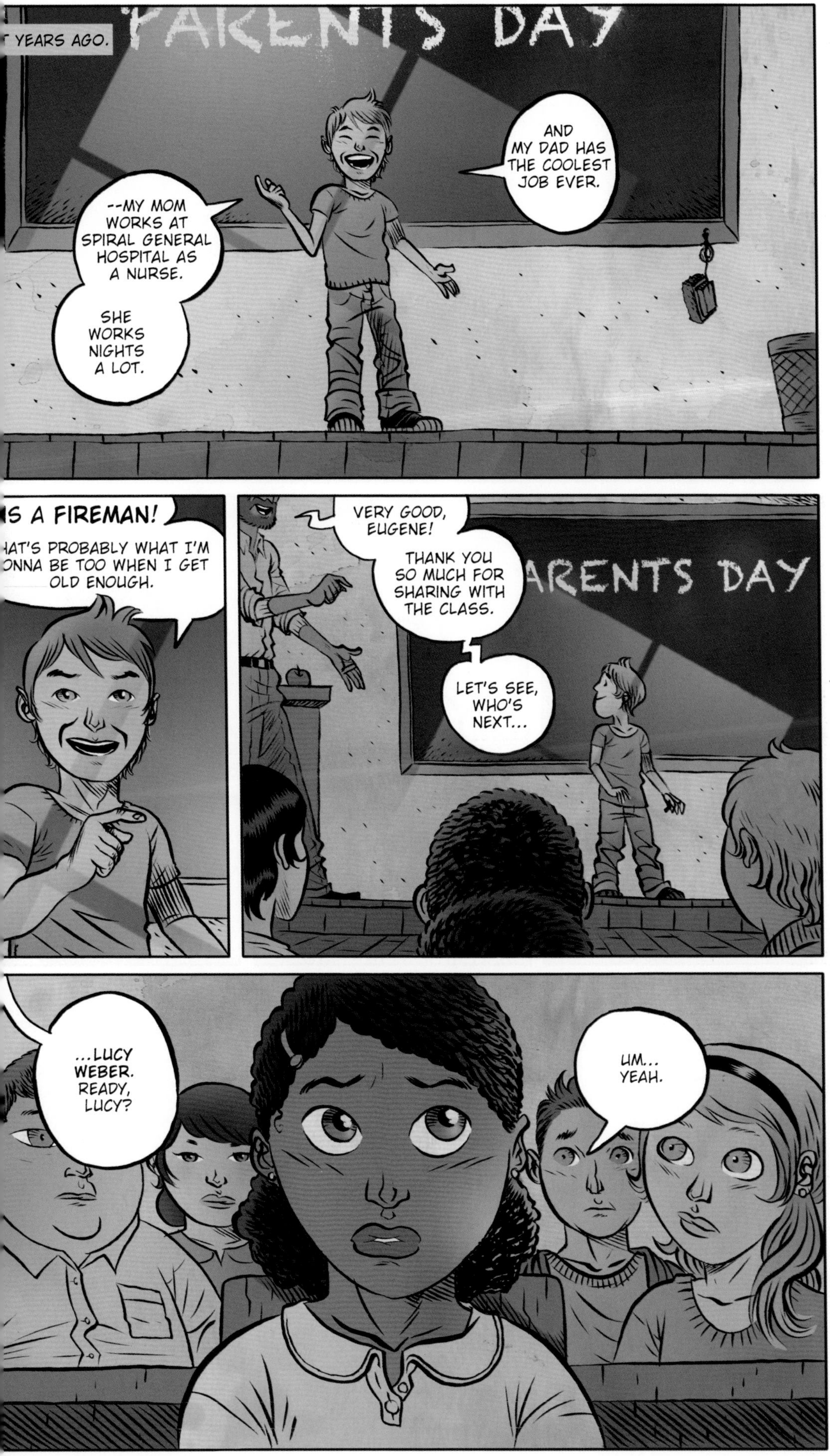

PARENTS DAY
YEARS AGO.
--MY MOM WORKS AT SPIRAL GENERAL HOSPITAL AS A NURSE.
SHE WORKS NIGHTS A LOT.
AND MY DAD HAS THE COOLEST JOB EVER.
S A FIREMAN!
HAT'S PROBABLY WHAT I'M ONNA BE TOO WHEN I GET OLD ENOUGH.
VERY GOOD, EUGENE!
THANK YOU SO MUCH FOR SHARING WITH THE CLASS.
LET'S SEE, WHO'S NEXT...
ARENTS DAY
...LUCY WEBER. READY, LUCY?
UM... YEAH.

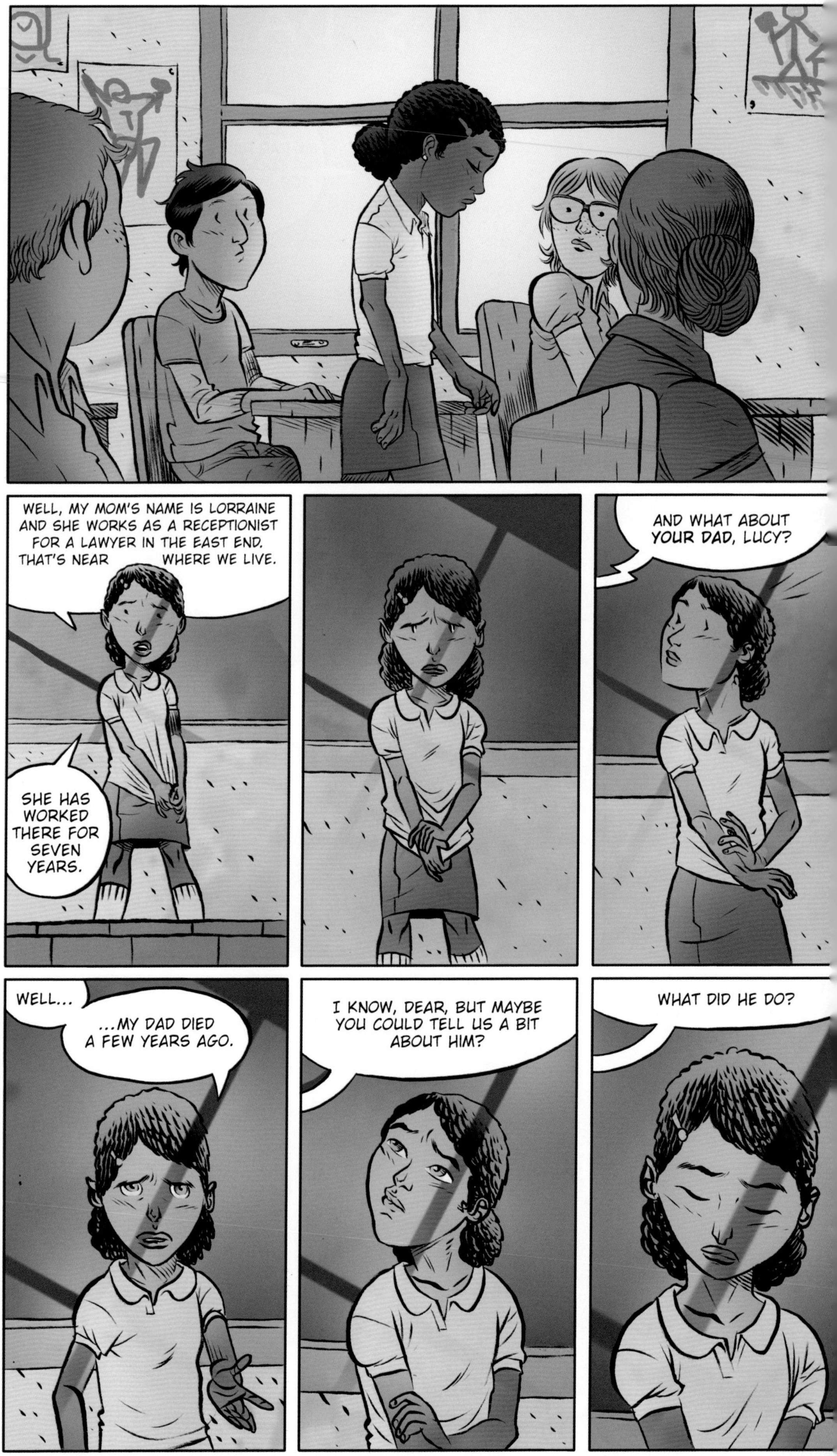

WELL, MY MOM'S NAME IS LORRAINE AND SHE WORKS AS A RECEPTIONIST FOR A LAWYER IN THE EAST END. THAT'S NEAR WHERE WE LIVE.
SHE HAS WORKED THERE FOR SEVEN YEARS.
AND WHAT ABOUT YOUR DAD, LUCY?
WELL...
...MY DAD DIED A FEW YEARS AGO.
I KNOW, DEAR, BUT MAYBE YOU COULD TELL US A BIT ABOUT HIM?
WHAT DID HE DO?

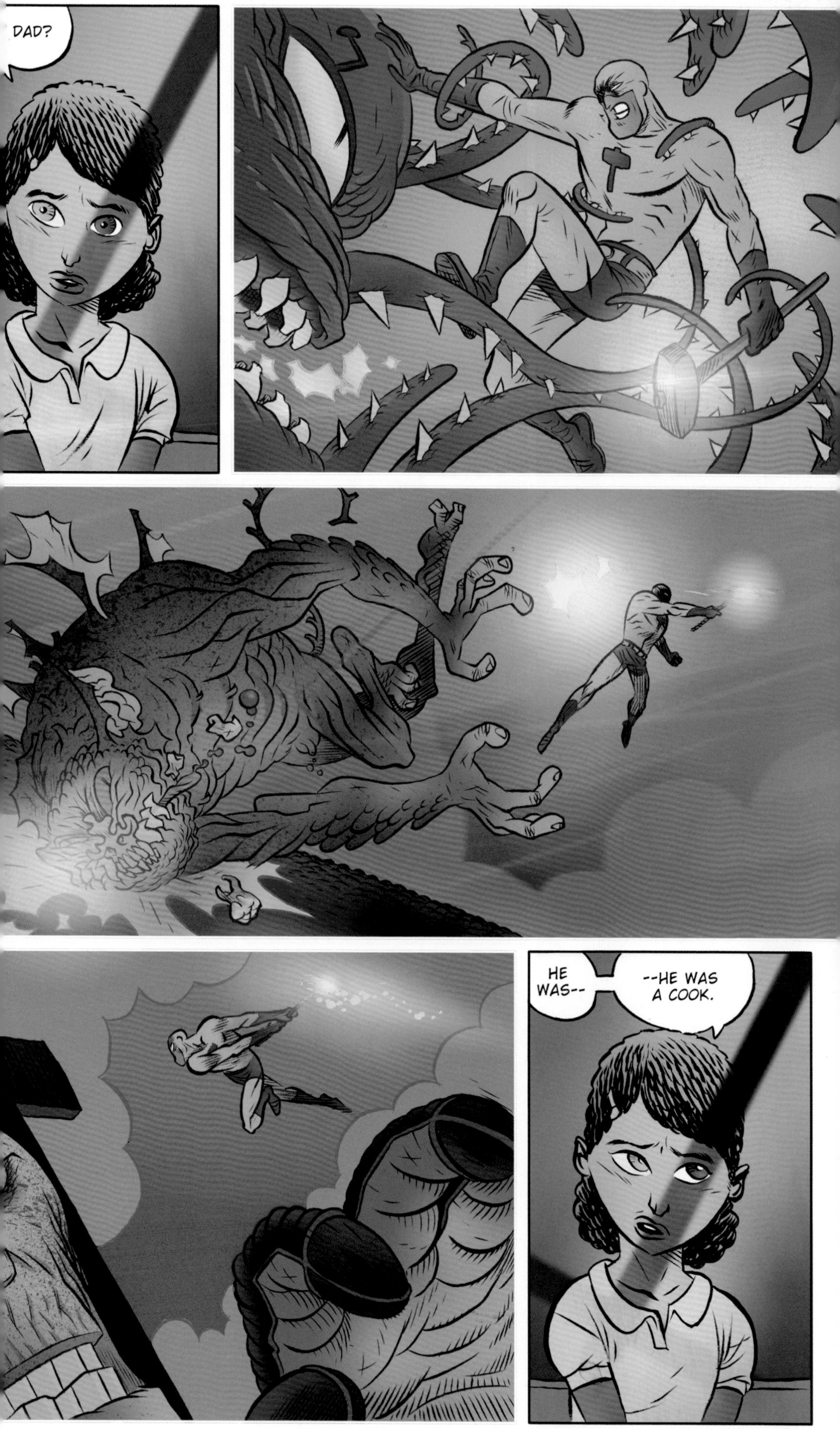
DAD?
HE WAS--
--HE WAS A COOK.

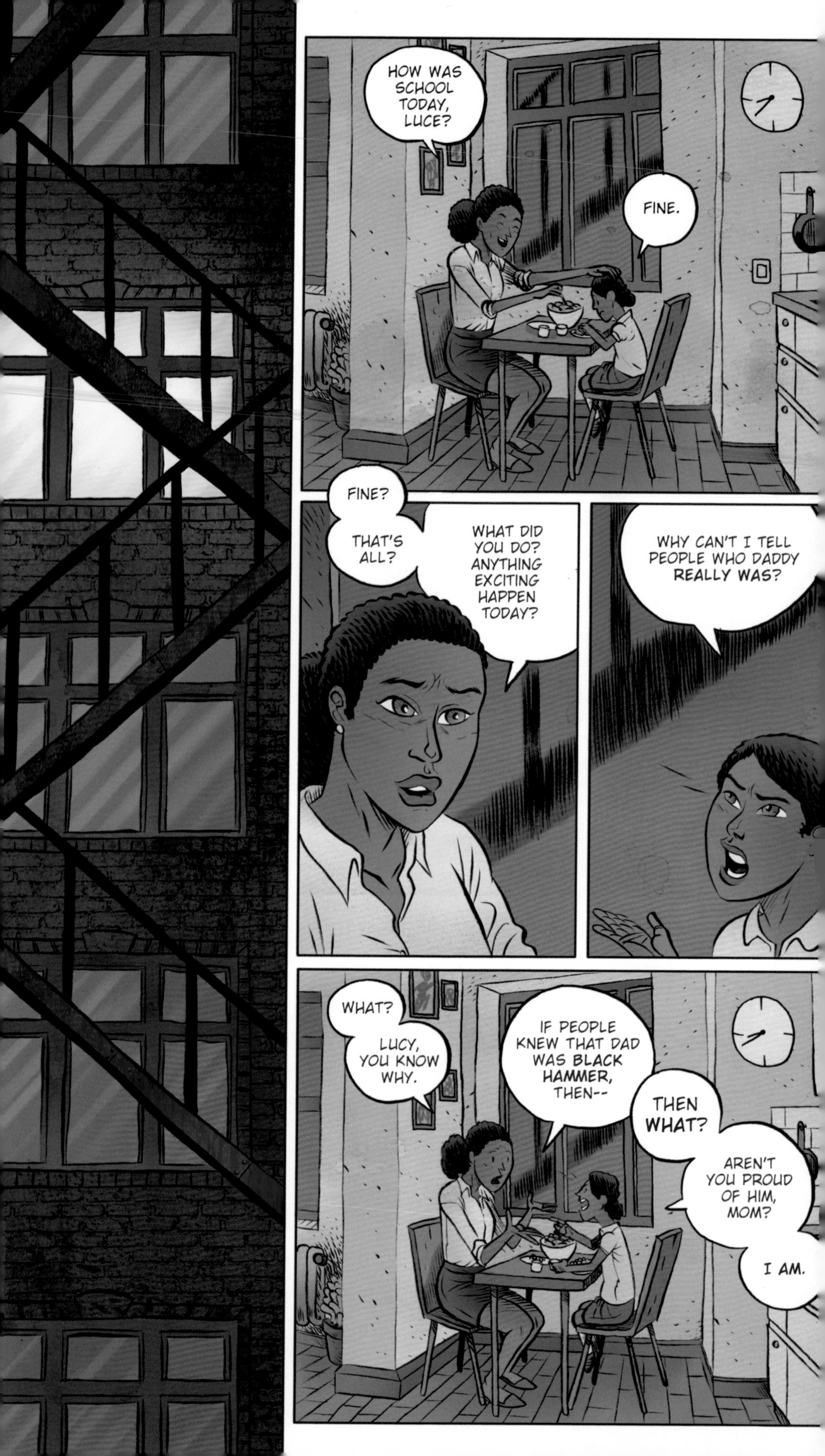

HOW WAS SCHOOL TODAY, LUCE?
FINE.
FINE?
THAT'S ALL?
WHAT DID YOU DO? ANYTHING EXCITING HAPPEN TODAY?
WHY CAN'T I TELL PEOPLE WHO DADDY REALLY WAS?
WHAT?
LUCY, YOU KNOW WHY.
IF PEOPLE KNEW THAT DAD WAS BLACK HAMMER, THEN--
THEN WHAT?
AREN'T YOU PROUD OF HIM, MOM?
I AM.

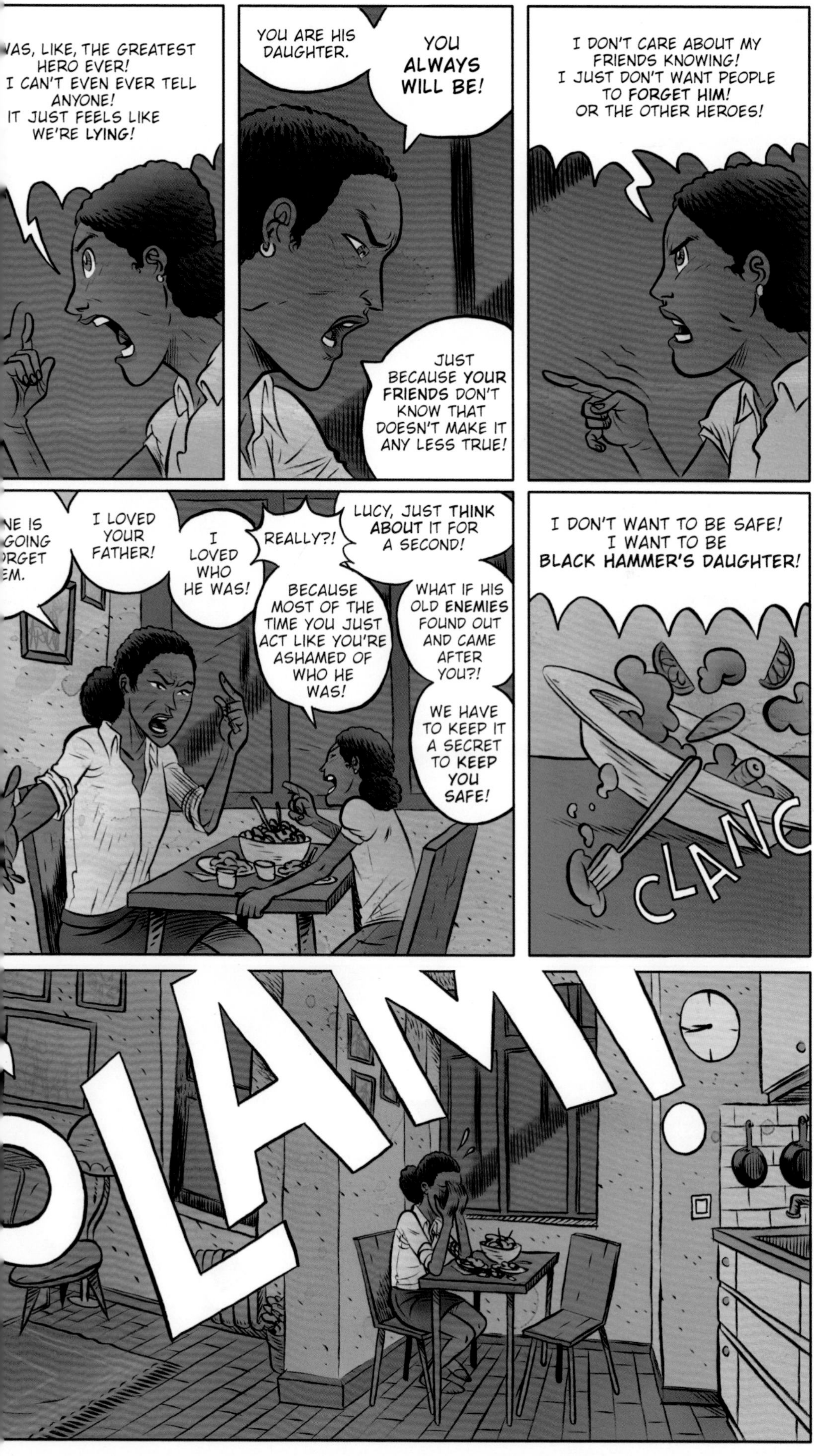

WAS, LIKE, THE GREATEST HERO EVER! I CAN'T EVEN EVER TELL ANYONE! IT JUST FEELS LIKE WE'RE LYING!
YOU ARE HIS DAUGHTER.
YOU ALWAYS WILL BE!
JUST BECAUSE YOUR FRIENDS DON'T KNOW THAT DOESN'T MAKE IT ANY LESS TRUE!
I DON'T CARE ABOUT MY FRIENDS KNOWING! I JUST DON'T WANT PEOPLE TO FORGET HIM! OR THE OTHER HEROES!
NE IS GOING RGET EM.
I LOVED YOUR FATHER!
I LOVED WHO HE WAS!
REALLY?!
BECAUSE MOST OF THE TIME YOU JUST ACT LIKE YOU'RE ASHAMED OF WHO HE WAS!
LUCY, JUST THINK ABOUT IT FOR A SECOND!
WHAT IF HIS OLD ENEMIES FOUND OUT AND CAME AFTER YOU?!
WE HAVE TO KEEP IT A SECRET TO KEEP YOU SAFE!
I DON'T WANT TO BE SAFE! I WANT TO BE BLACK HAMMER'S DAUGHTER!
CLANG
SLAM!

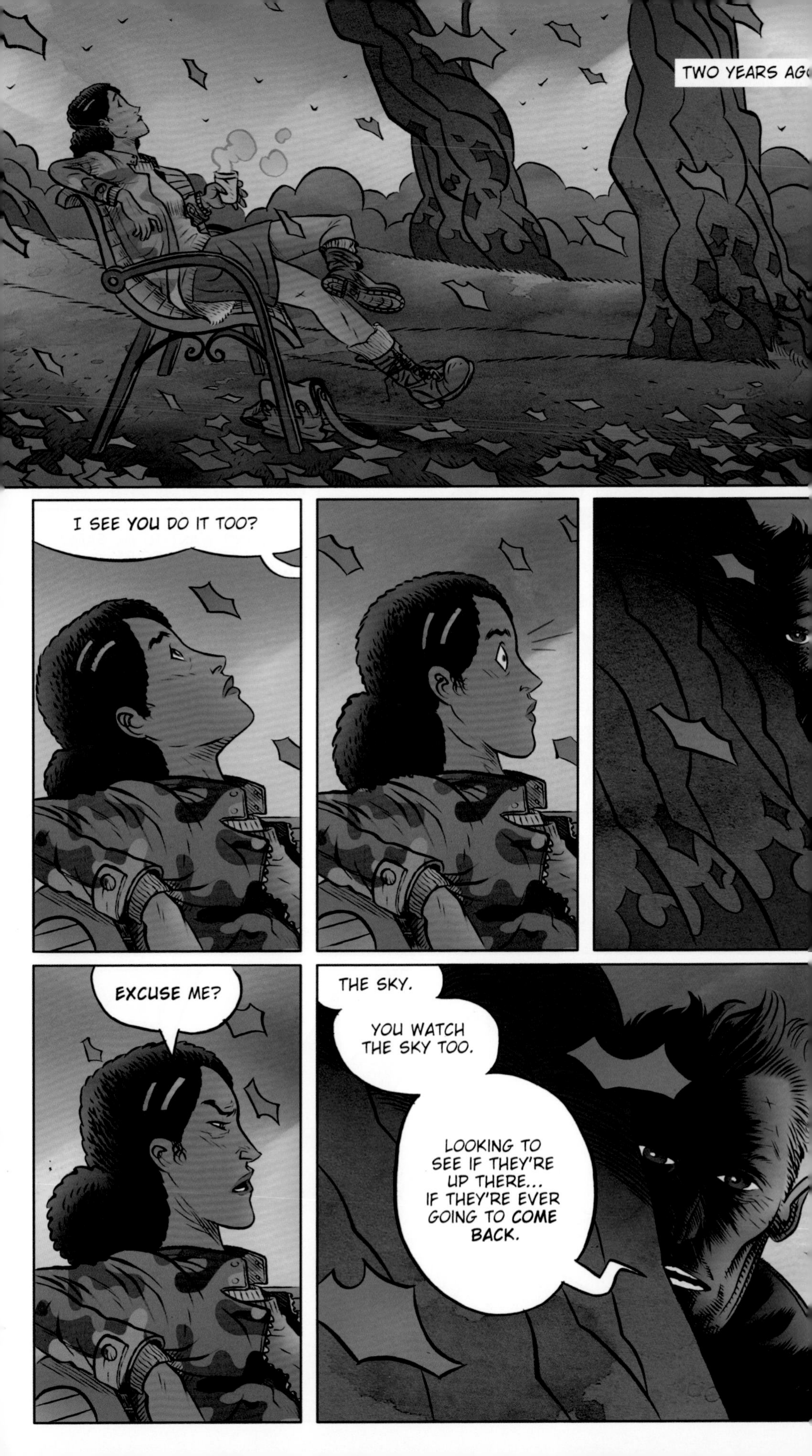
TWO YEARS AG
I SEE YOU DO IT TOO?
EXCUSE ME?
THE SKY.
YOU WATCH THE SKY TOO.
LOOKING TO SEE IF THEY'RE UP THERE... IF THEY'RE EVER GOING TO COME BACK.

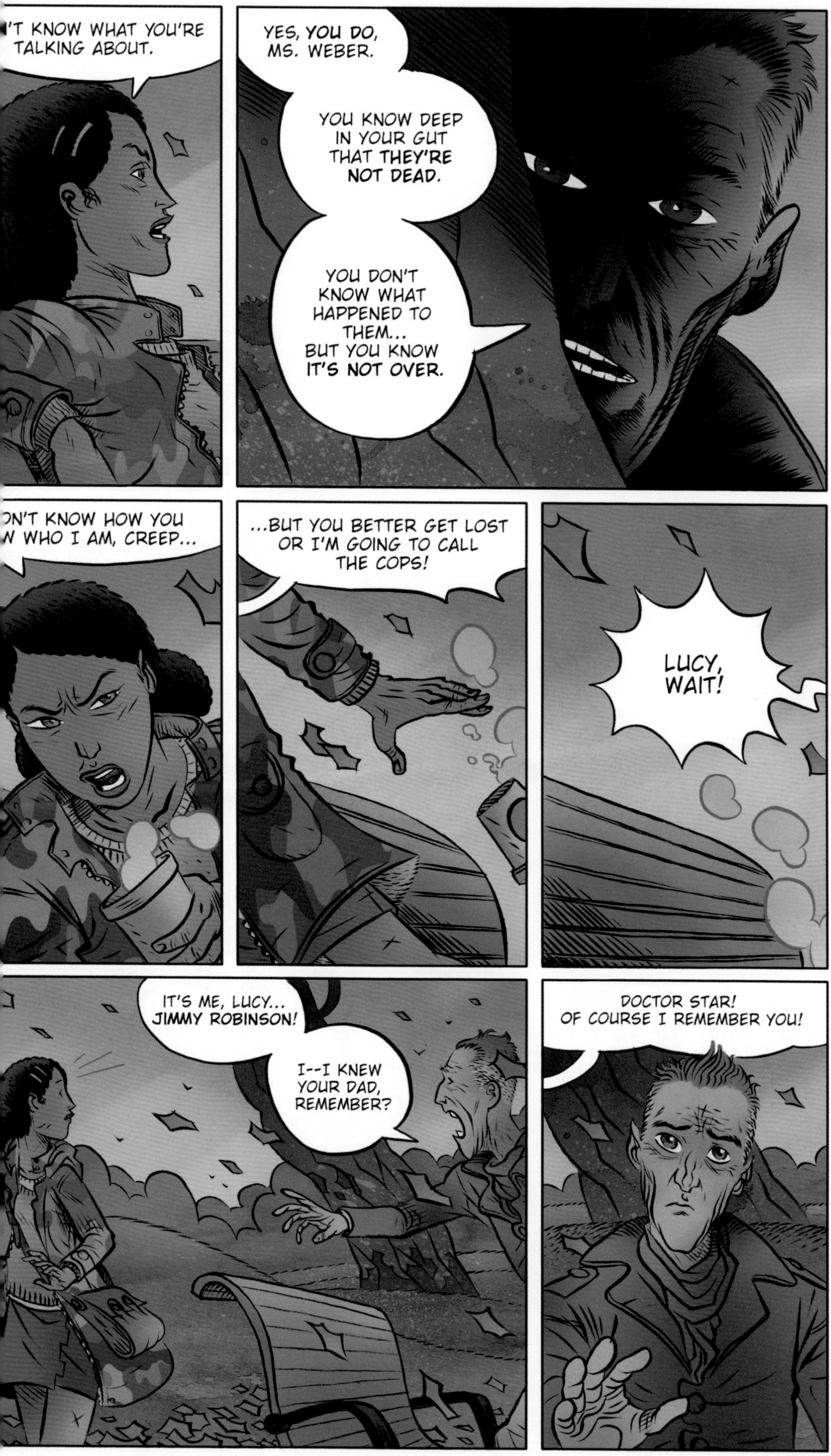
'T KNOW WHAT YOU'RE TALKING ABOUT.
YES, YOU DO, MS. WEBER.
YOU KNOW DEEP IN YOUR GUT THAT THEY'RE NOT DEAD.
YOU DON'T KNOW WHAT HAPPENED TO THEM... BUT YOU KNOW IT'S NOT OVER.
ON'T KNOW HOW YOU W WHO I AM, CREEP...
...BUT YOU BETTER GET LOST OR I'M GOING TO CALL THE COPS!
LUCY, WAIT!
IT'S ME, LUCY... JIMMY ROBINSON!
I--I KNEW YOUR DAD, REMEMBER?
DOCTOR STAR! OF COURSE I REMEMBER YOU!

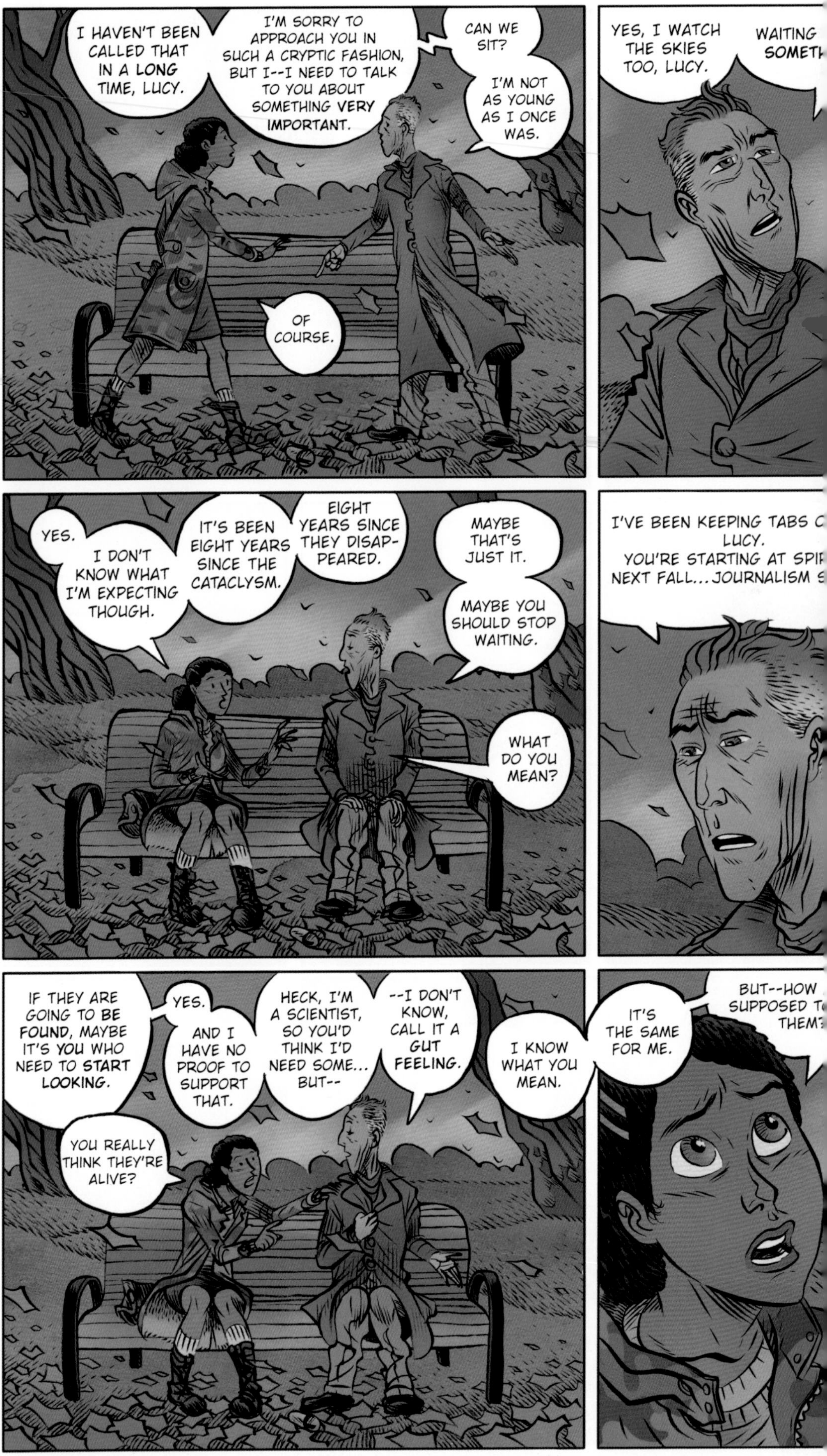
I HAVEN'T BEEN CALLED THAT IN A LONG TIME, LUCY.
I'M SORRY TO APPROACH YOU IN SUCH A CRYPTIC FASHION, BUT I--I NEED TO TALK TO YOU ABOUT SOMETHING VERY IMPORTANT.
CAN WE SIT?
I'M NOT AS YOUNG AS I ONCE WAS.
OF COURSE.
YES, I WATCH THE SKIES TOO, LUCY.
WAITING SOMETH
YES.
I DON'T KNOW WHAT I'M EXPECTING THOUGH.
IT'S BEEN EIGHT YEARS SINCE THE CATACLYSM.
EIGHT YEARS SINCE THEY DISAP-PEARED.
MAYBE THAT'S JUST IT.
MAYBE YOU SHOULD STOP WAITING.
WHAT DO YOU MEAN?
I'VE BEEN KEEPING TABS O LUCY.
YOU'RE STARTING AT SPIR NEXT FALL... JOURNALISM S
IF THEY ARE GOING TO BE FOUND, MAYBE IT'S YOU WHO NEED TO START LOOKING.
YOU REALLY THINK THEY'RE ALIVE?
YES.
AND I HAVE NO PROOF TO SUPPORT THAT.
HECK, I'M A SCIENTIST, SO YOU'D THINK I'D NEED SOME... BUT--
--I DON'T KNOW, CALL IT A GUT FEELING.
I KNOW WHAT YOU MEAN.
IT'S THE SAME FOR ME.
BUT--HOW SUPPOSED T THEM?

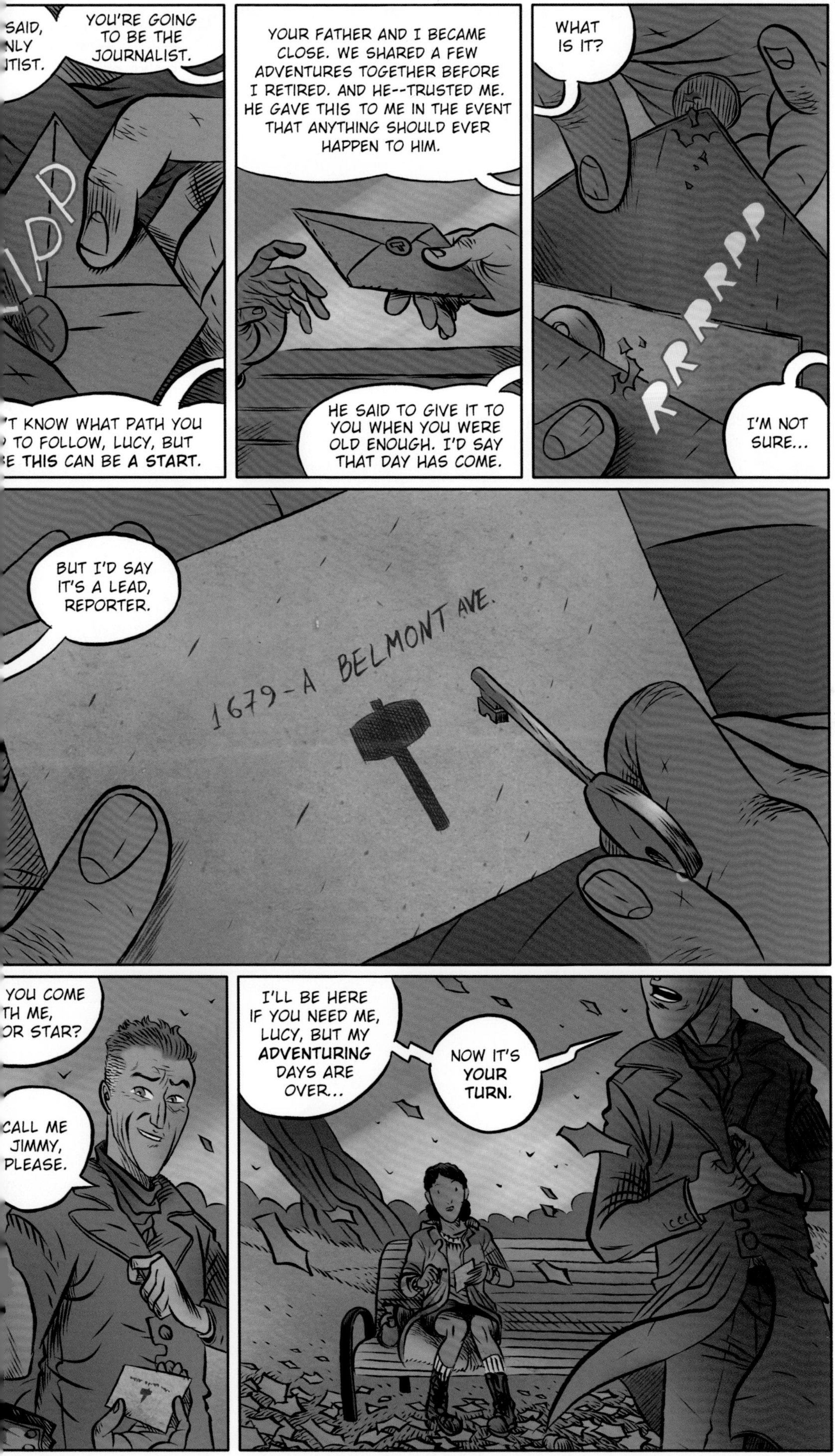
SAID,
NLY
TIST.
YOU'RE GOING TO BE THE JOURNALIST.
IPP
'T KNOW WHAT PATH YOU
TO FOLLOW, LUCY, BUT
E THIS CAN BE A START.
YOUR FATHER AND I BECAME CLOSE. WE SHARED A FEW ADVENTURES TOGETHER BEFORE I RETIRED. AND HE--TRUSTED ME. HE GAVE THIS TO ME IN THE EVENT THAT ANYTHING SHOULD EVER HAPPEN TO HIM.
HE SAID TO GIVE IT TO YOU WHEN YOU WERE OLD ENOUGH. I'D SAY THAT DAY HAS COME.
WHAT IS IT?
RRRRPP
I'M NOT SURE...
BUT I'D SAY IT'S A LEAD, REPORTER.
1679-A BELMONT AVE.
YOU COME
TH ME,
OR STAR?
CALL ME JIMMY, PLEASE.
I'LL BE HERE IF YOU NEED ME, LUCY, BUT MY ADVENTURING DAYS ARE OVER...
NOW IT'S YOUR TURN.

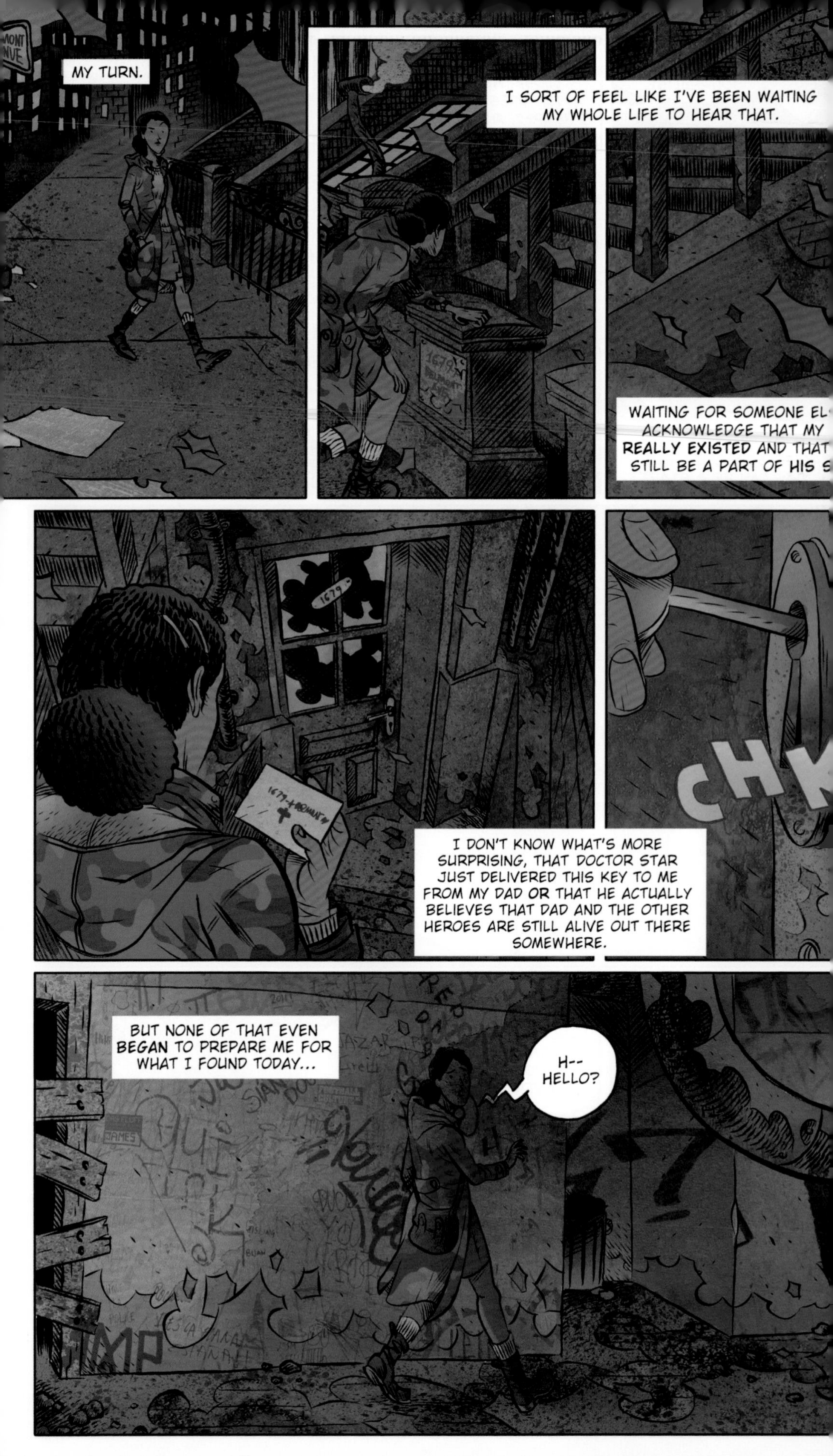
MY TURN.
I SORT OF FEEL LIKE I'VE BEEN WAITING MY WHOLE LIFE TO HEAR THAT.
WAITING FOR SOMEONE EL
ACKNOWLEDGE THAT MY
REALLY EXISTED AND THAT
STILL BE A PART OF HIS
I DON'T KNOW WHAT'S MORE SURPRISING, THAT DOCTOR STAR JUST DELIVERED THIS KEY TO ME FROM MY DAD OR THAT HE ACTUALLY BELIEVES THAT DAD AND THE OTHER HEROES ARE STILL ALIVE OUT THERE SOMEWHERE.
CHK
BUT NONE OF THAT EVEN BEGAN TO PREPARE ME FOR WHAT I FOUND TODAY...
H-- HELLO?

R DNA MATCH DETECTED.

T-WEEP!

WHOA!!

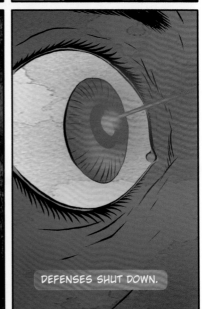

DEFENSES SHUT DOWN.

LUNG!!

WELCOME.

T-SS SKKKHHKK

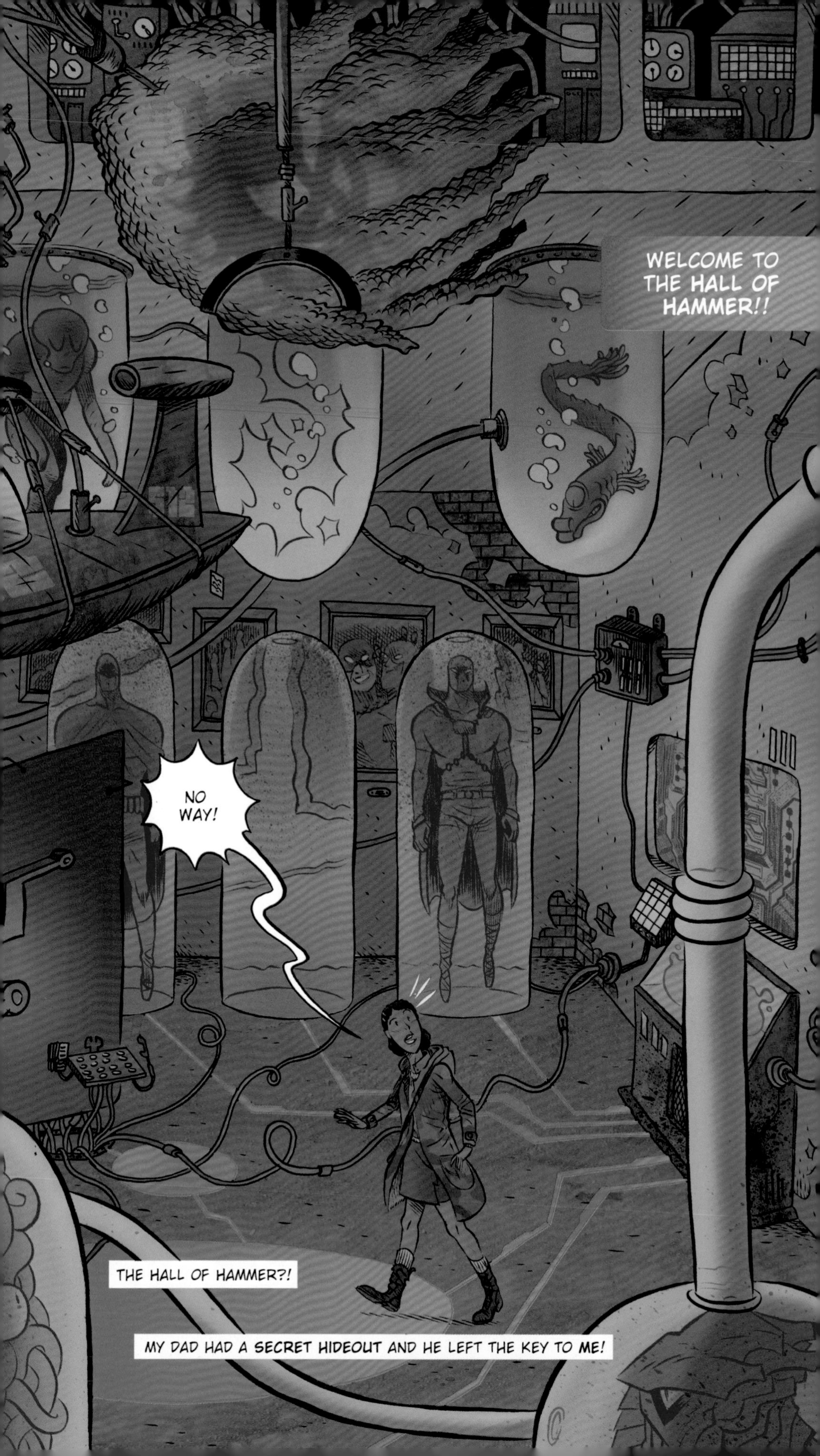
WELCOME TO THE HALL OF HAMMER!!
NO WAY!
THE HALL OF HAMMER?!
MY DAD HAD A SECRET HIDEOUT AND HE LEFT THE KEY TO ME!

MY WHOLE LIFE ALL I EVER WANTED WAS TO KNOW MORE ABOUT MY DAD.

WELL, HERE IT WAS, JUST WAITING FOR ME-- THE UNDISCOVERED WORLD OF BLACK HAMMER.

MACHINE 234: TURE E SE

VENUS FRY-TRA CASE#24 ADVENTURE OF THE BURNING PLANT MEN.

JUST BEING HERE I FELT CLOSER TO HIM THAN I HAD SINCE HE DISAPPEARED.

I KNEW I COULDN'T TELL MOM ABOUT THIS PLACE.

VILLAIN FILES #01

☐ SHER
☐ MAN ACONDA
☐ METAL MINOTAUR
☐ BLACK STALL
☐ ENTER TOOTS
☐ THU-LOU
☐ ULTRI

I KNOW SHE MEANS WELL, BUT SHE WOULD NEVER LET ME COME BACK HERE.

THIS PLACE HELD A LOT OF SECRETS.

AND IT HAD TO STAY THAT WAY.

CLIC!

BLEEPP!

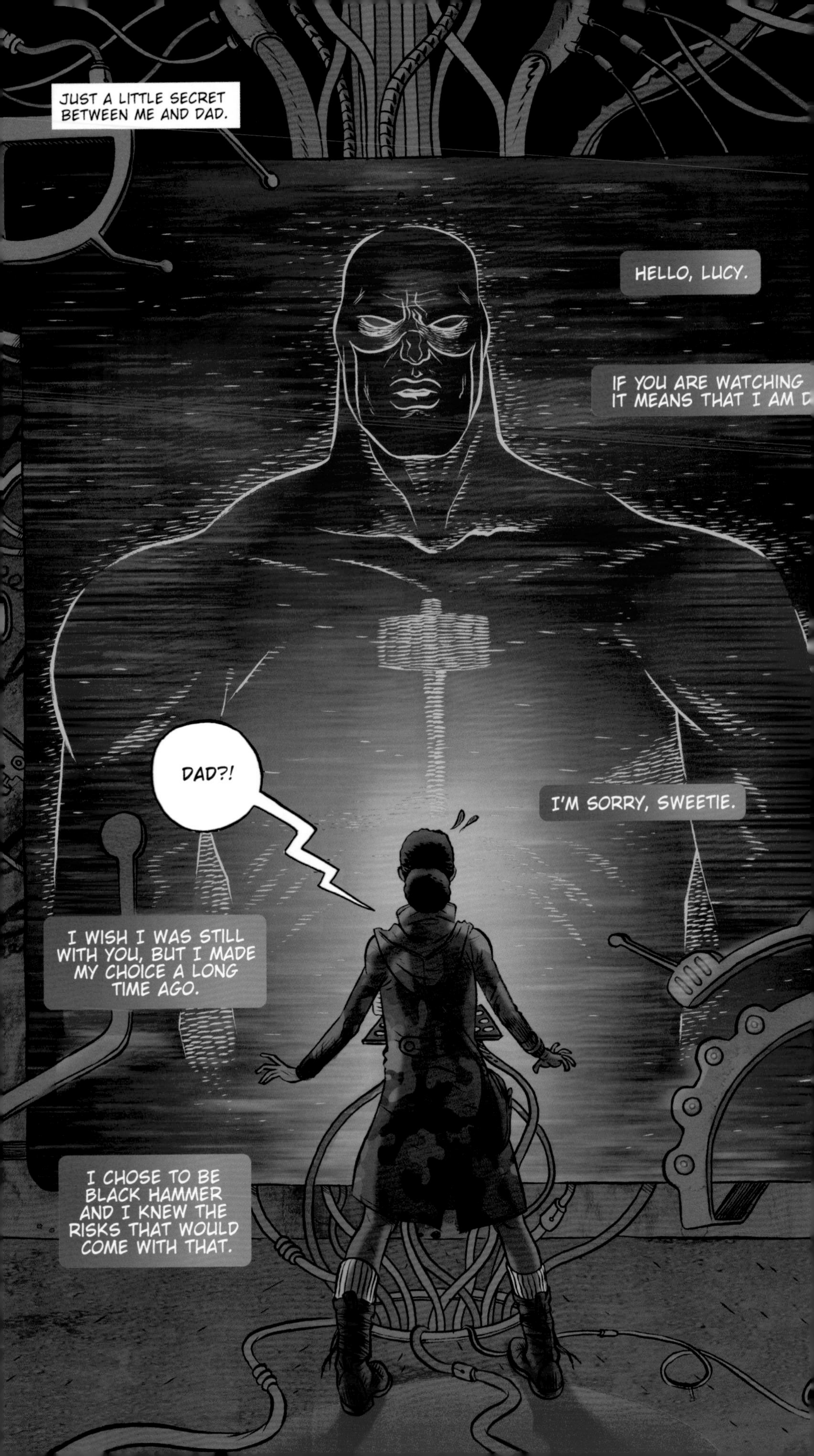

JUST A LITTLE SECRET BETWEEN ME AND DAD.
HELLO, LUCY.
IF YOU ARE WATCHING
IT MEANS THAT I AM
DAD?!
I'M SORRY, SWEETIE.
I WISH I WAS STILL WITH YOU, BUT I MADE MY CHOICE A LONG TIME AGO.
I CHOSE TO BE BLACK HAMMER AND I KNEW THE RISKS THAT WOULD COME WITH THAT.

F YOU'RE IN THE HALL OF
ER, IT ALSO MEANS THAT
CTOR STAR DID WHAT I
KED AND YOU'RE NOW
ALL GROWN UP.

UCY, THERE IS A VERY
RTANT REASON I WANTED
TO GIVE YOU THAT KEY.
U SEE, THIS BASEMENT
ADQUARTERS CONTAINS
ERY MEMENTO, FILE, AND
TRACE OF MY LIFE
AS BLACK HAMMER.

AND I NEED YOU TO
DESTROY IT ALL.

WHAT?!

LUCY, THIS LIFE...BEING BLACK
HAMMER...I DON'T WANT IT TO
EVER COME BACK ON YOU
OR YOUR MOM.

I DON'T WANT ANY TRACE LEFT
CONNECTING YOU TWO TO ME.

I'LL NEVER GET THAT TIME WITH
YOU BACK AND NEITHER WILL YOU.

N'T REGRET THE PATH MY
LIFE TOOK.
'M PROUD OF WHAT I
PLISHED IN THIS COSTUME.

PED A LOT OF PEOPLE AND
SAVED A LOT OF LIVES.

..I ALSO MISSED A LOT.

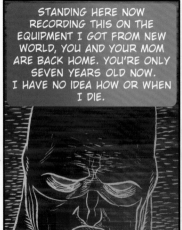

STANDING HERE NOW
RECORDING THIS ON THE
EQUIPMENT I GOT FROM NEW
WORLD, YOU AND YOUR MOM
ARE BACK HOME. YOU'RE ONLY
SEVEN YEARS OLD NOW.
I HAVE NO IDEA HOW OR WHEN
I DIE.

BUT I DO KNOW THAT I
PROBABLY MISSED A LOT OF
YOUR LIFE.

DESTROY EVERYTHING IN
S PLACE AND LEAVE ME
BEHIND.

ON WITH YOUR OWN LIFE
DON'T WASTE ANOTHER
MINUTE ON ME OR ON
BLACK HAMMER.

MY LIFE IS OVER, BUT YOURS
IS JUST STARTING, LUCY.

SO GO AND LIVE IT.

GOODBYE, SWEETHEART.

I'LL ALWAYS BE WITH YOU.

beep!

BUT YOU NEED TO LET
BLACK HAMMER GO.

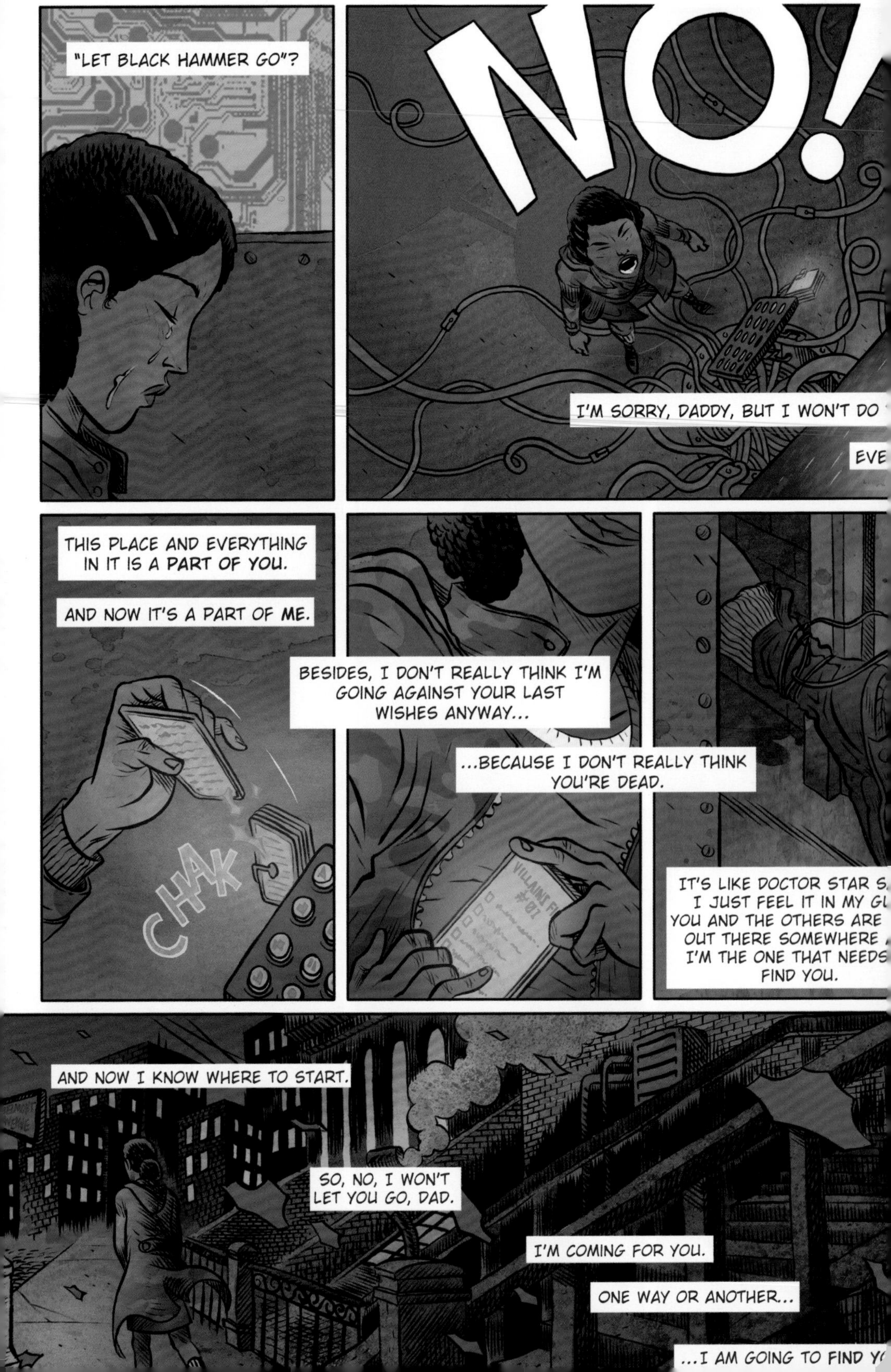
"LET BLACK HAMMER GO"?
NO!
I'M SORRY, DADDY, BUT I WON'T DO
EVE
THIS PLACE AND EVERYTHING IN IT IS A PART OF YOU.
AND NOW IT'S A PART OF ME.
CHAK
BESIDES, I DON'T REALLY THINK I'M GOING AGAINST YOUR LAST WISHES ANYWAY...
...BECAUSE I DON'T REALLY THINK YOU'RE DEAD.
IT'S LIKE DOCTOR STAR S
I JUST FEEL IT IN MY G
YOU AND THE OTHERS ARE
OUT THERE SOMEWHERE
I'M THE ONE THAT NEEDS
FIND YOU.
AND NOW I KNOW WHERE TO START.
SO, NO, I WON'T LET YOU GO, DAD.
I'M COMING FOR YOU.
ONE WAY OR ANOTHER...
...I AM GOING TO FIND Y

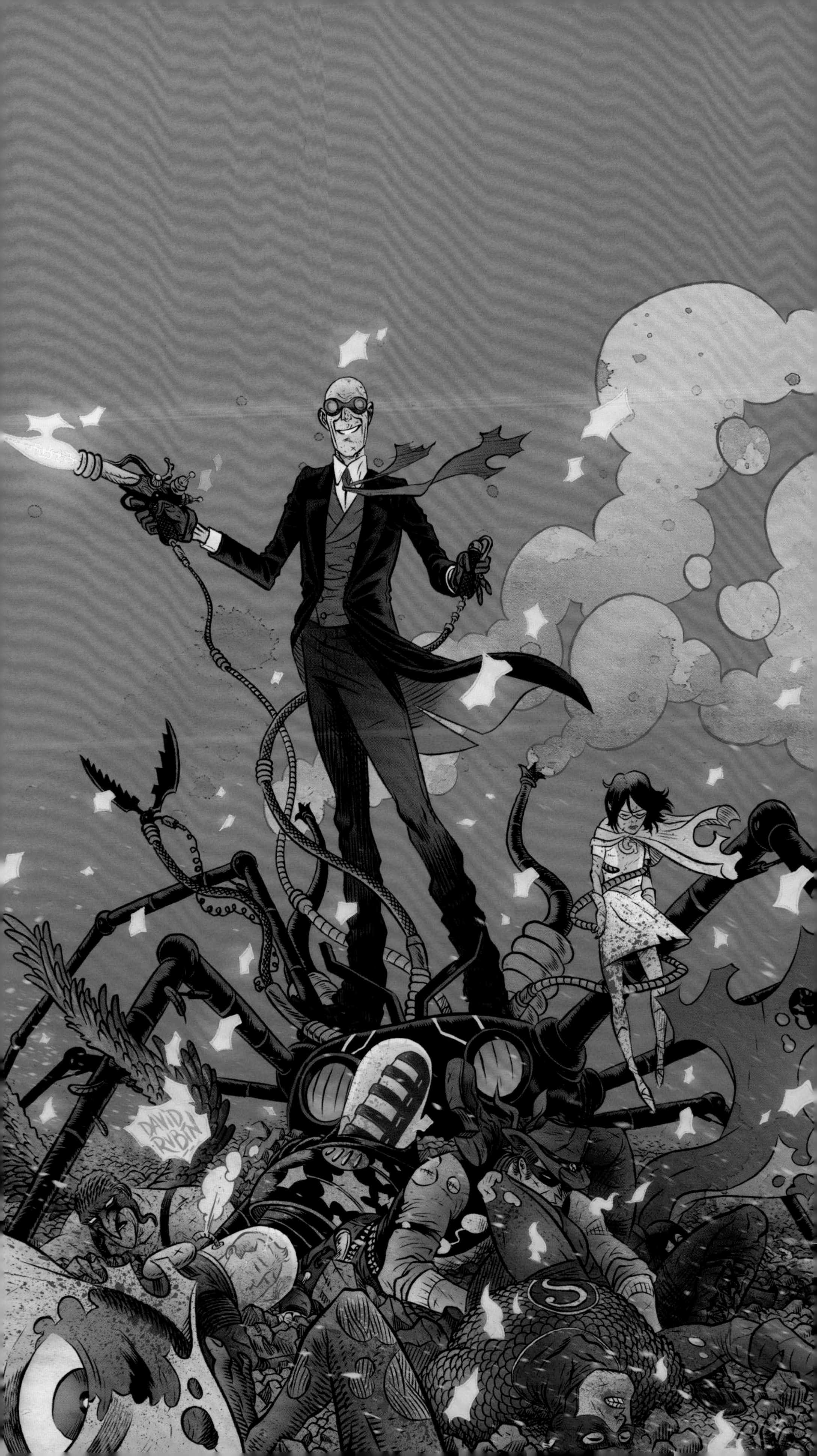
DAVID RUBIN

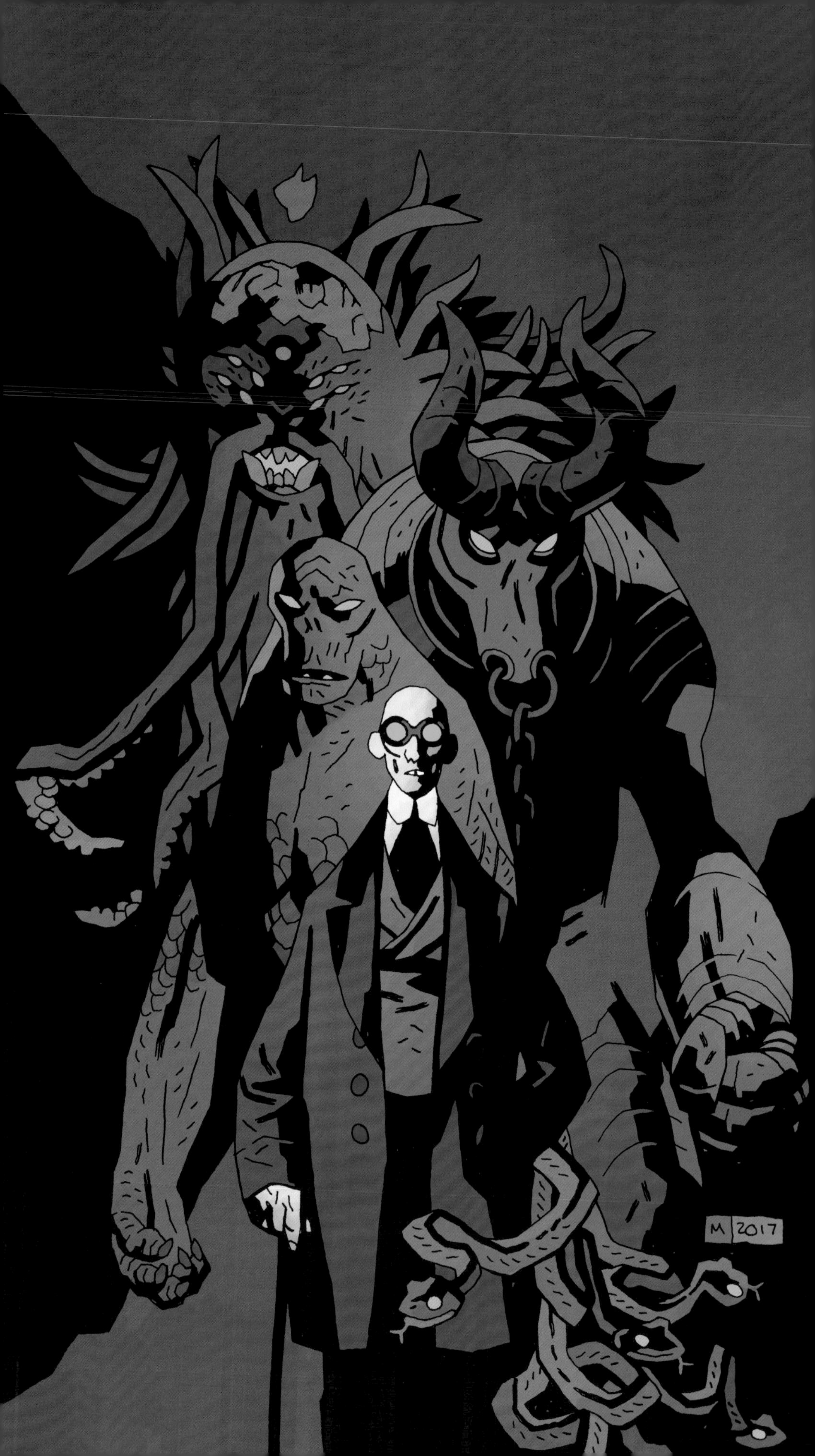
M 2017

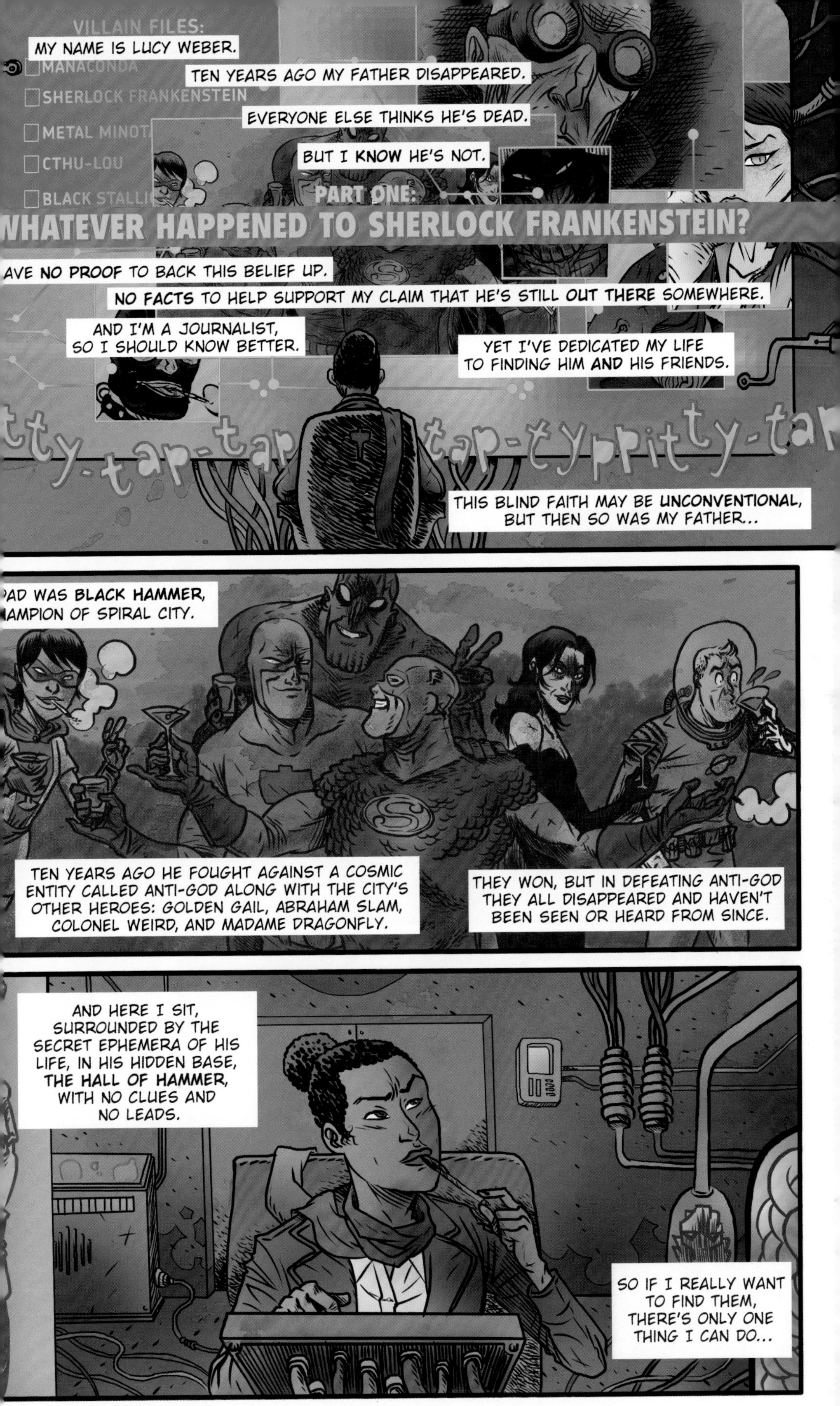
VILLAIN FILES:
MANACONDA
SHERLOCK FRANKENSTEIN
METAL MINOT
CTHU-LOU
BLACK STALLI
MY NAME IS LUCY WEBER.
TEN YEARS AGO MY FATHER DISAPPEARED.
EVERYONE ELSE THINKS HE'S DEAD.
BUT I KNOW HE'S NOT.
PART ONE:
WHATEVER HAPPENED TO SHERLOCK FRANKENSTEIN?
AVE NO PROOF TO BACK THIS BELIEF UP.
NO FACTS TO HELP SUPPORT MY CLAIM THAT HE'S STILL OUT THERE SOMEWHERE.
AND I'M A JOURNALIST, SO I SHOULD KNOW BETTER.
YET I'VE DEDICATED MY LIFE TO FINDING HIM AND HIS FRIENDS.
TTY-TAP-TAP TAP-TYPPITTY-TAP
THIS BLIND FAITH MAY BE UNCONVENTIONAL, BUT THEN SO WAS MY FATHER...
AD WAS BLACK HAMMER, AMPION OF SPIRAL CITY.
TEN YEARS AGO HE FOUGHT AGAINST A COSMIC ENTITY CALLED ANTI-GOD ALONG WITH THE CITY'S OTHER HEROES: GOLDEN GAIL, ABRAHAM SLAM, COLONEL WEIRD, AND MADAME DRAGONFLY.
THEY WON, BUT IN DEFEATING ANTI-GOD THEY ALL DISAPPEARED AND HAVEN'T BEEN SEEN OR HEARD FROM SINCE.
AND HERE I SIT, SURROUNDED BY THE SECRET EPHEMERA OF HIS LIFE, IN HIS HIDDEN BASE, THE HALL OF HAMMER, WITH NO CLUES AND NO LEADS.
SO IF I REALLY WANT TO FIND THEM, THERE'S ONLY ONE THING I CAN DO...

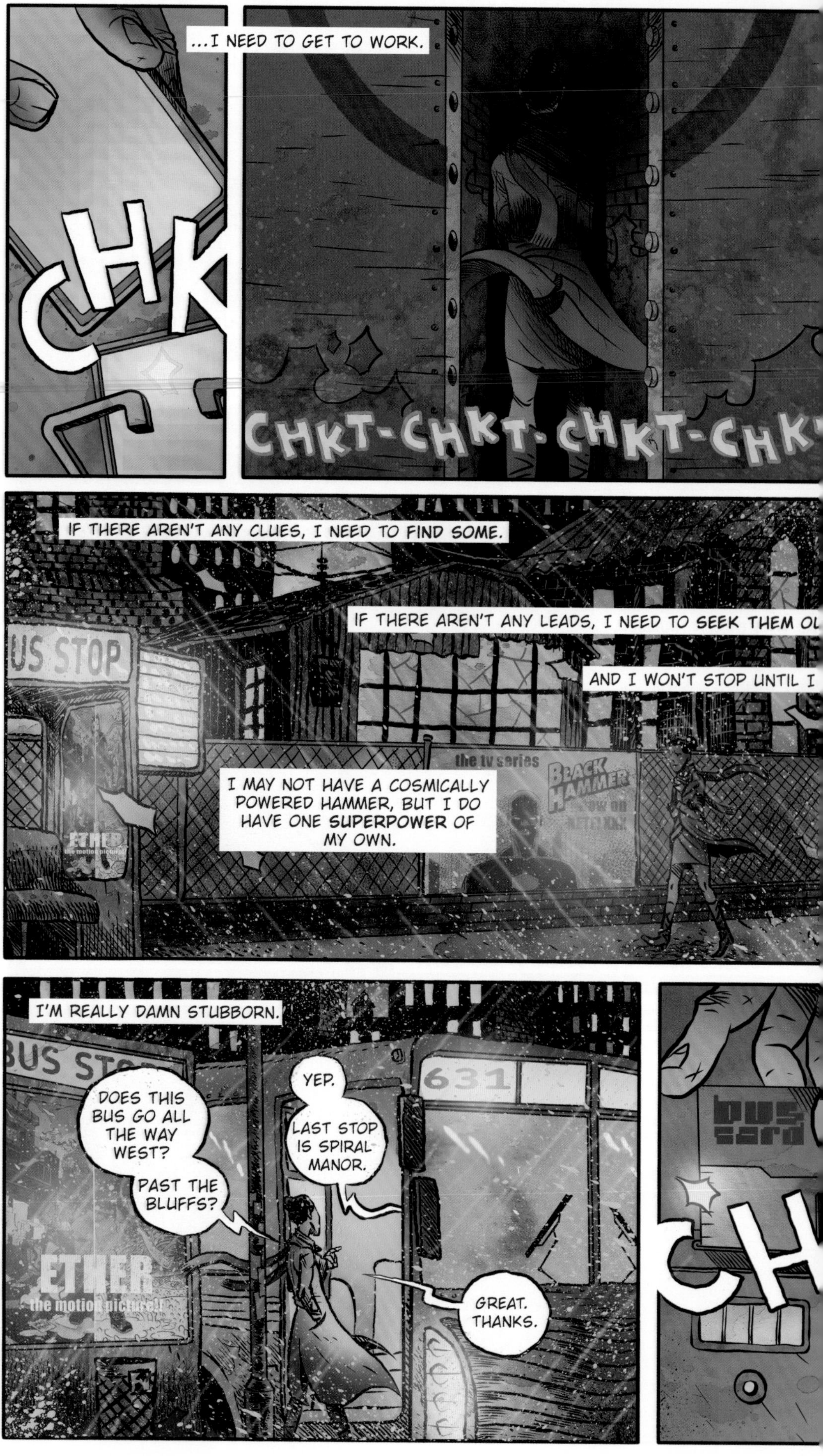
...I NEED TO GET TO WORK.
CHK
CHKT-CHKT-CHKT-CHK
IF THERE AREN'T ANY CLUES, I NEED TO FIND SOME.
IF THERE AREN'T ANY LEADS, I NEED TO SEEK THEM OU
AND I WON'T STOP UNTIL I
BUS STOP
the tv series
BLACK HAMMER
I MAY NOT HAVE A COSMICALLY POWERED HAMMER, BUT I DO HAVE ONE SUPERPOWER OF MY OWN.
ETHER the motion picture!!
I'M REALLY DAMN STUBBORN.
BUS STO
631
DOES THIS BUS GO ALL THE WAY WEST?
PAST THE BLUFFS?
YEP.
LAST STOP IS SPIRAL MANOR.
GREAT. THANKS.
ETHER the motion picture!!
bus card
CH

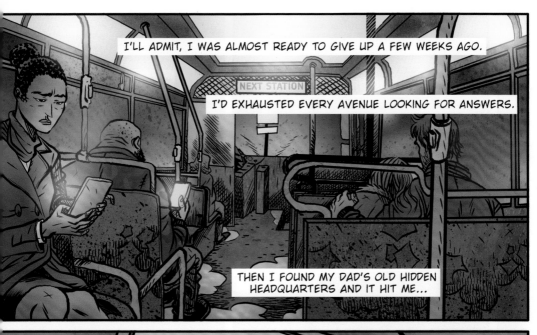

I'LL ADMIT, I WAS ALMOST READY TO GIVE UP A FEW WEEKS AGO.

NEXT STATION

I'D EXHAUSTED EVERY AVENUE LOOKING FOR ANSWERS.

THEN I FOUND MY DAD'S OLD HIDDEN HEADQUARTERS AND IT HIT ME...

...OU WANT TO FIND A BUNCH OF SUPERHEROES ...T CAN'T, THE NEXT BEST PLACE TO START IS WITH THEIR SUPERVILLAINS.

...N FILES:

...ANACONDA

☐ SHERLOCK FRANKENSTEIN

☐ METAL MINOTAUR

☐ CTHU-LOU

☐ BLACK STALLION

☐ SULTRIX

☐ TENTER...

AND IF YOU ARE GOING TO START WITH VILLAINS, THEN WHY NOT START WITH THE BIGGEST, BADDEST VILLAIN OF THEM ALL...

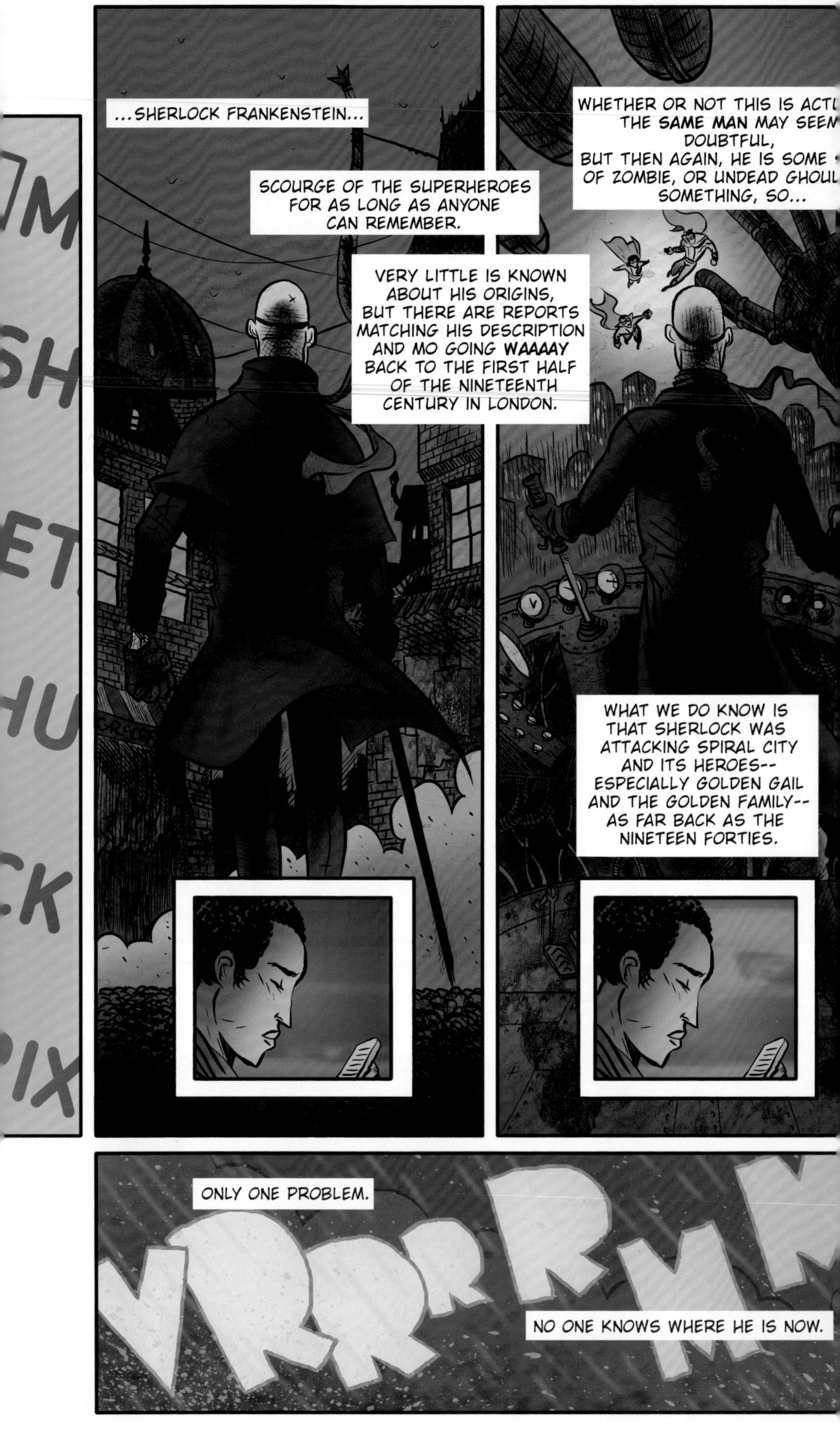
...SHERLOCK FRANKENSTEIN...
SCOURGE OF THE SUPERHEROES FOR AS LONG AS ANYONE CAN REMEMBER.
VERY LITTLE IS KNOWN ABOUT HIS ORIGINS, BUT THERE ARE REPORTS MATCHING HIS DESCRIPTION AND MO GOING WAAAAY BACK TO THE FIRST HALF OF THE NINETEENTH CENTURY IN LONDON.
WHETHER OR NOT THIS IS ACTU THE SAME MAN MAY SEEM DOUBTFUL, BUT THEN AGAIN, HE IS SOME OF ZOMBIE, OR UNDEAD GHOUL SOMETHING, SO...
WHAT WE DO KNOW IS THAT SHERLOCK WAS ATTACKING SPIRAL CITY AND ITS HEROES--ESPECIALLY GOLDEN GAIL AND THE GOLDEN FAMILY--AS FAR BACK AS THE NINETEEN FORTIES.
ONLY ONE PROBLEM.
VRRRRRMM
NO ONE KNOWS WHERE HE IS NOW.

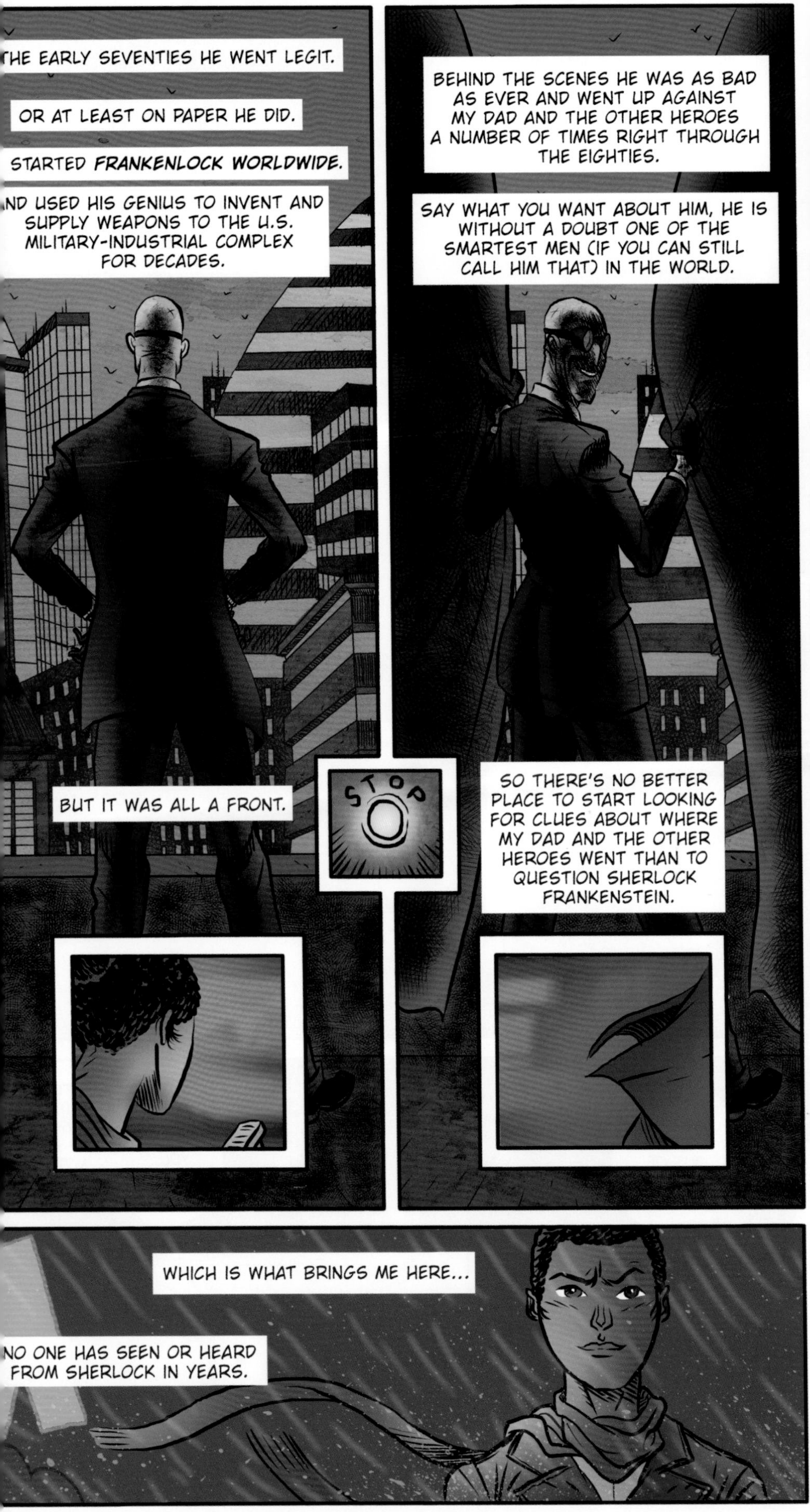
THE EARLY SEVENTIES HE WENT LEGIT.
OR AT LEAST ON PAPER HE DID.
STARTED FRANKENLOCK WORLDWIDE.
ND USED HIS GENIUS TO INVENT AND SUPPLY WEAPONS TO THE U.S. MILITARY-INDUSTRIAL COMPLEX FOR DECADES.
BEHIND THE SCENES HE WAS AS BAD AS EVER AND WENT UP AGAINST MY DAD AND THE OTHER HEROES A NUMBER OF TIMES RIGHT THROUGH THE EIGHTIES.
SAY WHAT YOU WANT ABOUT HIM, HE IS WITHOUT A DOUBT ONE OF THE SMARTEST MEN (IF YOU CAN STILL CALL HIM THAT) IN THE WORLD.
BUT IT WAS ALL A FRONT.
STOP
SO THERE'S NO BETTER PLACE TO START LOOKING FOR CLUES ABOUT WHERE MY DAD AND THE OTHER HEROES WENT THAN TO QUESTION SHERLOCK FRANKENSTEIN.
WHICH IS WHAT BRINGS ME HERE...
NO ONE HAS SEEN OR HEARD FROM SHERLOCK IN YEARS.

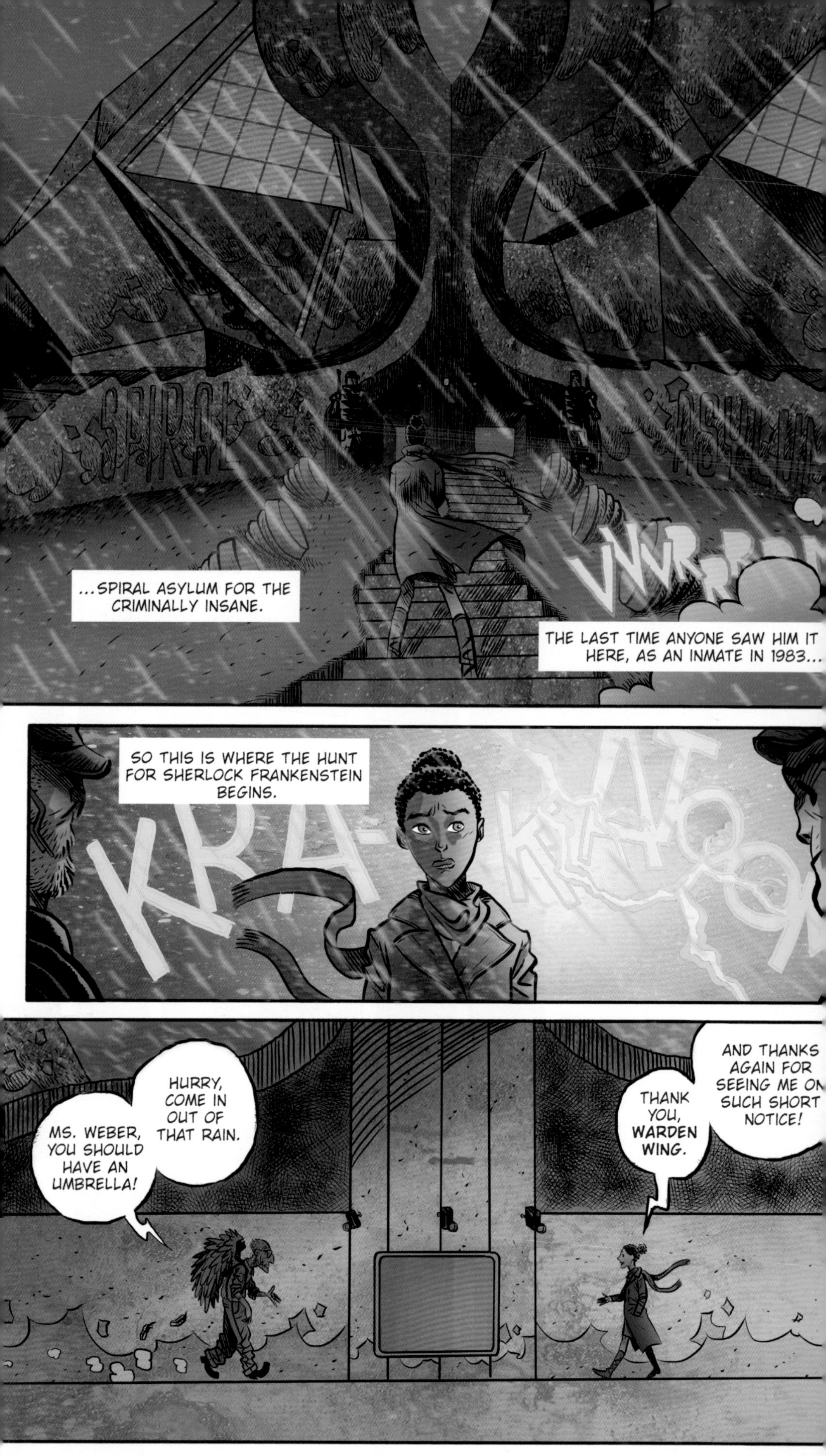
SPIRAL
ASYLUM
VVVRRRROOM
...SPIRAL ASYLUM FOR THE CRIMINALLY INSANE.
THE LAST TIME ANYONE SAW HIM IT HERE, AS AN INMATE IN 1983...
SO THIS IS WHERE THE HUNT FOR SHERLOCK FRANKENSTEIN BEGINS.
KRA-
MS. WEBER, YOU SHOULD HAVE AN UMBRELLA!
HURRY, COME IN OUT OF THAT RAIN.
THANK YOU, WARDEN WING.
AND THANKS AGAIN FOR SEEING ME ON SUCH SHORT NOTICE!

I HAVE TO SAY, IT'S QUITE AN HONOR MEETING THE GREAT "WINGMAN"!

I THINK YOU WERE ALREADY RETIRED WHEN MY DAD WAS ACTIVE AS BLACK HAMMER...

...BUT I KNOW ALL ABOUT YOUR ADVENTURES WITH THE LIBERTY SQUADRON...

...AND I KNOW MY DAD REALLY RESPECTED YOU.

scanning... CLEAR

scanning... CLEAR

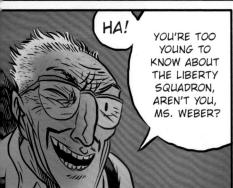

HA! YOU'RE TOO YOUNG TO KNOW ABOUT THE LIBERTY SQUADRON, AREN'T YOU, MS. WEBER?

ARE YOU KIDDING...

.I'VE READ EVERY ACCOUNT OF YOUR ADVENTURES IN EUROPE DURING THE WAR."

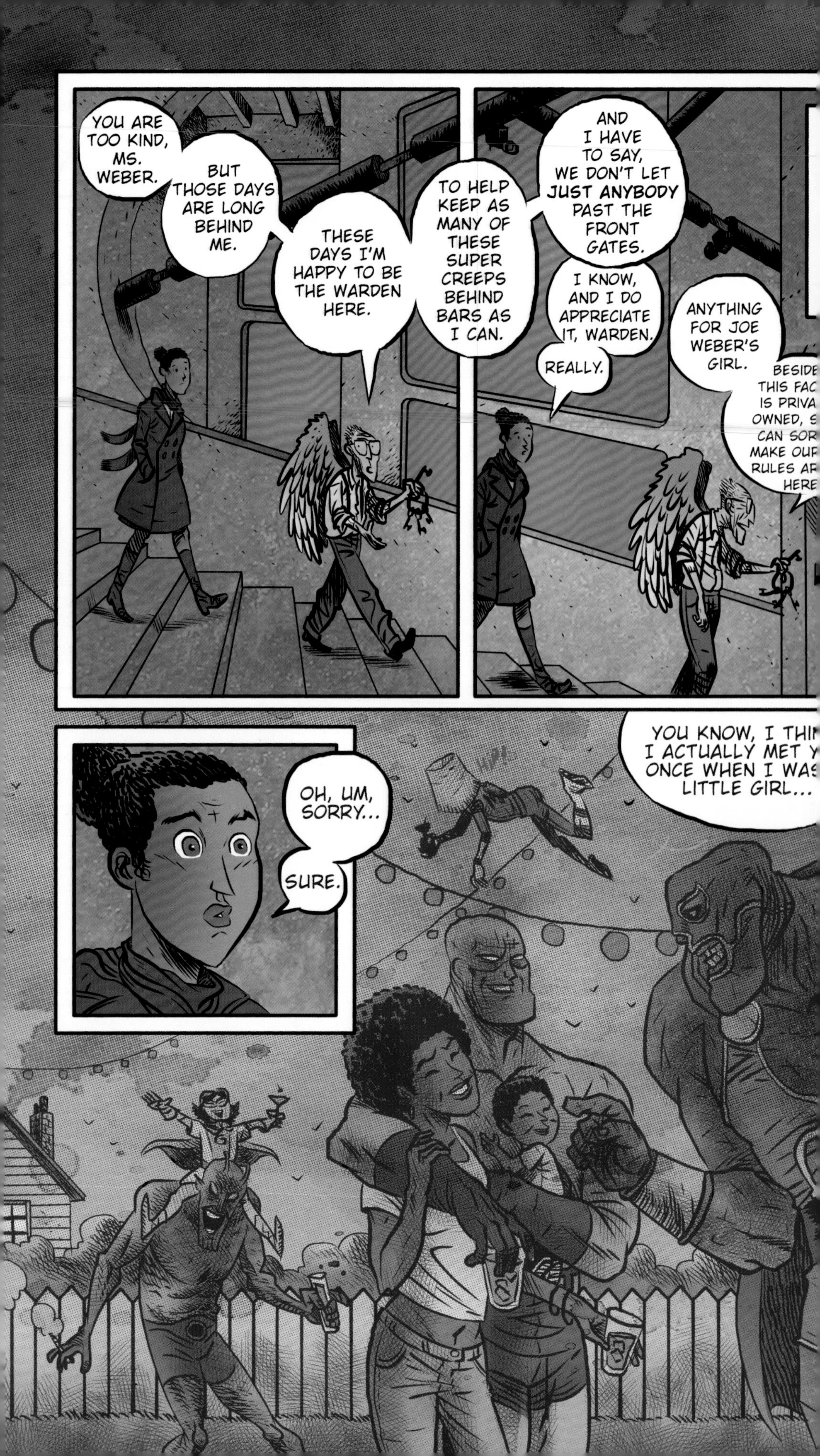

YOU ARE TOO KIND, MS. WEBER.
BUT THOSE DAYS ARE LONG BEHIND ME.
THESE DAYS I'M HAPPY TO BE THE WARDEN HERE.
TO HELP KEEP AS MANY OF THESE SUPER CREEPS BEHIND BARS AS I CAN.
AND I HAVE TO SAY, WE DON'T LET **JUST ANYBODY** PAST THE FRONT GATES.
I KNOW, AND I DO APPRECIATE IT, WARDEN.
REALLY.
ANYTHING FOR JOE WEBER'S GIRL.
BESIDE THIS FAC IS PRIVA OWNED, S CAN SOR MAKE OUR RULES AR HERE
YOU KNOW, I THI I ACTUALLY MET Y ONCE WHEN I WAS LITTLE GIRL...
OH, UM, SORRY...
SURE.

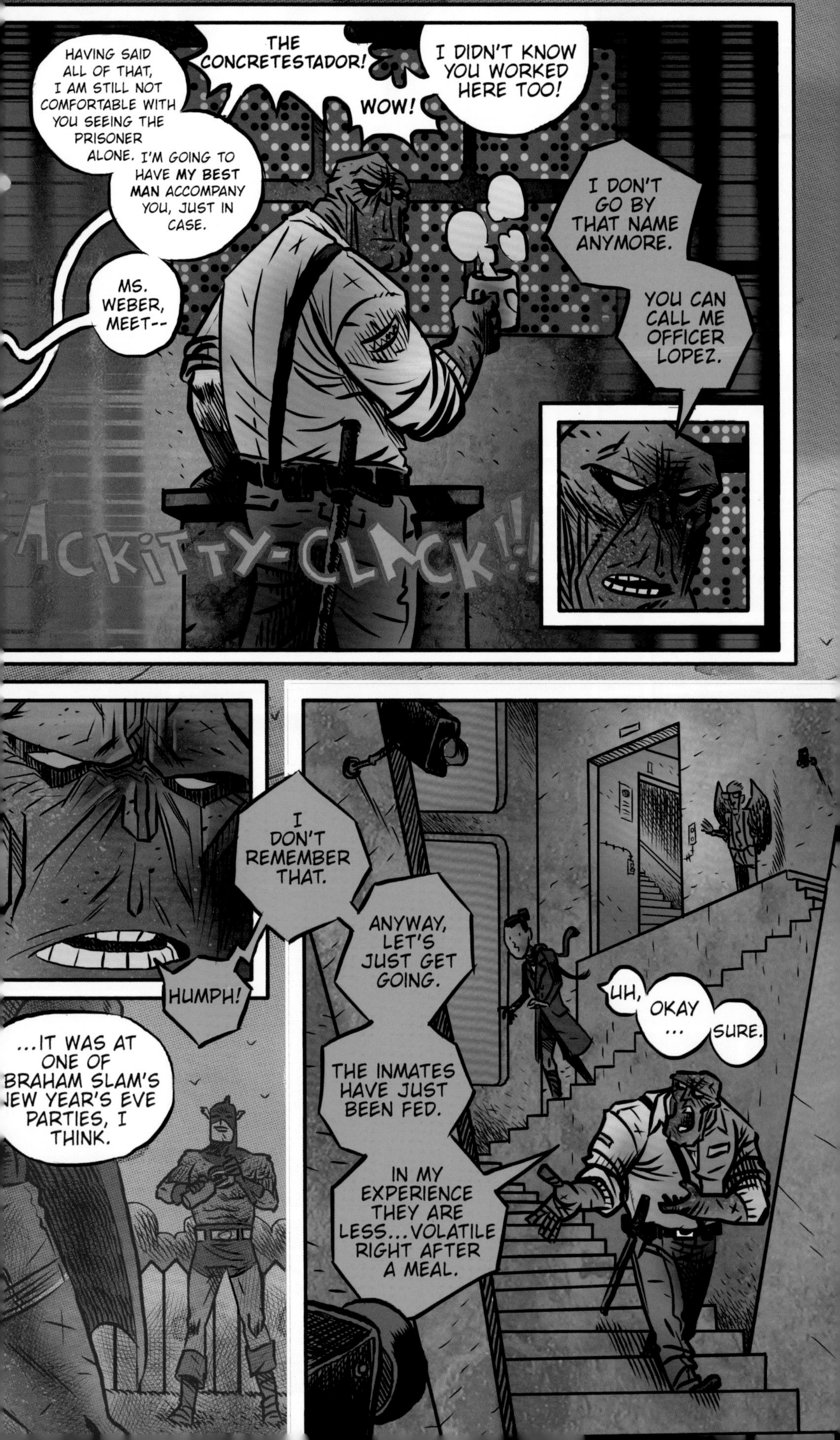
HAVING SAID ALL OF THAT, I AM STILL NOT COMFORTABLE WITH YOU SEEING THE PRISONER ALONE.
I'M GOING TO HAVE MY BEST MAN ACCOMPANY YOU, JUST IN CASE.
MS. WEBER, MEET--
THE CONCRETESTADOR!
WOW!
I DIDN'T KNOW YOU WORKED HERE TOO!
I DON'T GO BY THAT NAME ANYMORE.
YOU CAN CALL ME OFFICER LOPEZ.
CKITTY-CLACK!!!
HUMPH!
...IT WAS AT ONE OF BRAHAM SLAM'S NEW YEAR'S EVE PARTIES, I THINK.
I DON'T REMEMBER THAT.
ANYWAY, LET'S JUST GET GOING.
THE INMATES HAVE JUST BEEN FED.
IN MY EXPERIENCE THEY ARE LESS...VOLATILE RIGHT AFTER A MEAL.
UH, OKAY ... SURE.

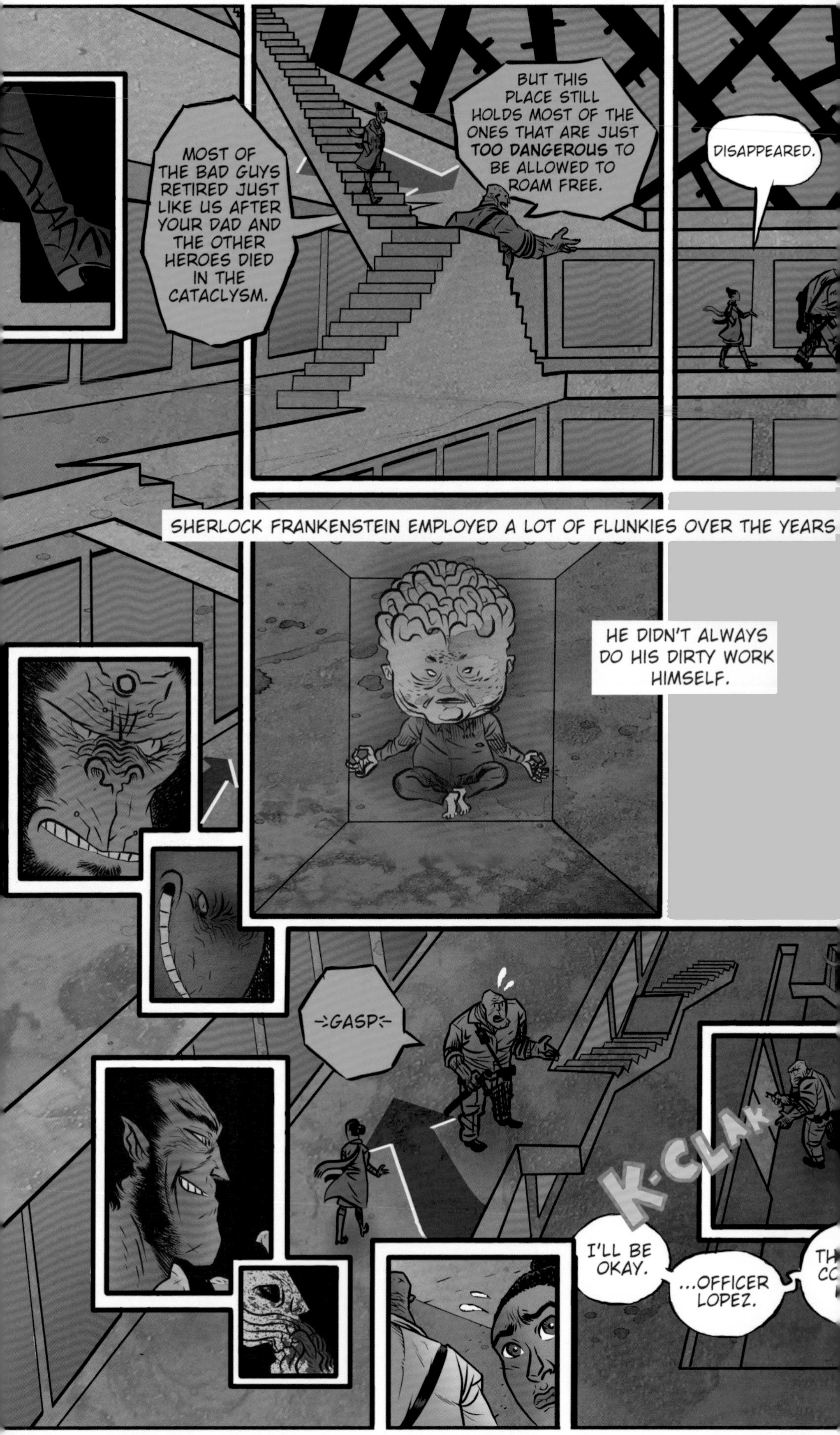
MOST OF THE BAD GUYS RETIRED JUST LIKE US AFTER YOUR DAD AND THE OTHER HEROES DIED IN THE CATACLYSM.
BUT THIS PLACE STILL HOLDS MOST OF THE ONES THAT ARE JUST TOO DANGEROUS TO BE ALLOWED TO ROAM FREE.
DISAPPEARED.
SHERLOCK FRANKENSTEIN EMPLOYED A LOT OF FLUNKIES OVER THE YEARS
HE DIDN'T ALWAYS DO HIS DIRTY WORK HIMSELF.
GASP
K-CLAK
I'LL BE OKAY.
...OFFICER LOPEZ.

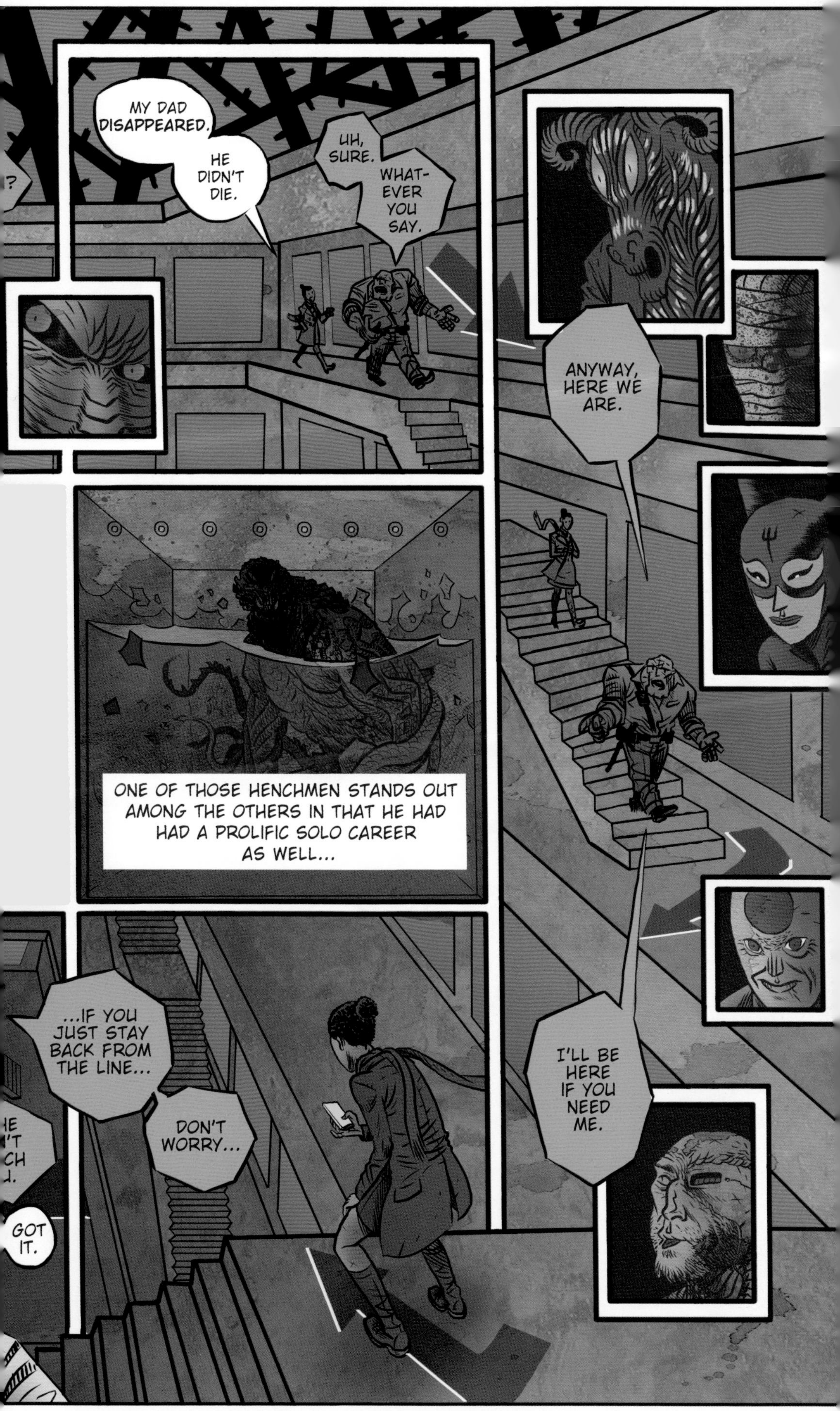
?
MY DAD DISAPPEARED.
HE DIDN'T DIE.
UH, SURE.
WHAT-EVER YOU SAY.
ANYWAY, HERE WE ARE.
ONE OF THOSE HENCHMEN STANDS OUT AMONG THE OTHERS IN THAT HE HAD HAD A PROLIFIC SOLO CAREER AS WELL...
I'LL BE HERE IF YOU NEED ME.
...IF YOU JUST STAY BACK FROM THE LINE...
DON'T WORRY...
GOT IT.

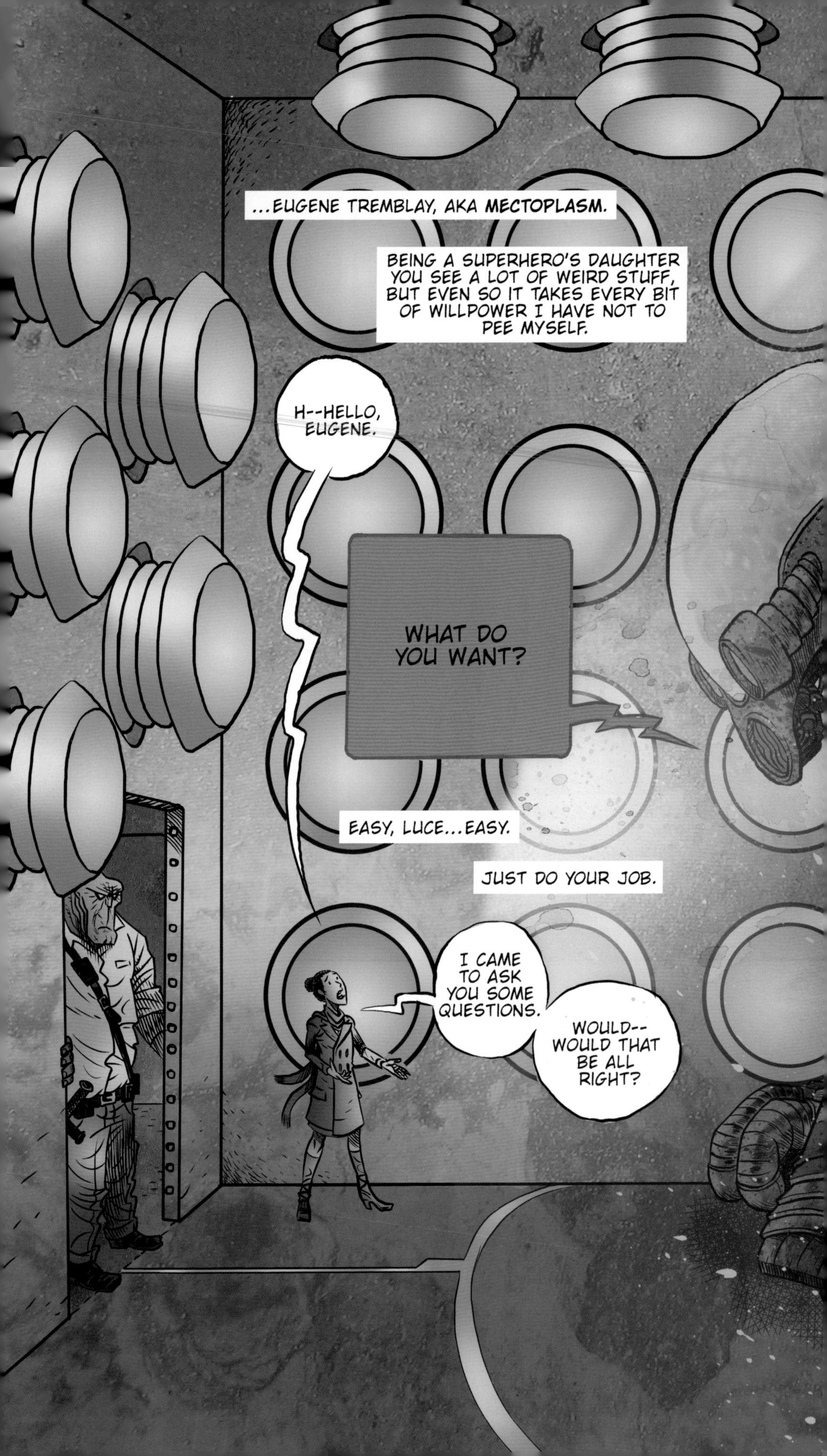
...EUGENE TREMBLAY, AKA MECTOPLASM.
BEING A SUPERHERO'S DAUGHTER YOU SEE A LOT OF WEIRD STUFF, BUT EVEN SO IT TAKES EVERY BIT OF WILLPOWER I HAVE NOT TO PEE MYSELF.
H--HELLO, EUGENE.
WHAT DO YOU WANT?
EASY, LUCE...EASY.
JUST DO YOUR JOB.
I CAME TO ASK YOU SOME QUESTIONS.
WOULD--WOULD THAT BE ALL RIGHT?

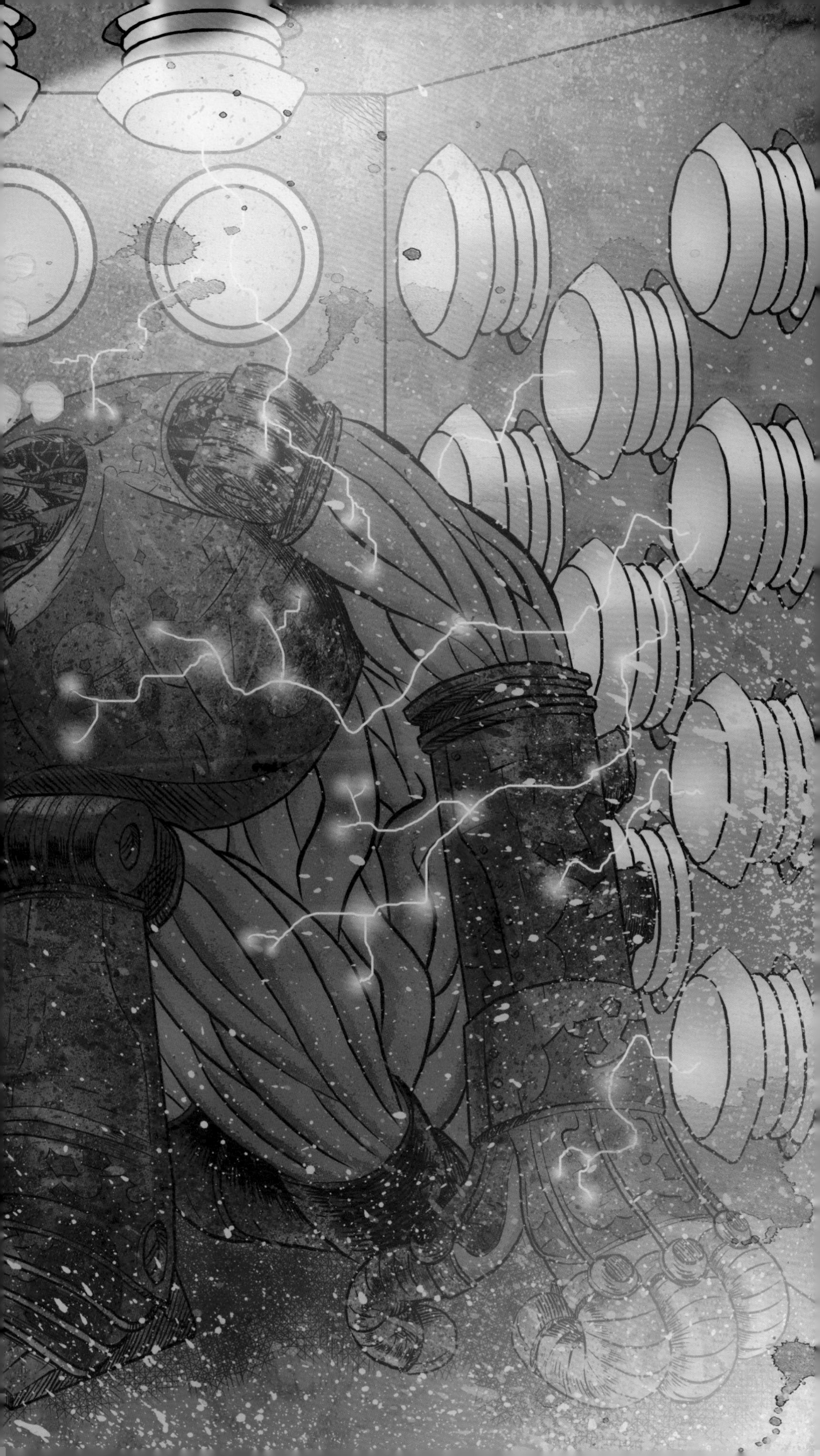

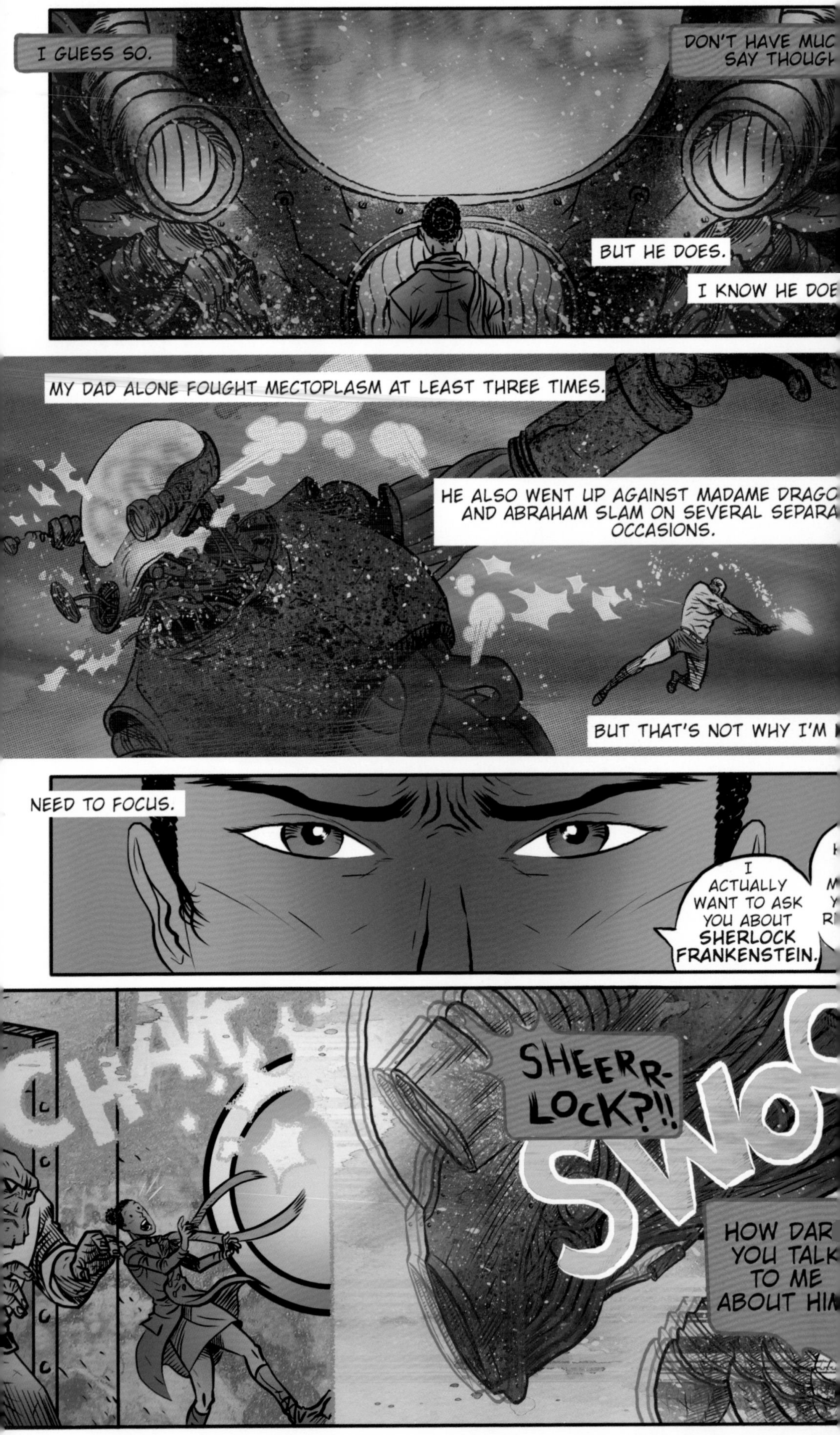

I GUESS SO.
DON'T HAVE MUC
SAY THOUG
BUT HE DOES.
I KNOW HE DOE
MY DAD ALONE FOUGHT MECTOPLASM AT LEAST THREE TIMES.
HE ALSO WENT UP AGAINST MADAME DRAGO AND ABRAHAM SLAM ON SEVERAL SEPARA OCCASIONS.
BUT THAT'S NOT WHY I'M
NEED TO FOCUS.
I ACTUALLY WANT TO ASK YOU ABOUT SHERLOCK FRANKENSTEIN.
SHEERR-LOCK?!!
HOW DAR YOU TALK TO ME ABOUT HIM

M
Y.

I KNOW IT MUST BE PAINFUL TO TALK ABOUT THAT.

I JUST--I'M TRYING TO FIND MY FATHER. AND I THINK IF I CAN FIND SHERLOCK, I MIGHT BE ABLE TO GET SOME CLUES AS TO WHERE HE WENT.

I DON'T TELL HIM MY FATHER WAS ONE OF HIS ARCHENEMIES, HOPING A LITTLE LIE OF OMISSION WILL HELP MY CAUSE.

DID--DID SHERLOCK HURT YOUR DADDY?

I DON'T KNOW.

BUT I'M HOPING TO FIND OUT.

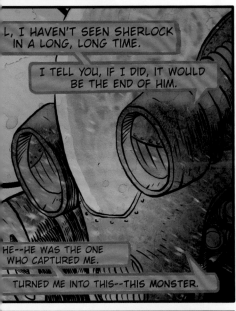

L, I HAVEN'T SEEN SHERLOCK IN A LONG, LONG TIME.

I TELL YOU, IF I DID, IT WOULD BE THE END OF HIM.

HE--HE WAS THE ONE WHO CAPTURED ME.

TURNED ME INTO THIS--THIS MONSTER.

I READ ABOUT THAT.

YOU CLAIM THAT YOU WERE-- YOU WERE DEAD AND HE BROUGHT YOU BACK?

MAYBE IF YOU CAN EXPLAIN.

WHAT DOES WHAT HAPPENED TO ME HAVE TO DO WITH YOUR DADDY?

MAYBE NOTHING.

BUT ANY DETAIL COULD BE A CLUE.

PLEASE.

I DON'T REMEMBER MUCH ABOUT WHO I WAS.

I KNOW I WASN'T VERY OLD.

I REMEMBER BEING A KID.

PLAYING.

I REMEMBER MY MOM AND DAD.

THEN THERE WAS SOME KIND OF ACCIDENT.

I REMEMBER THAT IT HURT REAL BAD...

...JUS

...AND THEN IT WAS DARK.

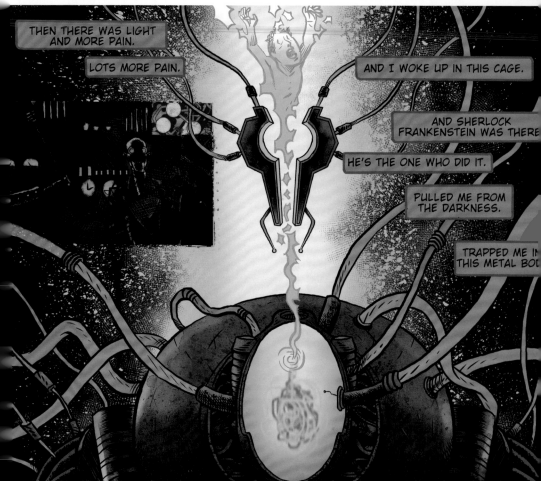

THEN THERE WAS LIGHT AND MORE PAIN.

LOTS MORE PAIN.

AND I WOKE UP IN THIS CAGE.

AND SHERLOCK FRANKENSTEIN WAS THERE

HE'S THE ONE WHO DID IT.

PULLED ME FROM THE DARKNESS.

TRAPPED ME IN THIS METAL BOD

YOU-- YOU WERE JUST A CHILD WHEN YOU DIED!

JUST A BOY!

DON'T KNOW.

I THINK SO.

LIKE I SAID, I DON'T REMEMBER MUCH.

BUT AFTER HE BROUGHT ME BACK AND TRAPPED ME IN THIS BODY, SHERLOCK MADE ME DO LOTS OF BAD STUFF.

BUT I LEARNED HOW TO RESIST HIM AND I RAN AWAY. HE TRIED TO CONVINCE ME TO JOIN HIM AGAIN A FEW TIMES. BUT--

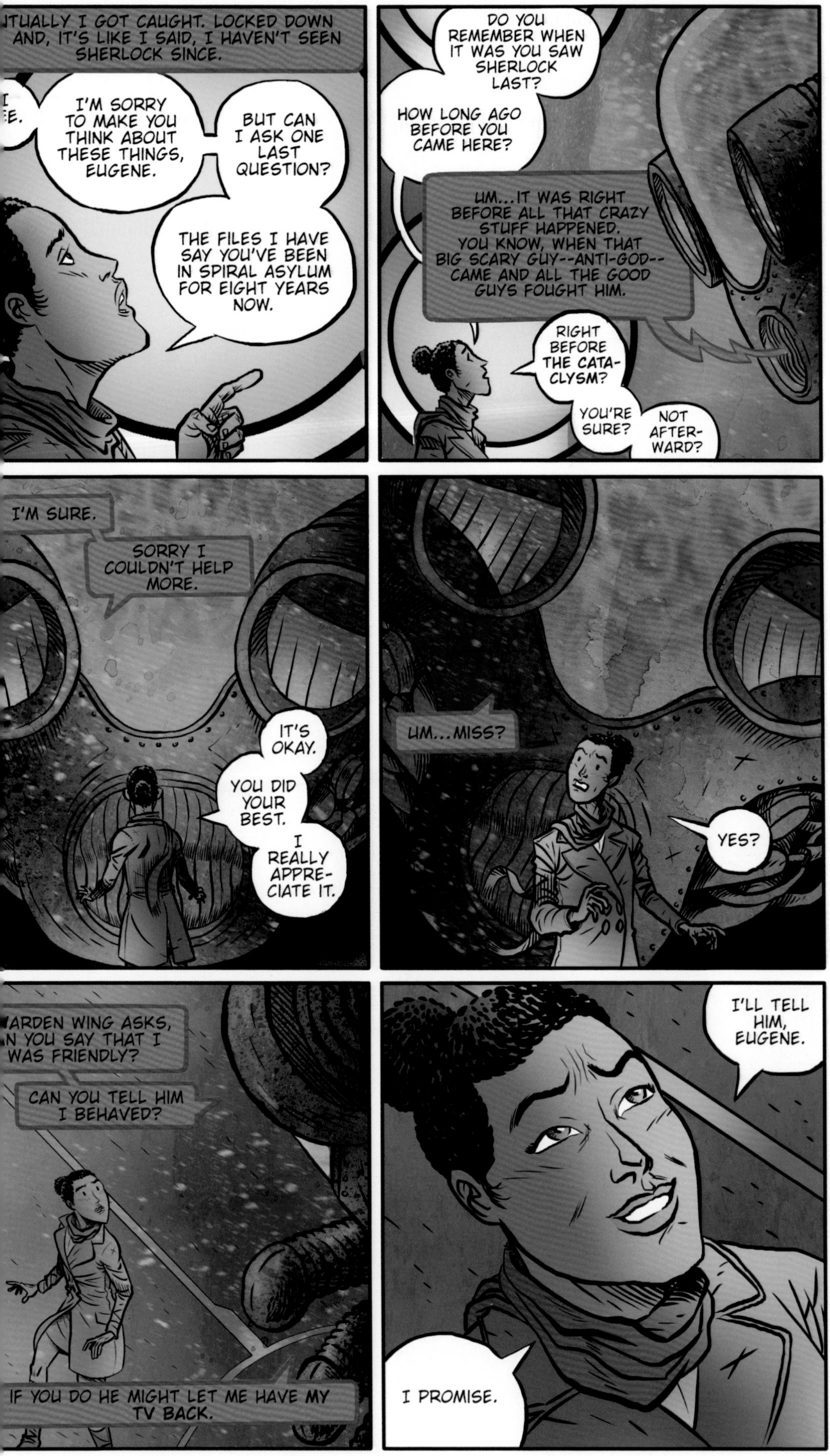
...NTUALLY I GOT CAUGHT. LOCKED DOWN AND, IT'S LIKE I SAID, I HAVEN'T SEEN SHERLOCK SINCE.
I'M SORRY TO MAKE YOU THINK ABOUT THESE THINGS, EUGENE.
BUT CAN I ASK ONE LAST QUESTION?
THE FILES I HAVE SAY YOU'VE BEEN IN SPIRAL ASYLUM FOR EIGHT YEARS NOW.
DO YOU REMEMBER WHEN IT WAS YOU SAW SHERLOCK LAST?
HOW LONG AGO BEFORE YOU CAME HERE?
UM...IT WAS RIGHT BEFORE ALL THAT CRAZY STUFF HAPPENED. YOU KNOW, WHEN THAT BIG SCARY GUY--ANTI-GOD--CAME AND ALL THE GOOD GUYS FOUGHT HIM.
RIGHT BEFORE THE CATACLYSM?
YOU'RE SURE?
NOT AFTERWARD?
I'M SURE.
SORRY I COULDN'T HELP MORE.
IT'S OKAY.
YOU DID YOUR BEST.
I REALLY APPRECIATE IT.
UM...MISS?
YES?
...ARDEN WING ASKS, ...N YOU SAY THAT I WAS FRIENDLY?
CAN YOU TELL HIM I BEHAVED?
IF YOU DO HE MIGHT LET ME HAVE MY TV BACK.
I'LL TELL HIM, EUGENE.
I PROMISE.

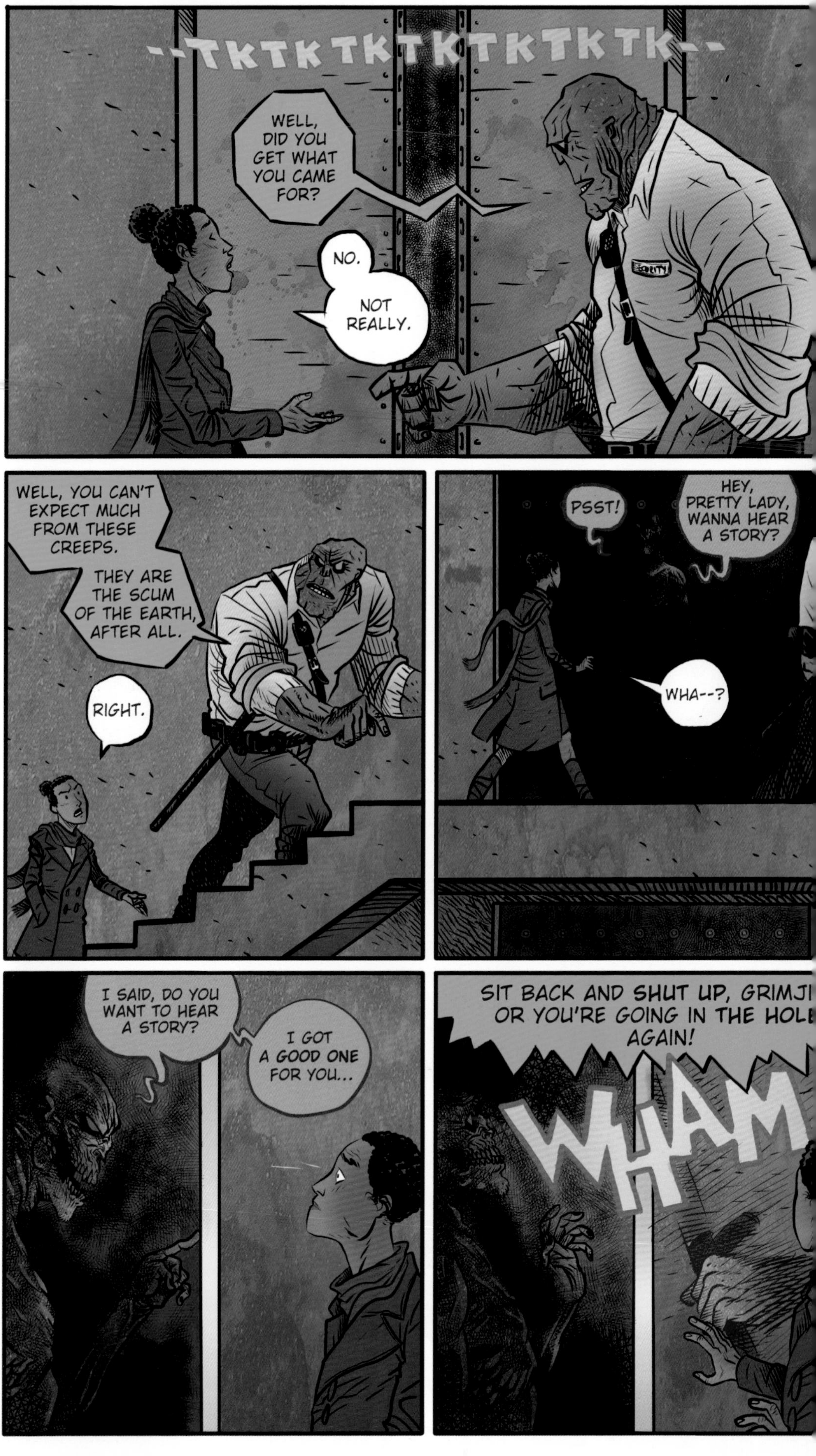
--TKTKTKTKTKTKTK--
WELL, DID YOU GET WHAT YOU CAME FOR?
NO.
NOT REALLY.
SECURITY
WELL, YOU CAN'T EXPECT MUCH FROM THESE CREEPS.
THEY ARE THE SCUM OF THE EARTH, AFTER ALL.
RIGHT.
PSST!
HEY, PRETTY LADY, WANNA HEAR A STORY?
WHA--?
I SAID, DO YOU WANT TO HEAR A STORY?
I GOT A GOOD ONE FOR YOU...
SIT BACK AND SHUT UP, GRIMJI
OR YOU'RE GOING IN THE HOL
AGAIN!
WHAM

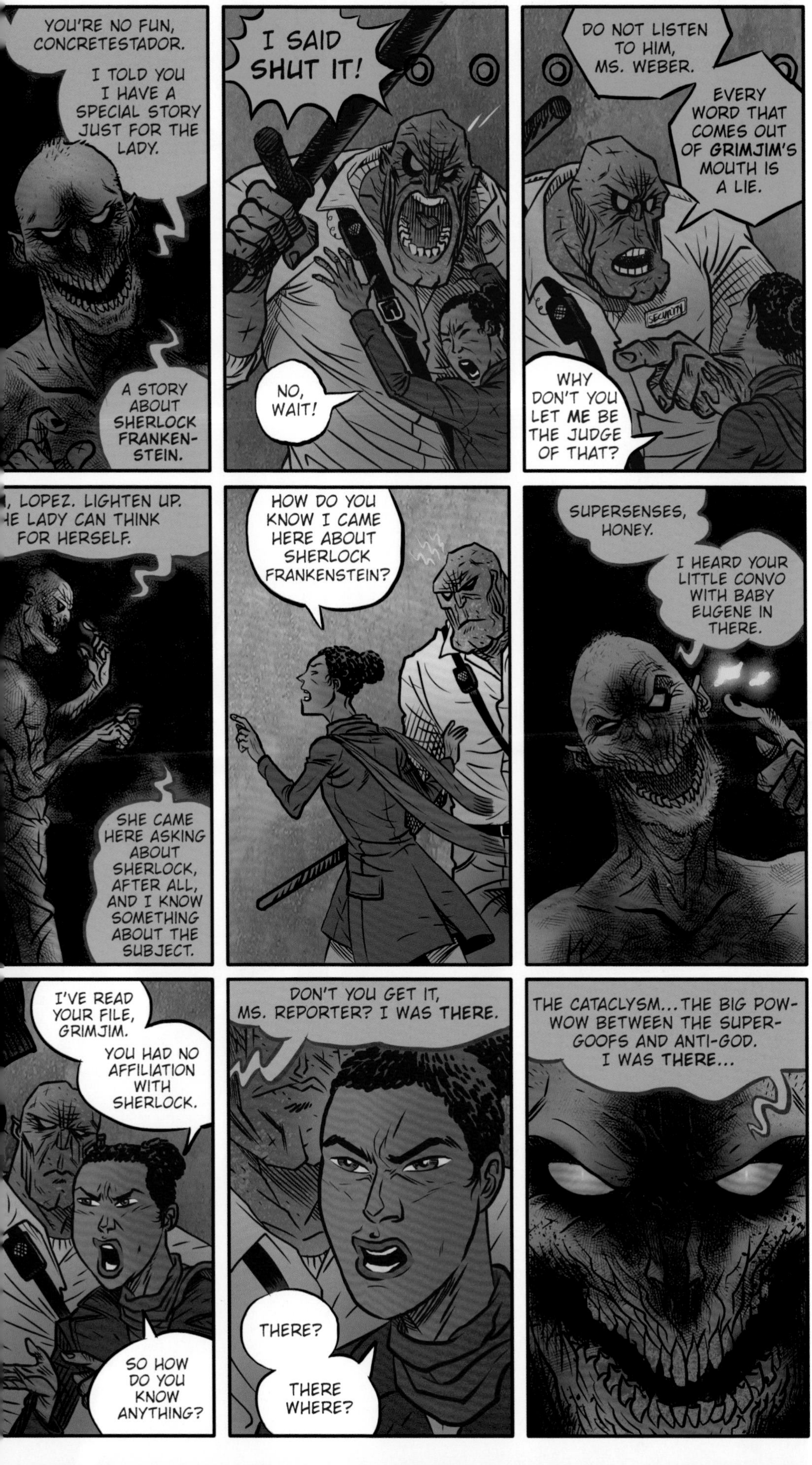

YOU'RE NO FUN, CONCRETESTADOR.
I TOLD YOU I HAVE A SPECIAL STORY JUST FOR THE LADY.
A STORY ABOUT SHERLOCK FRANKEN-STEIN.
I SAID SHUT IT!
NO, WAIT!
DO NOT LISTEN TO HIM, MS. WEBER.
EVERY WORD THAT COMES OUT OF GRIMJIM'S MOUTH IS A LIE.
SECURITY
WHY DON'T YOU LET ME BE THE JUDGE OF THAT?
, LOPEZ. LIGHTEN UP. HE LADY CAN THINK FOR HERSELF.
SHE CAME HERE ASKING ABOUT SHERLOCK, AFTER ALL, AND I KNOW SOMETHING ABOUT THE SUBJECT.
HOW DO YOU KNOW I CAME HERE ABOUT SHERLOCK FRANKENSTEIN?
SUPERSENSES, HONEY.
I HEARD YOUR LITTLE CONVO WITH BABY EUGENE IN THERE.
I'VE READ YOUR FILE, GRIMJIM.
YOU HAD NO AFFILIATION WITH SHERLOCK.
SO HOW DO YOU KNOW ANYTHING?
DON'T YOU GET IT, MS. REPORTER? I WAS THERE.
THERE?
THERE WHERE?
THE CATACLYSM...THE BIG POW-WOW BETWEEN THE SUPER-GOOFS AND ANTI-GOD. I WAS THERE...

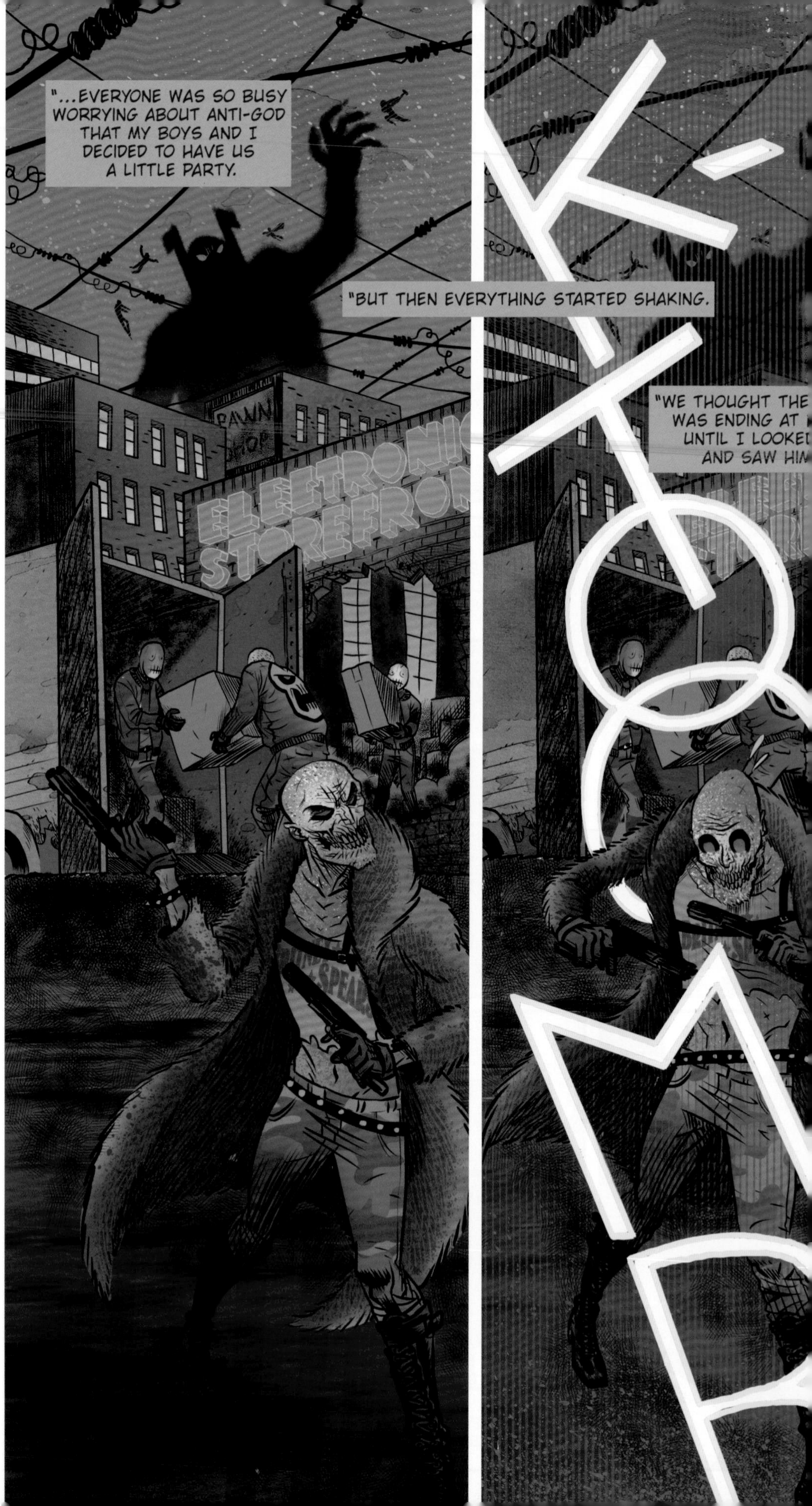
"...EVERYONE WAS SO BUSY WORRYING ABOUT ANTI-GOD THAT MY BOYS AND I DECIDED TO HAVE US A LITTLE PARTY.
"BUT THEN EVERYTHING STARTED SHAKING.
"WE THOUGHT THE WAS ENDING AT UNTIL I LOOKE AND SAW HI

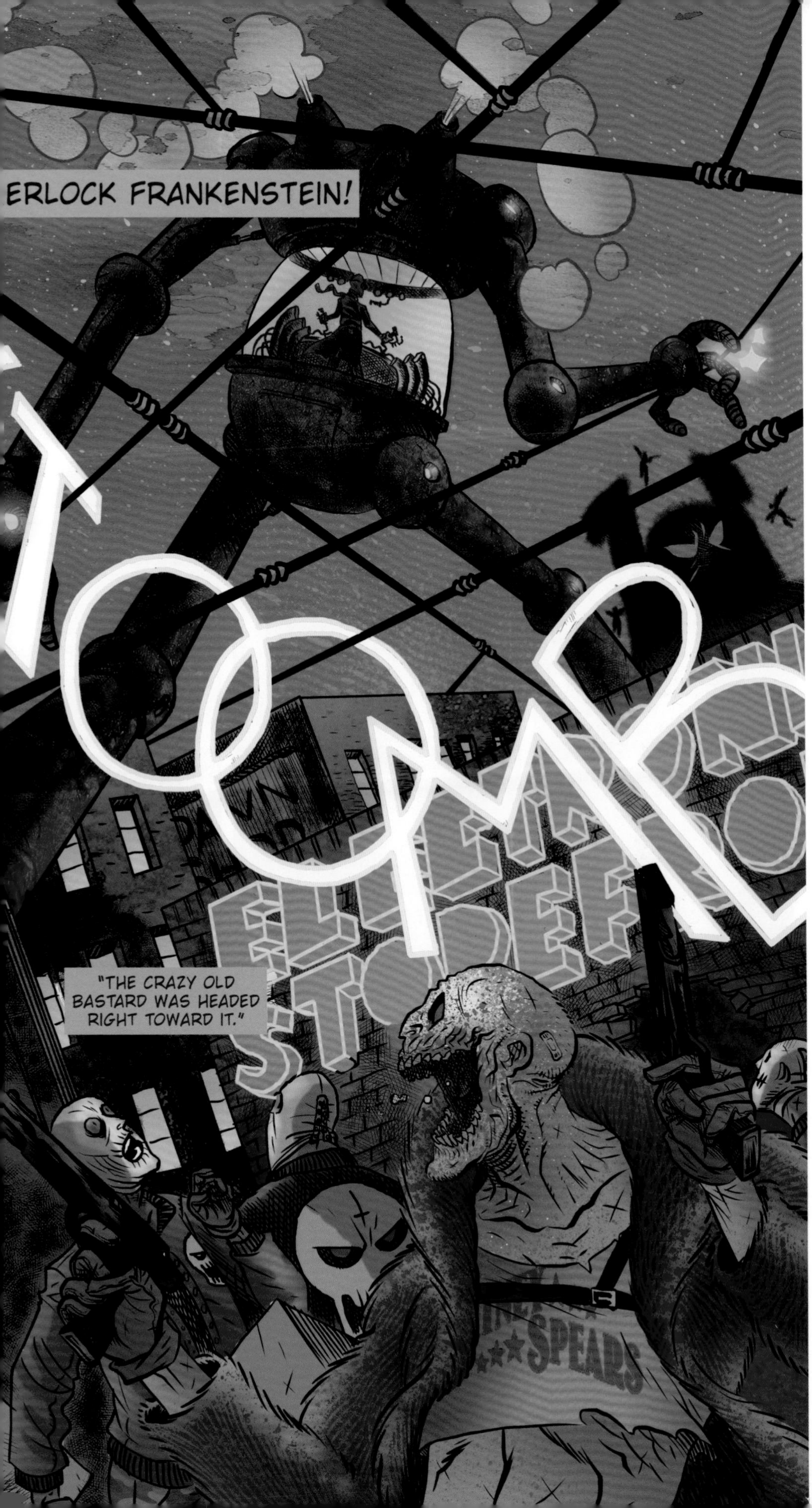
ERLOCK FRANKENSTEIN!
TOOMP
"THE CRAZY OLD BASTARD WAS HEADED RIGHT TOWARD IT."
SPEARS

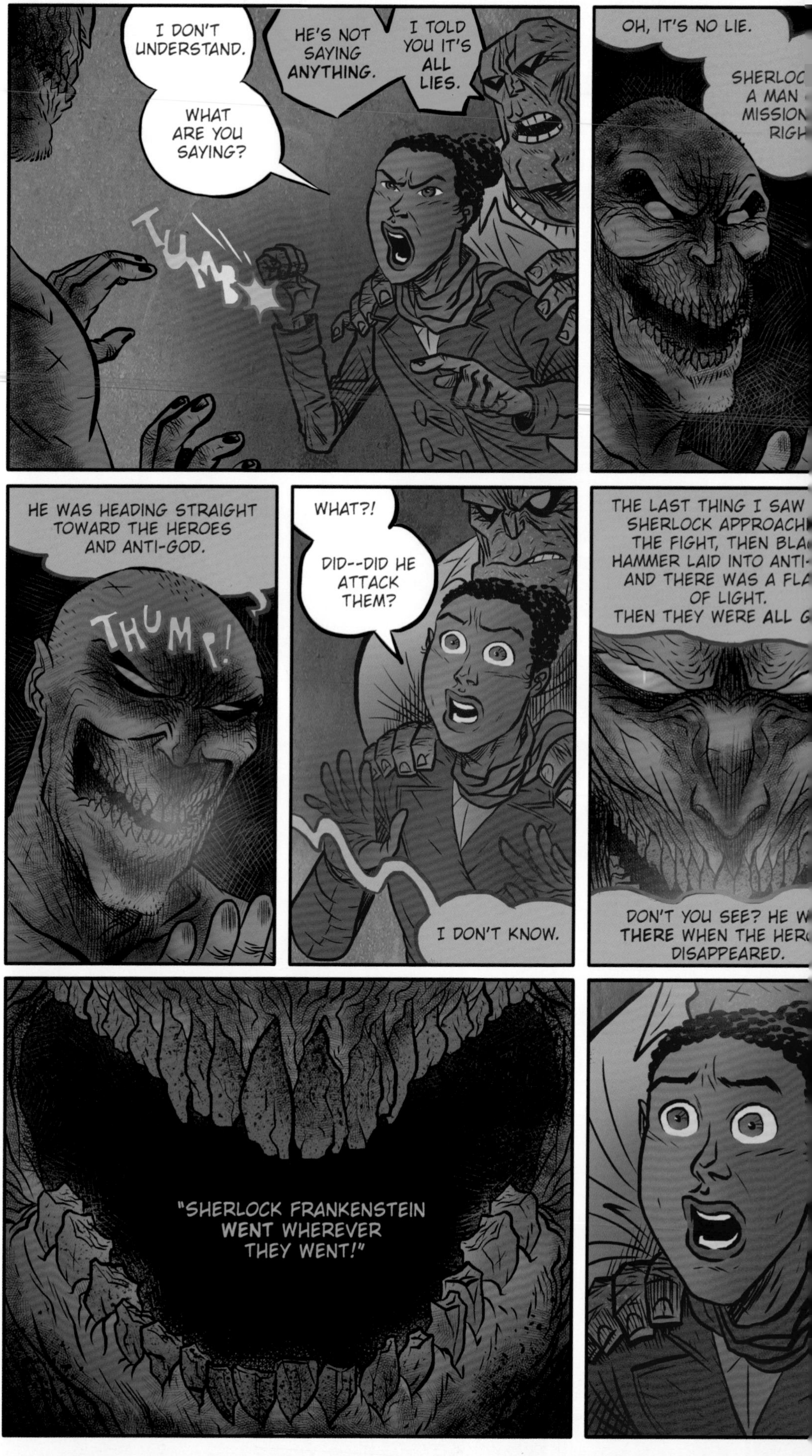
I DON'T UNDERSTAND.
WHAT ARE YOU SAYING?
HE'S NOT SAYING ANYTHING.
I TOLD YOU IT'S ALL LIES.
TUMP
OH, IT'S NO LIE.
SHERLOC
A MAN
MISSION
RIGH
HE WAS HEADING STRAIGHT TOWARD THE HEROES AND ANTI-GOD.
THUMP!
WHAT?!
DID--DID HE ATTACK THEM?
I DON'T KNOW.
THE LAST THING I SAW
SHERLOCK APPROACH
THE FIGHT, THEN BLA
HAMMER LAID INTO ANTI-
AND THERE WAS A FLA
OF LIGHT.
THEN THEY WERE ALL G
DON'T YOU SEE? HE W
THERE WHEN THE HER
DISAPPEARED.
"SHERLOCK FRANKENSTEIN WENT WHEREVER THEY WENT!"

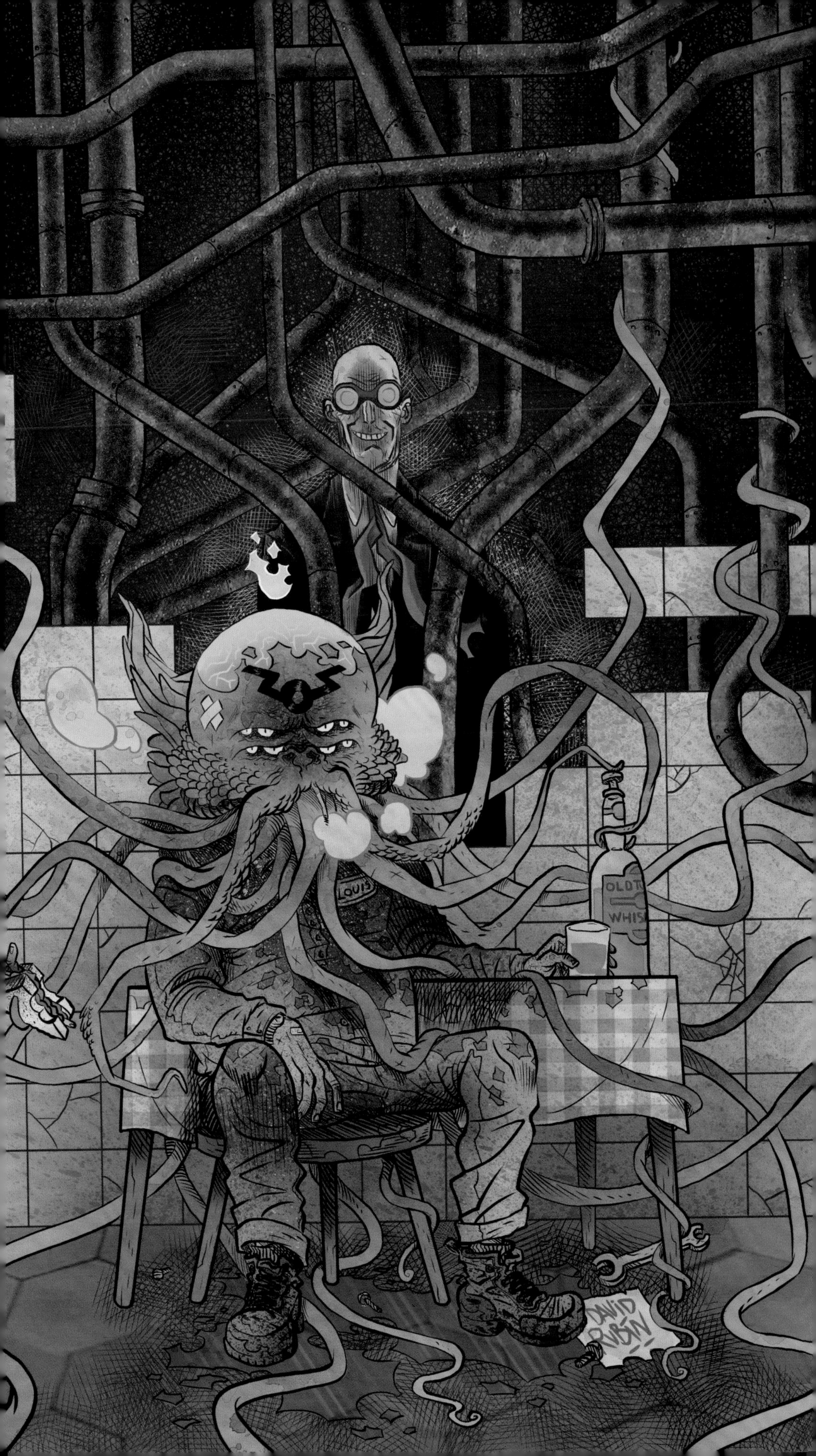
LOUIS
OLD T
WHIS
DAVID RUBÍN

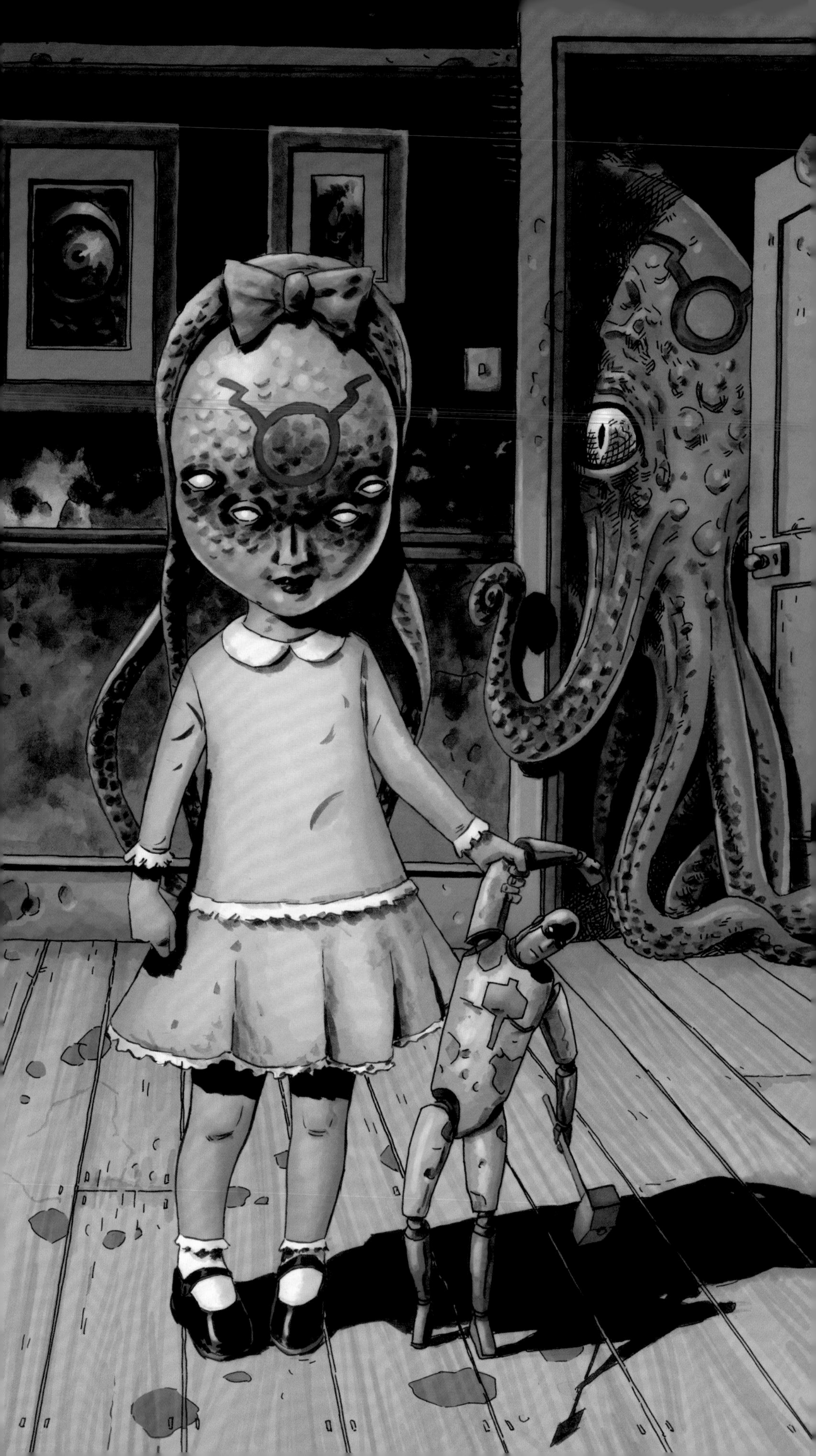

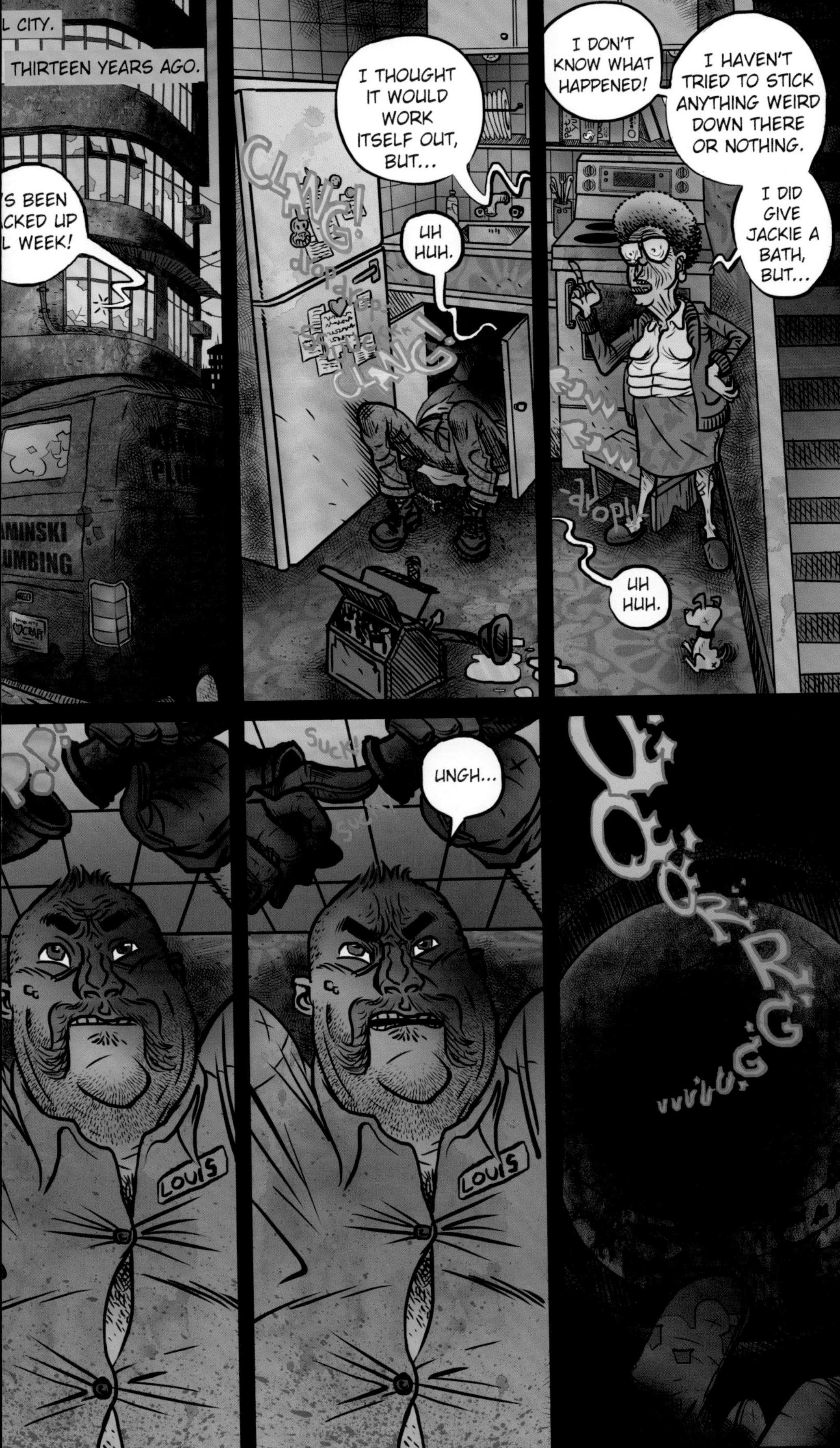
L CITY.
THIRTEEN YEARS AGO.
'S BEEN
CKED UP
L WEEK!
AMINSKI
UMBING
I THOUGHT IT WOULD WORK ITSELF OUT, BUT...
CLNG!
UH HUH.
CLNG!
I DON'T KNOW WHAT HAPPENED!
I HAVEN'T TRIED TO STICK ANYTHING WEIRD DOWN THERE OR NOTHING.
I DID GIVE JACKIE A BATH, BUT...
UH HUH.
LOUIS
SUCK!
UNGH...
LOUIS
VVVLUGG

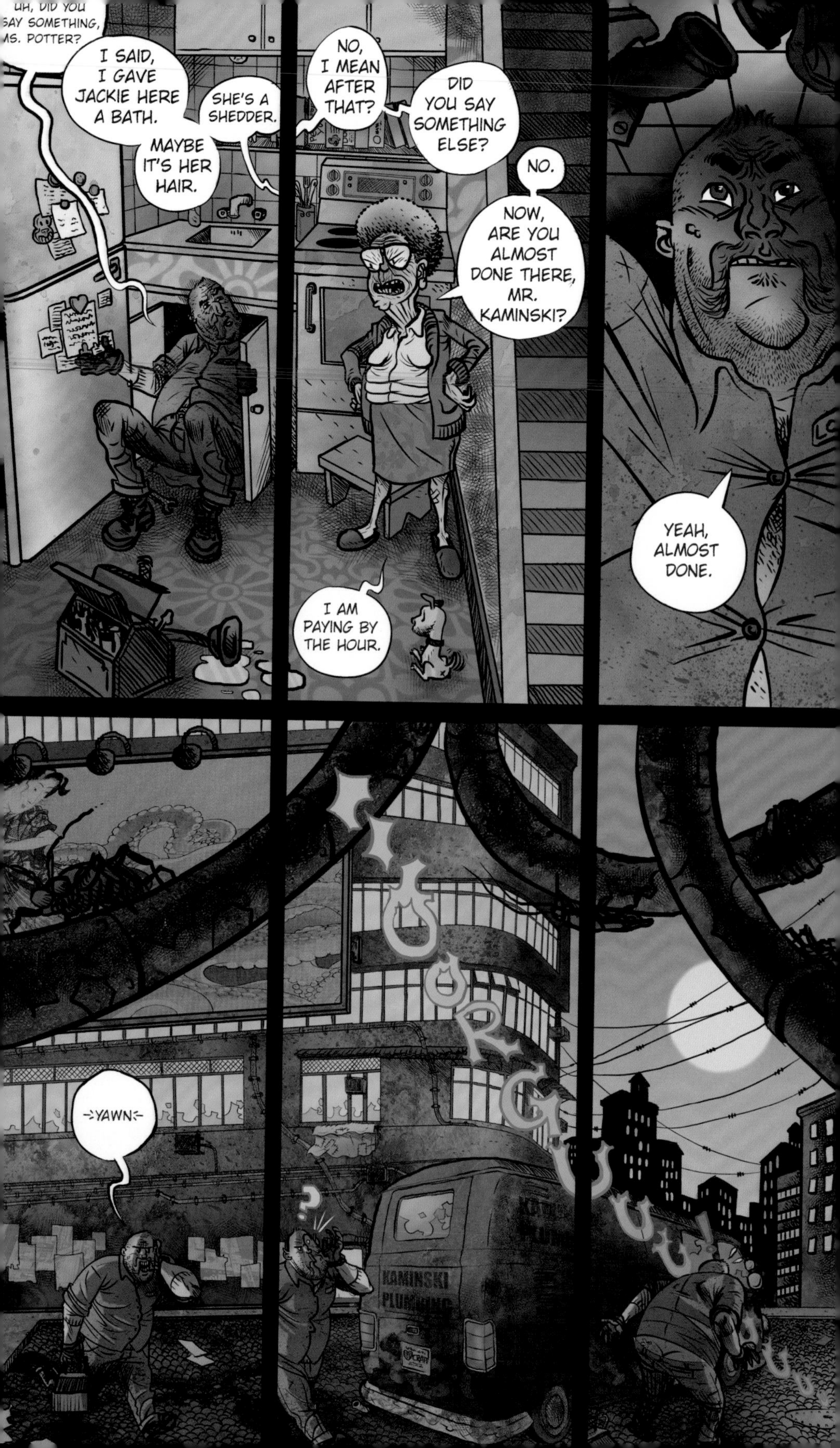
UH, DID YOU SAY SOMETHING, MS. POTTER?
I SAID, I GAVE JACKIE HERE A BATH.
MAYBE IT'S HER HAIR.
SHE'S A SHEDDER.
NO, I MEAN AFTER THAT?
DID YOU SAY SOMETHING ELSE?
NO.
NOW, ARE YOU ALMOST DONE THERE, MR. KAMINSKI?
I AM PAYING BY THE HOUR.
YEAH, ALMOST DONE.
~YAWN~
?
KAMINSKI PLUMBING
UORGUUU!

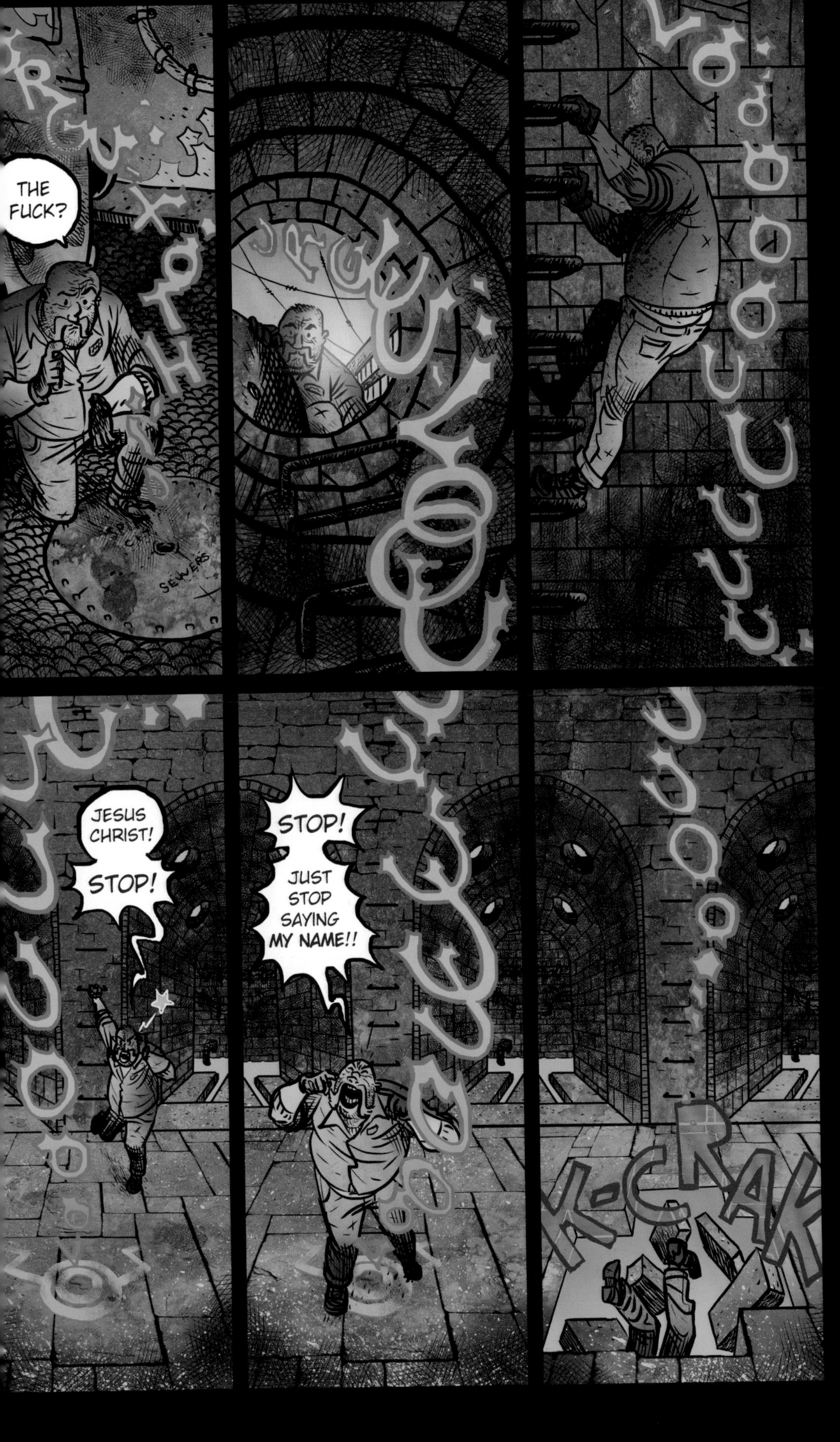
THE FUCK?
SEWERS
JESUS CHRIST!
STOP!
STOP!
JUST STOP SAYING MY NAME!!
K-CRAK

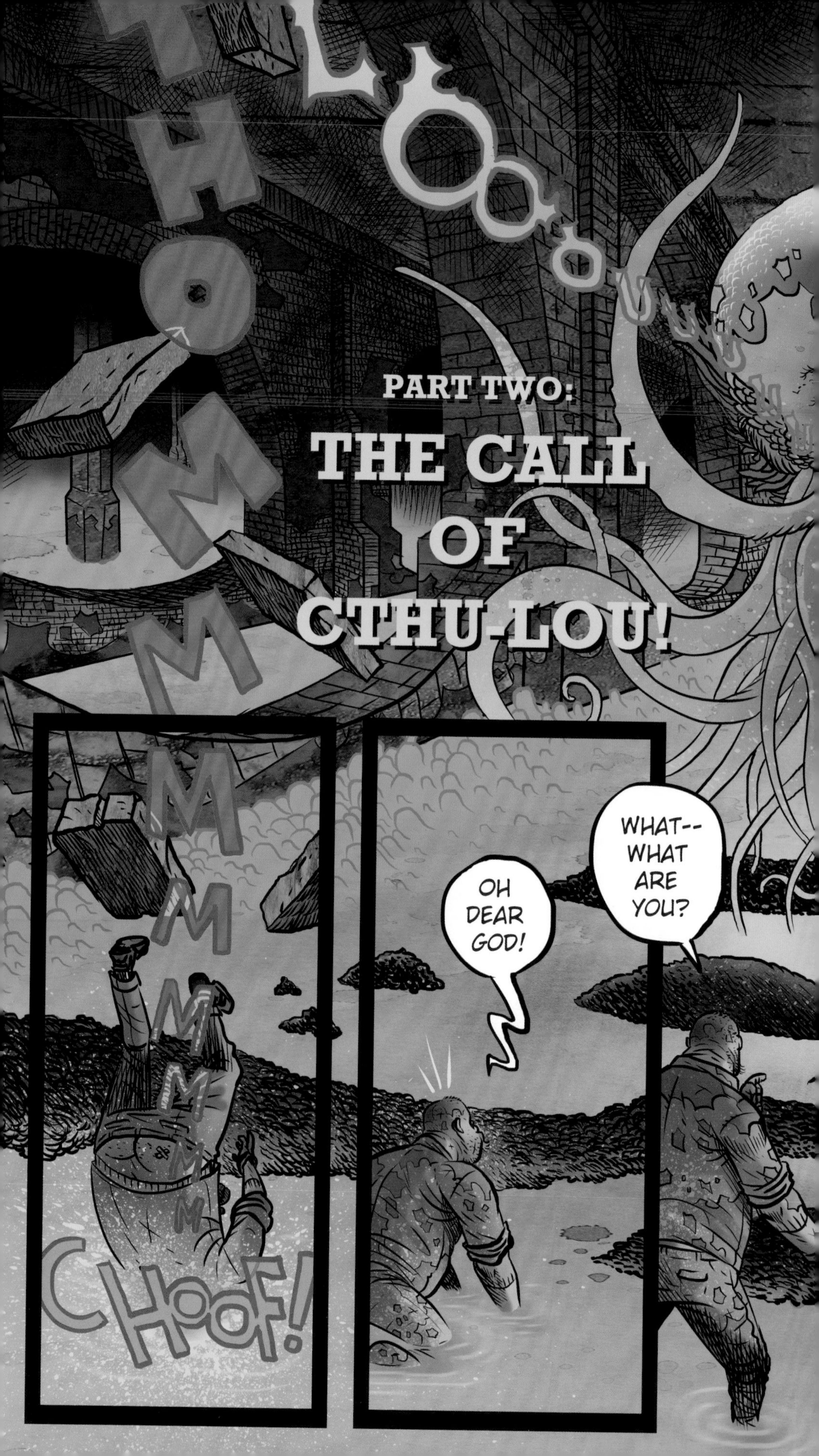

PART TWO:
THE CALL OF CTHU-LOU!
OH DEAR GOD!
WHAT--WHAT ARE YOU?
CHOOF!

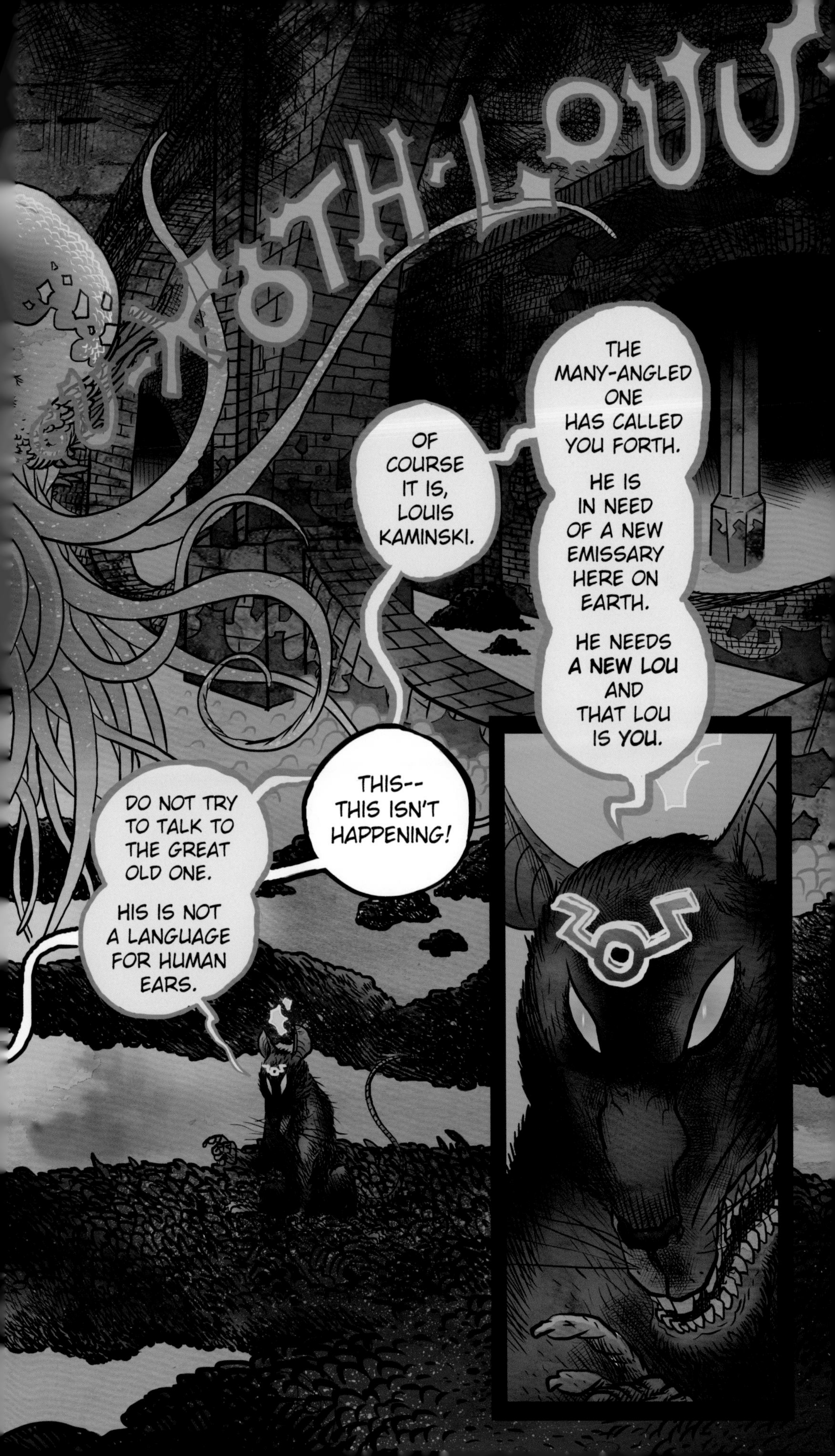
OTH'LOUU
OF COURSE IT IS, LOUIS KAMINSKI.
THE MANY-ANGLED ONE HAS CALLED YOU FORTH.
HE IS IN NEED OF A NEW EMISSARY HERE ON EARTH.
HE NEEDS A NEW LOU AND THAT LOU IS YOU.
DO NOT TRY TO TALK TO THE GREAT OLD ONE.
HIS IS NOT A LANGUAGE FOR HUMAN EARS.
THIS-- THIS ISN'T HAPPENING!

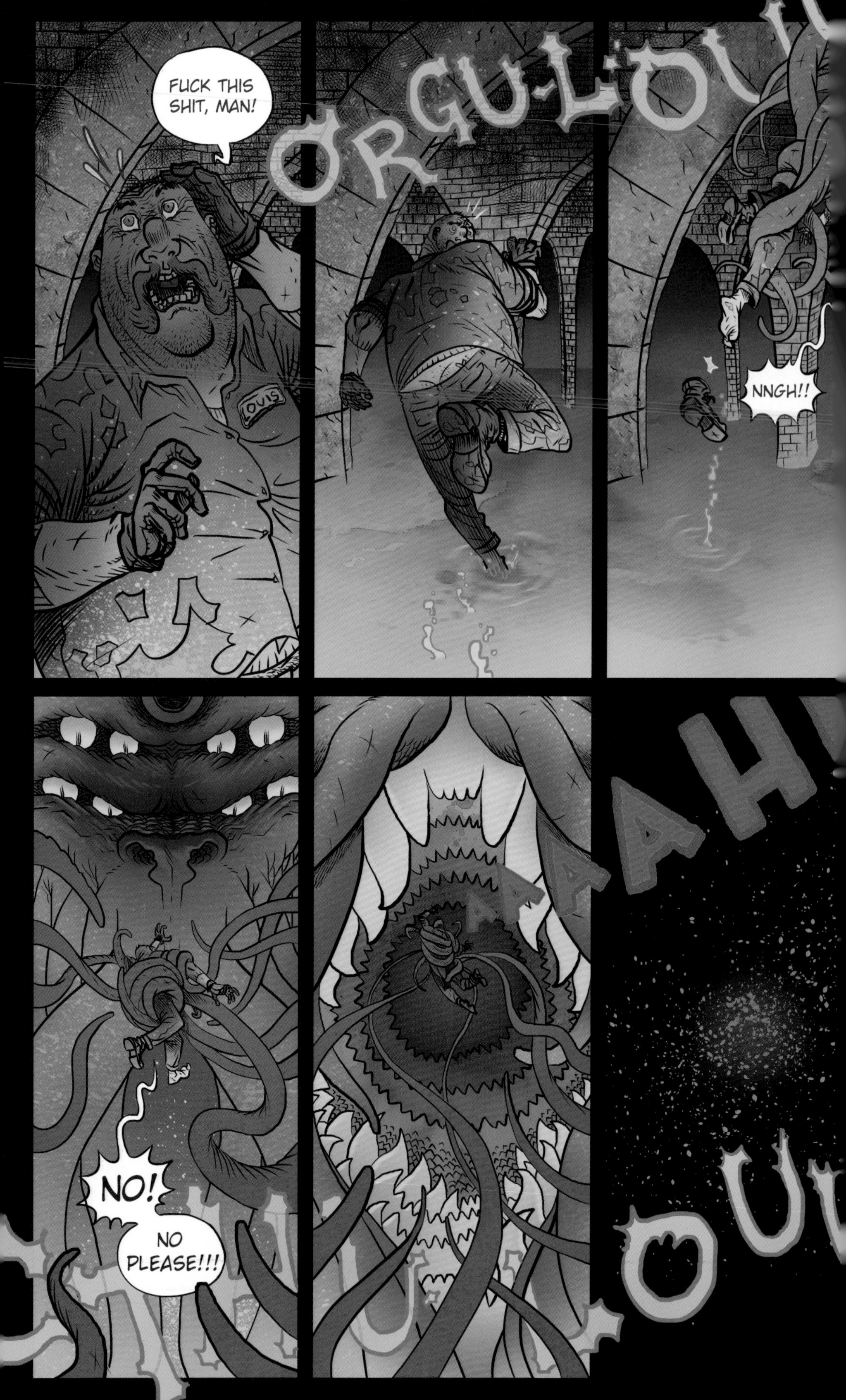
FUCK THIS SHIT, MAN!
ORGU-L'OU
LOUIS
NNGH!!
NO!
NO PLEASE!!!
AAAH

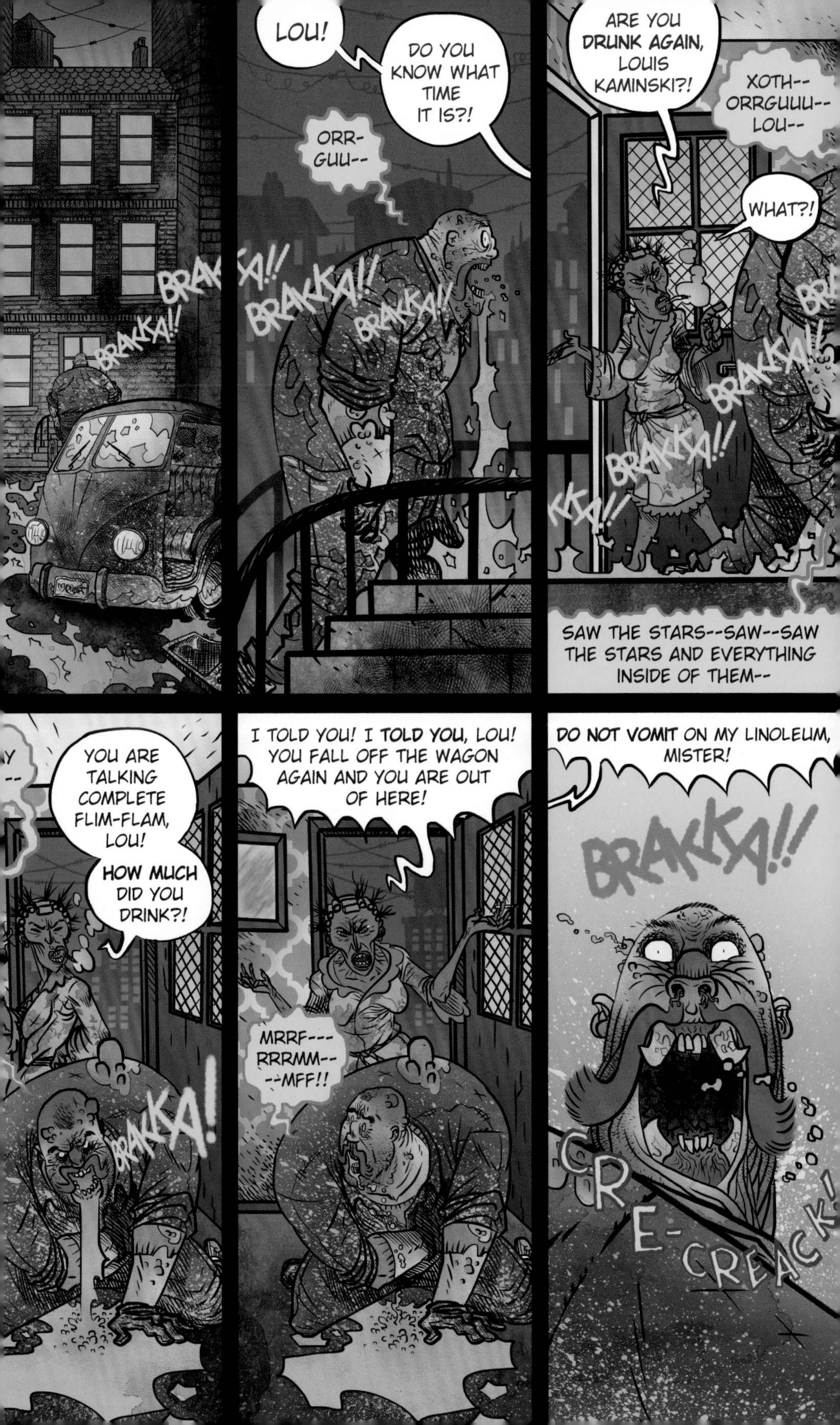

BRAKKA!!
BRAKKA!!
LOU!
DO YOU KNOW WHAT TIME IT IS?!
ORR-GUU--
BRAKKA!!
BRAKKA!!
ARE YOU DRUNK AGAIN, LOUIS KAMINSKI?!
XOTH--ORRGUUU--LOU--
WHAT?!
BRAKKA!!
BRAKKA!!
SAW THE STARS--SAW--SAW THE STARS AND EVERYTHING INSIDE OF THEM--
YOU ARE TALKING COMPLETE FLIM-FLAM, LOU!
HOW MUCH DID YOU DRINK?!
BRAKKA!
I TOLD YOU! I TOLD YOU, LOU! YOU FALL OFF THE WAGON AGAIN AND YOU ARE OUT OF HERE!
MRRF---RRRMM----MFF!!
DO NOT VOMIT ON MY LINOLEUM, MISTER!
BRAKKA!!
CRE-CREACK!

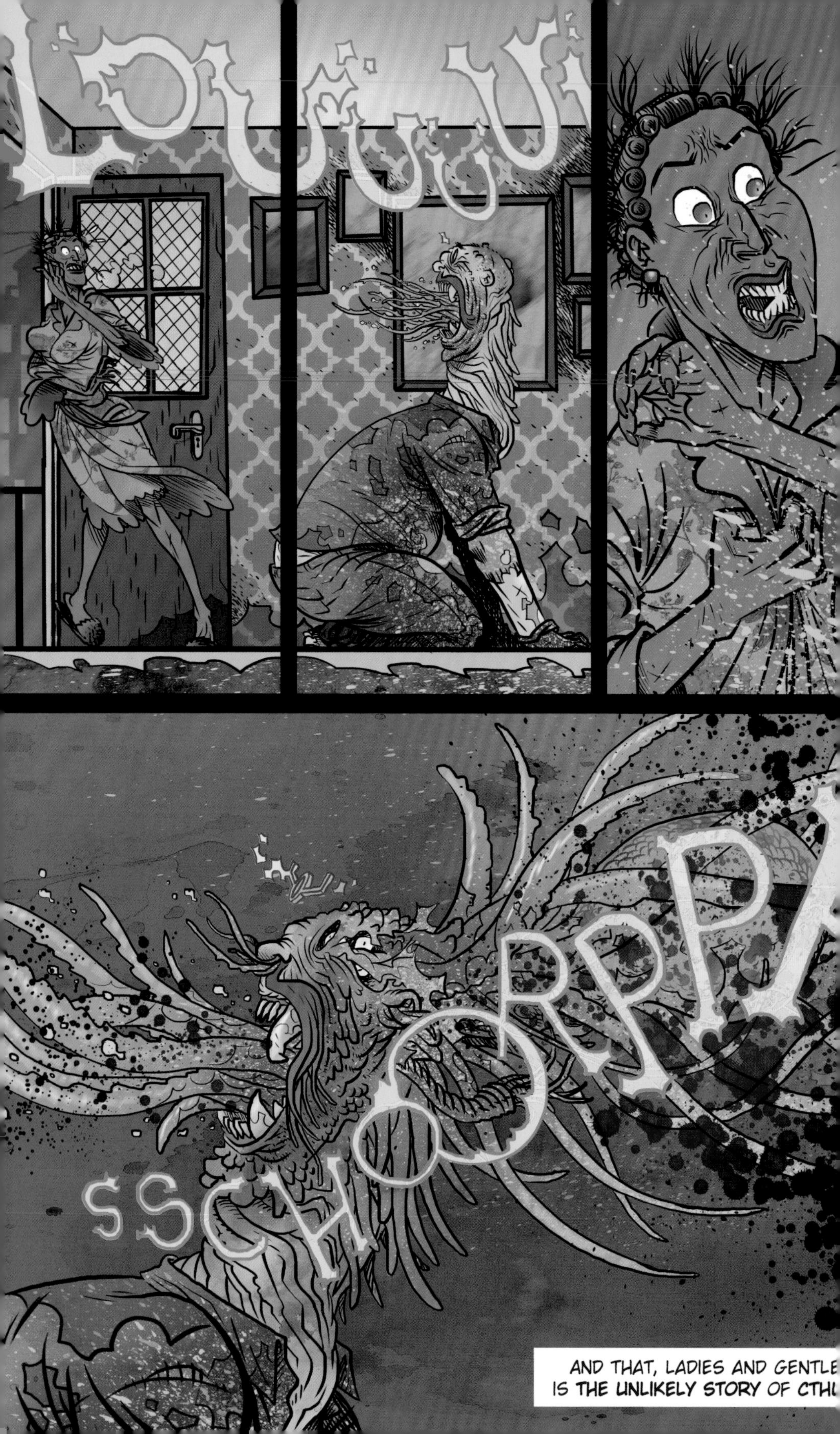
SSCHOORRPP
AND THAT, LADIES AND GENTLE
IS THE UNLIKELY STORY OF CTHU

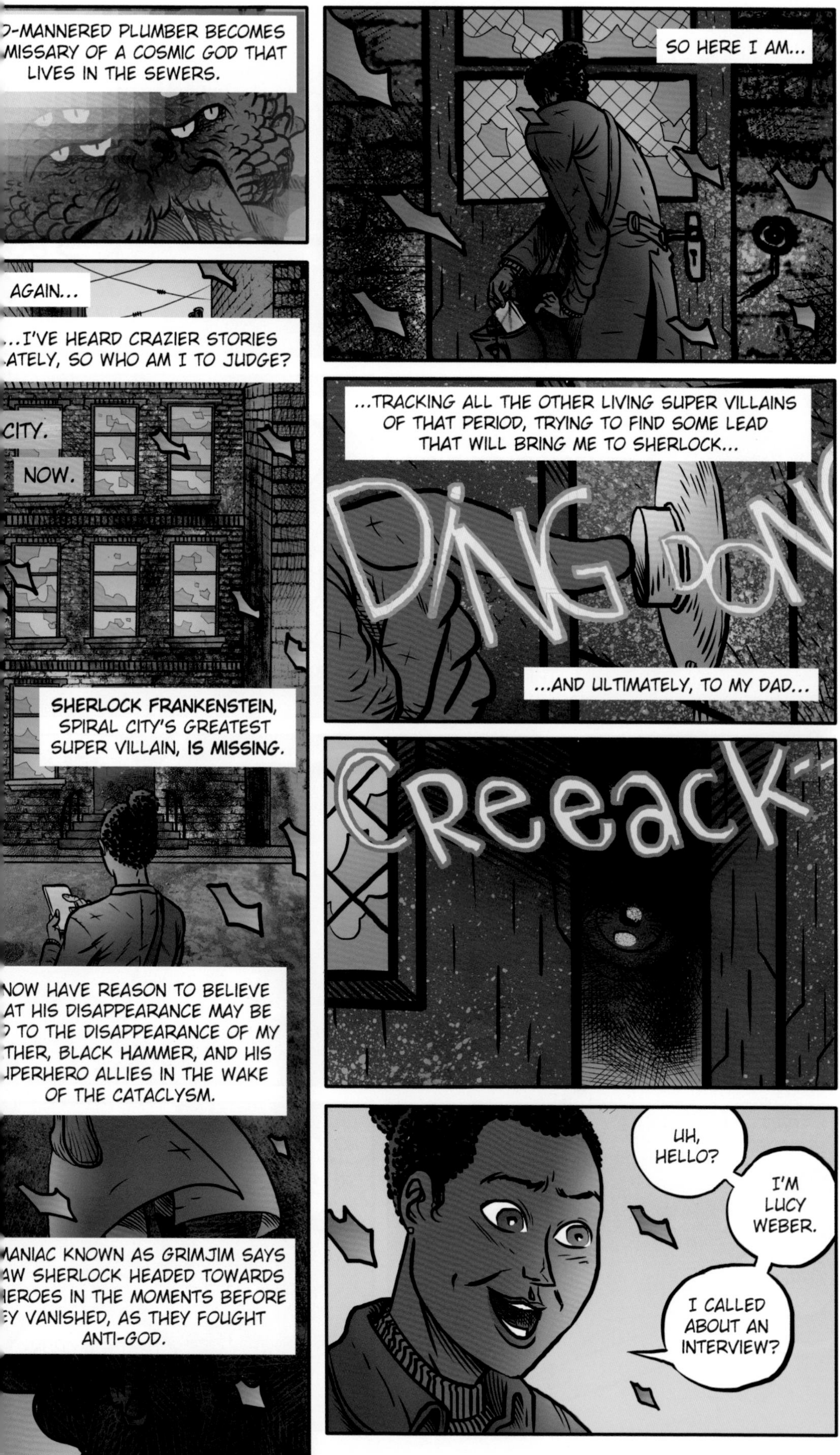

-MANNERED PLUMBER BECOMES
MISSARY OF A COSMIC GOD THAT LIVES IN THE SEWERS.
AGAIN...
...I'VE HEARD CRAZIER STORIES ATELY, SO WHO AM I TO JUDGE?
CITY.
NOW.
SHERLOCK FRANKENSTEIN, SPIRAL CITY'S GREATEST SUPER VILLAIN, IS MISSING.
NOW HAVE REASON TO BELIEVE AT HIS DISAPPEARANCE MAY BE TO THE DISAPPEARANCE OF MY THER, BLACK HAMMER, AND HIS UPERHERO ALLIES IN THE WAKE OF THE CATACLYSM.
MANIAC KNOWN AS GRIMJIM SAYS AW SHERLOCK HEADED TOWARDS HEROES IN THE MOMENTS BEFORE EY VANISHED, AS THEY FOUGHT ANTI-GOD.
SO HERE I AM...
...TRACKING ALL THE OTHER LIVING SUPER VILLAINS OF THAT PERIOD, TRYING TO FIND SOME LEAD THAT WILL BRING ME TO SHERLOCK...
DING DON
...AND ULTIMATELY, TO MY DAD...
CREEACK
UH, HELLO?
I'M LUCY WEBER.
I CALLED ABOUT AN INTERVIEW?

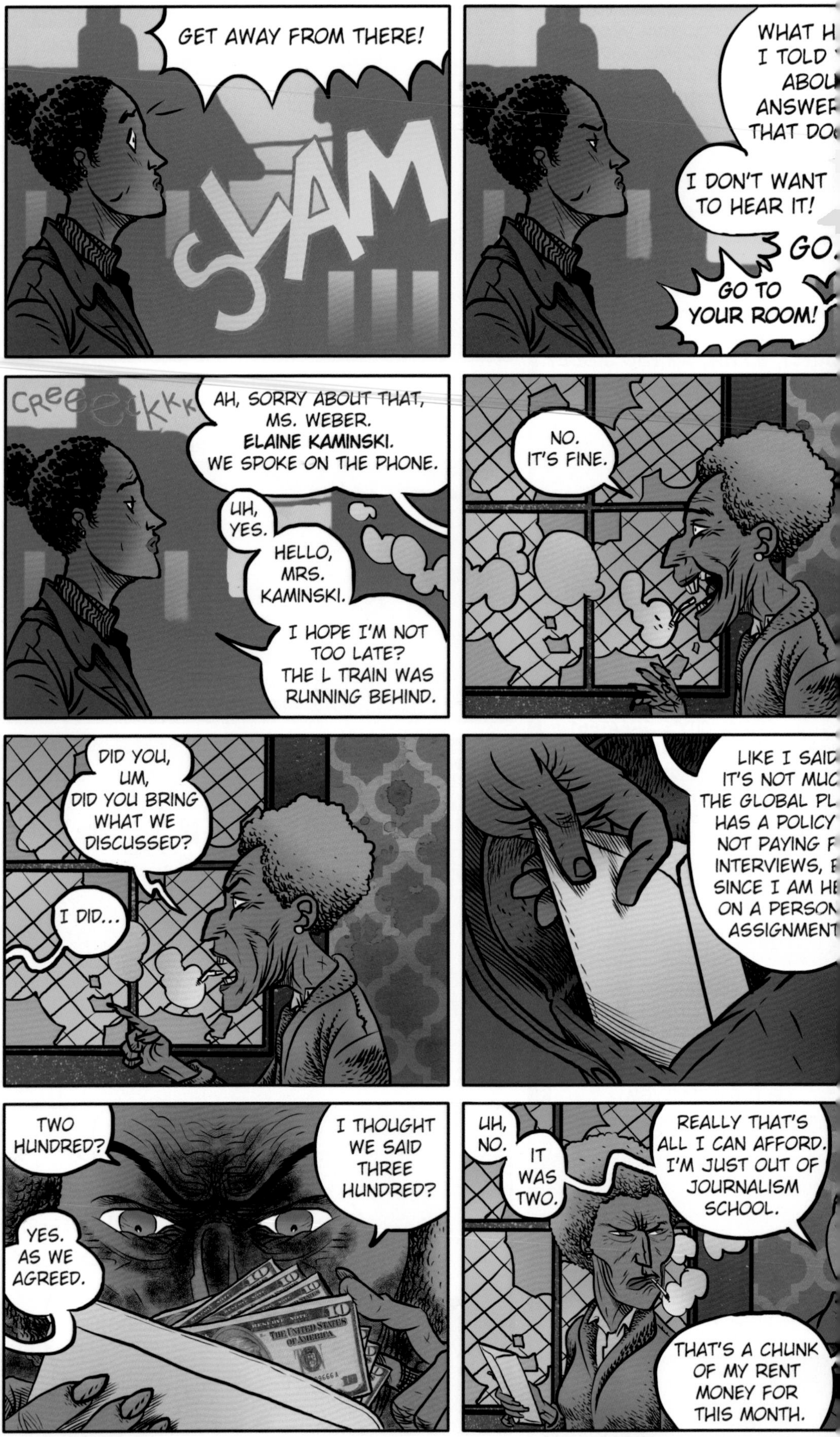
GET AWAY FROM THERE!
SLAM
I DON'T WANT TO HEAR IT!
GO TO YOUR ROOM!
CREEEKKK
AH, SORRY ABOUT THAT, MS. WEBER. ELAINE KAMINSKI. WE SPOKE ON THE PHONE.
UH, YES.
HELLO, MRS. KAMINSKI.
I HOPE I'M NOT TOO LATE? THE L TRAIN WAS RUNNING BEHIND.
NO. IT'S FINE.
DID YOU, UM, DID YOU BRING WHAT WE DISCUSSED?
I DID...
TWO HUNDRED?
I THOUGHT WE SAID THREE HUNDRED?
YES. AS WE AGREED.
UH, NO.
IT WAS TWO.
REALLY THAT'S ALL I CAN AFFORD. I'M JUST OUT OF JOURNALISM SCHOOL.
THAT'S A CHUNK OF MY RENT MONEY FOR THIS MONTH.

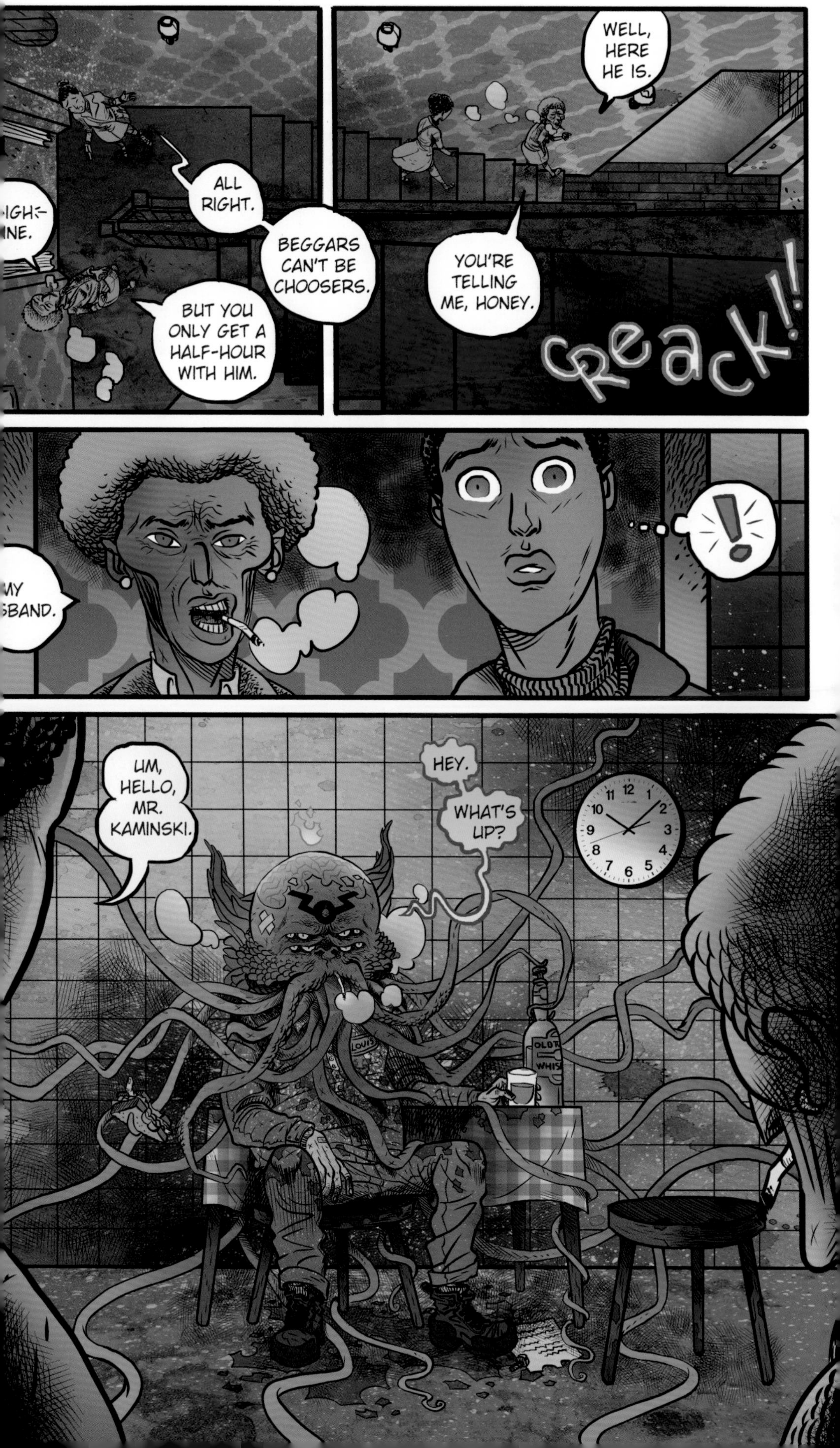

-IGH-
-NE.
ALL RIGHT.
BEGGARS CAN'T BE CHOOSERS.
BUT YOU ONLY GET A HALF-HOUR WITH HIM.
WELL, HERE HE IS.
YOU'RE TELLING ME, HONEY.
CREACK!!
MY
-SBAND.
!
UM, HELLO, MR. KAMINSKI.
HEY.
WHAT'S UP?

SO, MR. KAMINSKI, AS I TOLD YOUR WIFE ON THE PHONE, I WAS HOPING TO SPEAK TO YOU ABOUT YOUR PAST AS CTHU-LOU AND ALSO ABOUT ANY DEALING YOU MAY HAVE HAD WITH SHERLOCK FRANKENSTEIN.

AND I TOLD HER TO TELL YOU, I DON'T KNOW MUCH ABOUT SHERLOCK FRANKENSTEIN.

NEVER EVEN MET HIM.

I KNOW, BUT I'D STILL LIKE TO ASK YOU SOME QUESTIONS.

YOU NEVER KNOW WHAT LITTLE THINGS MAY END UP BEING CLUES.

SURE, SURE.

SO, YO REALLY HAMM DAUGH

YE

HUH.

C
W

WHAT'S THAT FOR?

OH, IT'S JUST FOR TAKING NOTES.

YOU NEVER SAID ANYTHING ABOUT RECORDING THIS.

IT'S FINE.

LIKE HELL IT IS.

ELAINE, WHY DON'T YOU TAKE A WALK, HUH?

I AIN'T GOING NOWHERE, LOU!

ELAINE!!!

HUMPH!

FINE.

AIN'T
I DC
GOT B
THIN
TO
ANY

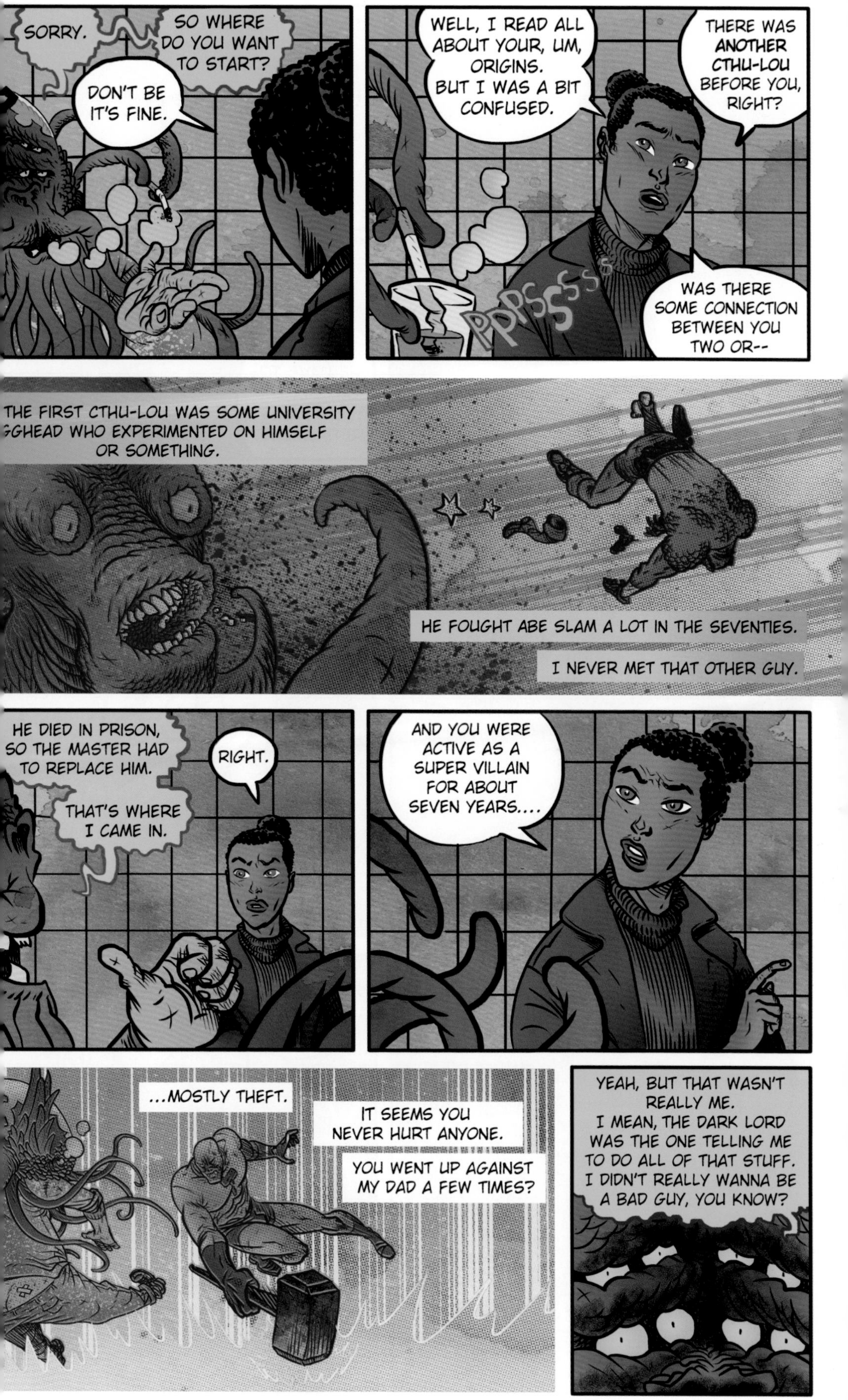

SORRY.
SO WHERE DO YOU WANT TO START?
DON'T BE IT'S FINE.
WELL, I READ ALL ABOUT YOUR, UM, ORIGINS. BUT I WAS A BIT CONFUSED.
THERE WAS ANOTHER CTHU-LOU BEFORE YOU, RIGHT?
PPPSSSSS
WAS THERE SOME CONNECTION BETWEEN YOU TWO OR--
THE FIRST CTHU-LOU WAS SOME UNIVERSITY GGHEAD WHO EXPERIMENTED ON HIMSELF OR SOMETHING.
HE FOUGHT ABE SLAM A LOT IN THE SEVENTIES.
I NEVER MET THAT OTHER GUY.
HE DIED IN PRISON, SO THE MASTER HAD TO REPLACE HIM.
RIGHT.
THAT'S WHERE I CAME IN.
AND YOU WERE ACTIVE AS A SUPER VILLAIN FOR ABOUT SEVEN YEARS....
...MOSTLY THEFT.
IT SEEMS YOU NEVER HURT ANYONE.
YOU WENT UP AGAINST MY DAD A FEW TIMES?
YEAH, BUT THAT WASN'T REALLY ME. I MEAN, THE DARK LORD WAS THE ONE TELLING ME TO DO ALL OF THAT STUFF. I DIDN'T REALLY WANNA BE A BAD GUY, YOU KNOW?

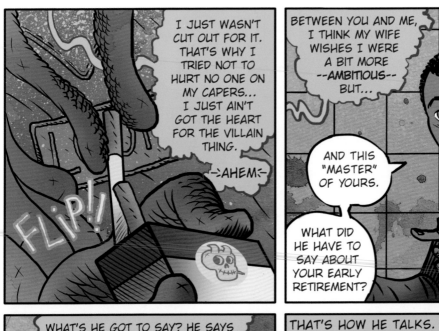

I JUST WASN'T CUT OUT FOR IT. THAT'S WHY I TRIED NOT TO HURT NO ONE ON MY CAPERS... I JUST AIN'T GOT THE HEART FOR THE VILLAIN THING.

->AHEM<-

FLIP!!

BETWEEN YOU AND ME, I THINK MY WIFE WISHES I WERE A BIT MORE --AMBITIOUS-- BUT...

AND THIS "MASTER" OF YOURS.

WHAT DID HE HAVE TO SAY ABOUT YOUR EARLY RETIREMENT?

WHAT'S HE GOT TO SAY? HE SAYS "ORRRGGUUUU-LOUUUUU--" AND SHIT LIKE THAT.

EXCUSE ME?

THAT'S HOW HE TALKS. I HEAR HIM IN MY HEAD ALL THE TIME, BUT I PRETTY MUCH LEARNED TO IGNORE HIM.

I MEA... HE ALRE... TURNED... INTO A GO... OCTOPUS... WHAT EL... HE GON... DO TO...

GOTTA SAY THOUGH, IT'S BEEN PRETTY HARD MAKING ENDS MEET. NO ONE WANTS TO HIRE A PLUMBER THAT LOOKS LIKE CALAMARI, YOU KNOW WHAT I MEAN?

BUT IT DON'T MATTER NOW. THOSE DAYS ARE OVER. I RETIRED RIGHT BEFORE THE CATACLYSM. SO, LIKE I SAID, I HAD NO PART IN WHAT SHERLOCK WAS PLANNING.

PLANNING?

HUH?

YOU SAID, "WHAT SHERLOCK WAS PLANNING." WHAT DID YOU MEAN BY THAT?

H, I DON'T KNOW. RD THAT HE CALLED A EETING WHEN THAT GOD GUY SHOWED UP STARTED DESTROYING EVERYTHING.

A MEETING? WHAT KIND OF MEETING, MR. KAMINSKI? PLEASE, THIS COULD BE VERY IMPORTANT.

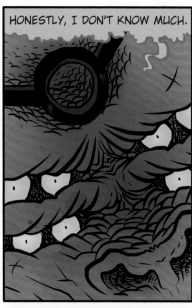

HONESTLY, I DON'T KNOW MUCH.

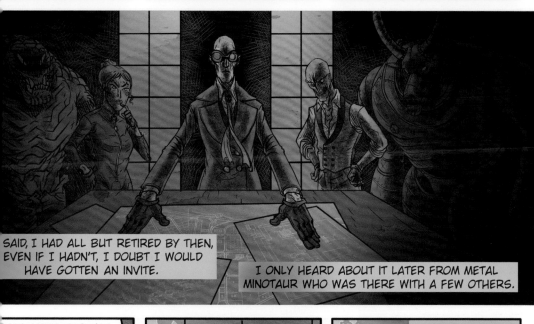

SAID, I HAD ALL BUT RETIRED BY THEN, EVEN IF I HADN'T, I DOUBT I WOULD HAVE GOTTEN AN INVITE.

I ONLY HEARD ABOUT IT LATER FROM METAL MINOTAUR WHO WAS THERE WITH A FEW OTHERS.

HAT HAPPENED? WAS LOCK PLANNING SOME OF ATTACK ON THE ES WHILE THEY WERE EADY PRE-OCCUPIED ITH ANTI-GOD?

I DON'T KNOW. HONESTLY. METAL MINOTAUR DIDN'T SAY ANYTHING ELSE ABOUT IT.

I'M REALLY SORRY, MS. WEBER...

...I WISH I COULD BE OF MORE HELP.

IT'S-- IT'S ALL RIGHT.

YOU'VE GIVEN ME SOMETHING ELSE TO WORK ON.

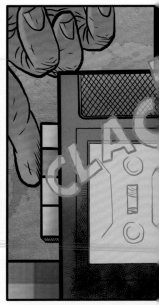

CLAC

THANK YOU AGAIN, MR. KAMINSKI.

CALL ME LOU.

AND REALLY, IT WAS NO BOTHER.

OH!

CREEEAACKK

WHAT ARE YOU DOING SKU
AROUND OUT THERE?
COME ON IN IF YOU WAN
DON'T MAKE NO DIFFERE

THIS IS MY LITTLE GIRL, LOUISE.

I LIKE CTHU-LOUISE BETTER.

HELLO, CTHU-LOUISE.

MY NAME IS LUCY.

SO, ARE YOU TALKING TO MY DAD 'CAUSE HE WAS A SUPER VILLAIN?

YEP.

AND YOU KNOW WHAT?

MY DAD USED TO BE A **SUPERHERO**.

YBE MEANS 'RE A BE NEMIES DAY.

HEH.

MAYBE.

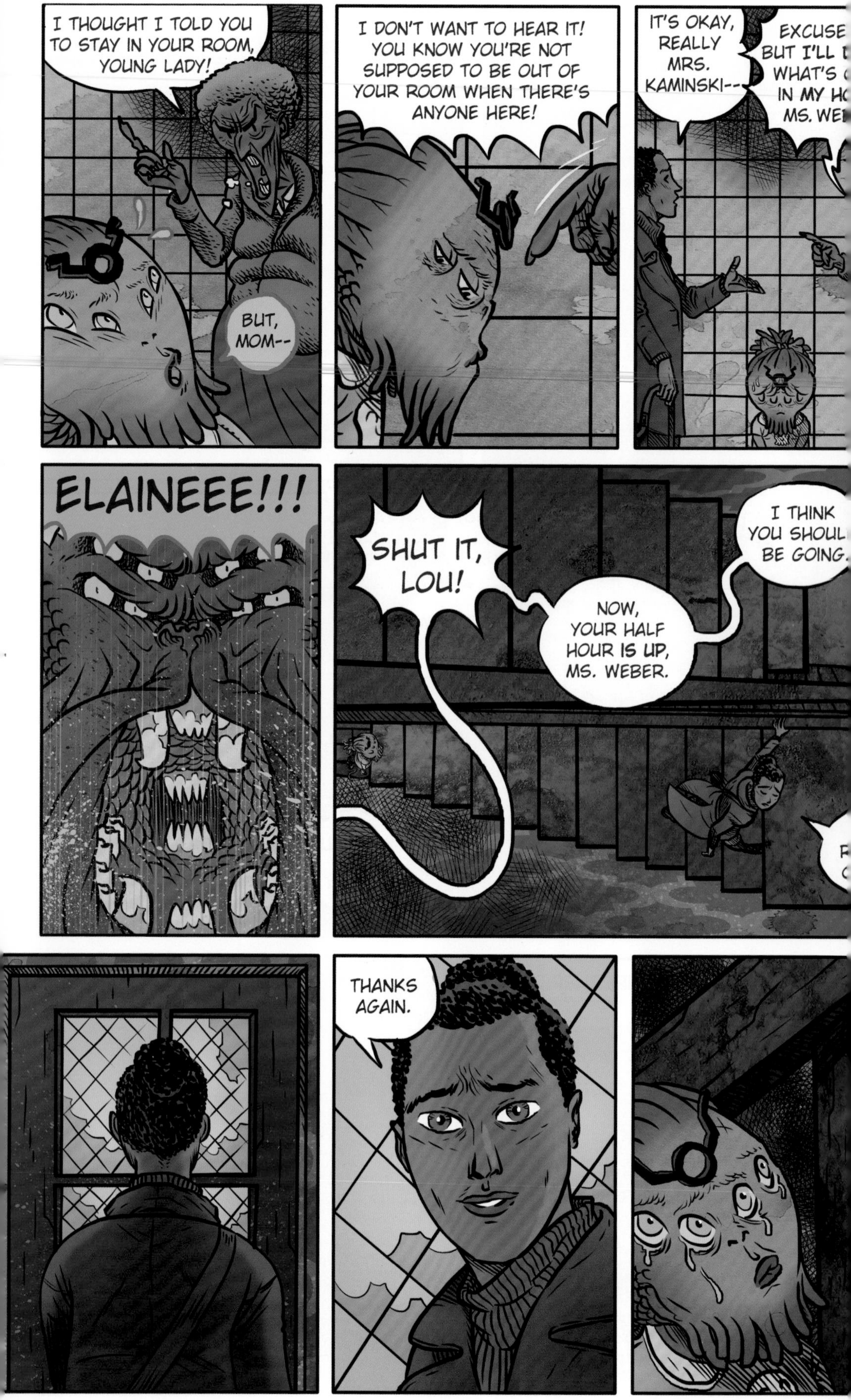
I THOUGHT I TOLD YOU TO STAY IN YOUR ROOM, YOUNG LADY!
BUT, MOM--
I DON'T WANT TO HEAR IT! YOU KNOW YOU'RE NOT SUPPOSED TO BE OUT OF YOUR ROOM WHEN THERE'S ANYONE HERE!
IT'S OKAY, REALLY MRS. KAMINSKI--
EXCUSE BUT I'LL WHAT'S IN MY MS.
ELAINEEE!!!
SHUT IT, LOU!
NOW, YOUR HALF HOUR IS UP, MS. WEBER.
I THINK YOU SHOUL BE GOING.
THANKS AGAIN.

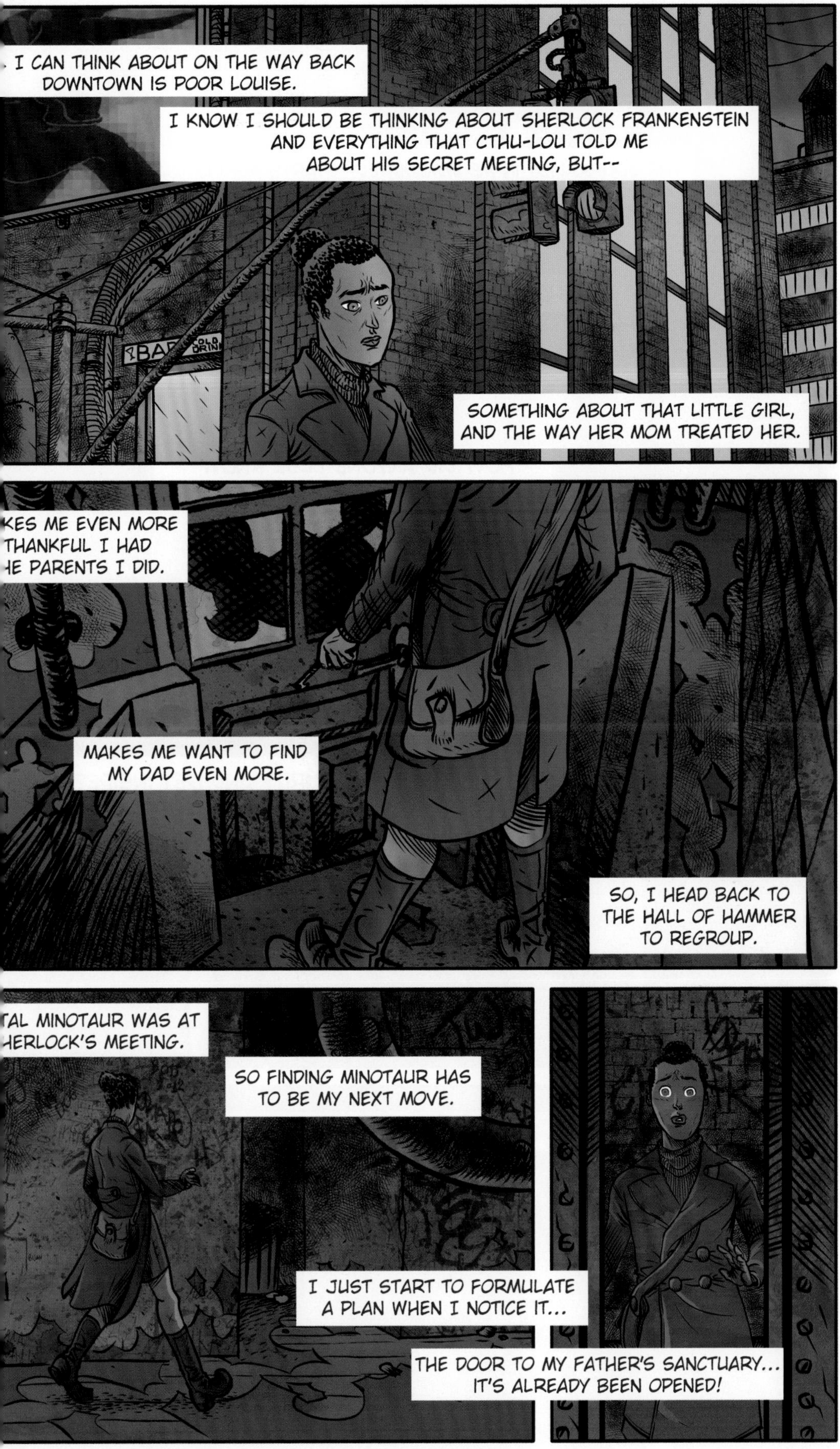
I CAN THINK ABOUT ON THE WAY BACK DOWNTOWN IS POOR LOUISE.
I KNOW I SHOULD BE THINKING ABOUT SHERLOCK FRANKENSTEIN AND EVERYTHING THAT CTHU-LOU TOLD ME ABOUT HIS SECRET MEETING, BUT--
SOMETHING ABOUT THAT LITTLE GIRL, AND THE WAY HER MOM TREATED HER.
KES ME EVEN MORE THANKFUL I HAD HE PARENTS I DID.
MAKES ME WANT TO FIND MY DAD EVEN MORE.
SO, I HEAD BACK TO THE HALL OF HAMMER TO REGROUP.
TAL MINOTAUR WAS AT HERLOCK'S MEETING.
SO FINDING MINOTAUR HAS TO BE MY NEXT MOVE.
I JUST START TO FORMULATE A PLAN WHEN I NOTICE IT...
THE DOOR TO MY FATHER'S SANCTUARY... IT'S ALREADY BEEN OPENED!

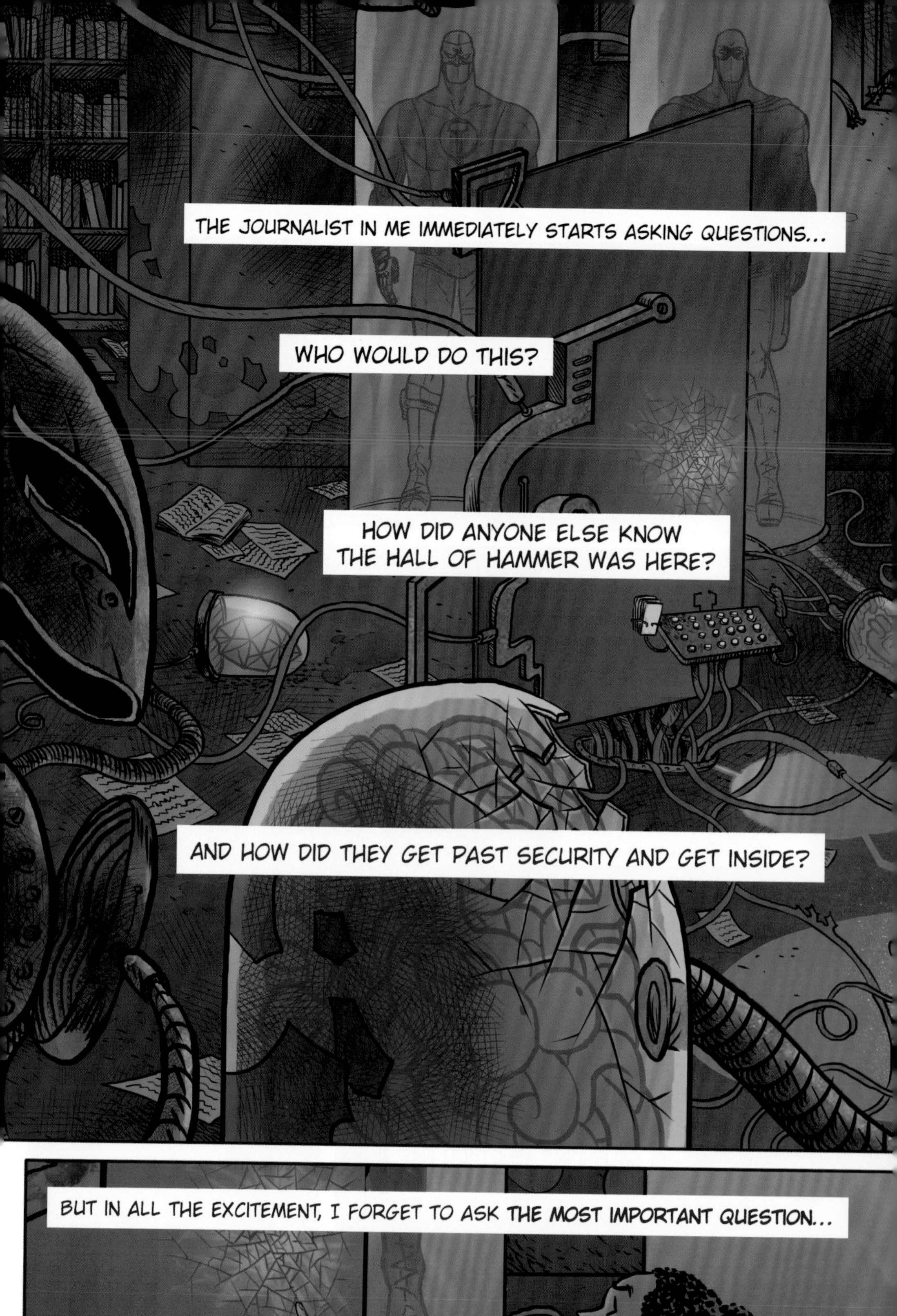
THE JOURNALIST IN ME IMMEDIATELY STARTS ASKING QUESTIONS...
WHO WOULD DO THIS?
HOW DID ANYONE ELSE KNOW THE HALL OF HAMMER WAS HERE?
AND HOW DID THEY GET PAST SECURITY AND GET INSIDE?

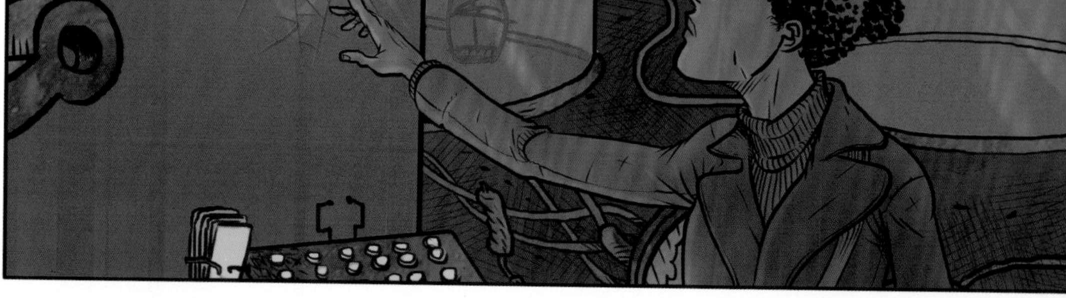
BUT IN ALL THE EXCITEMENT, I FORGET TO ASK THE MOST IMPORTANT QUESTION...

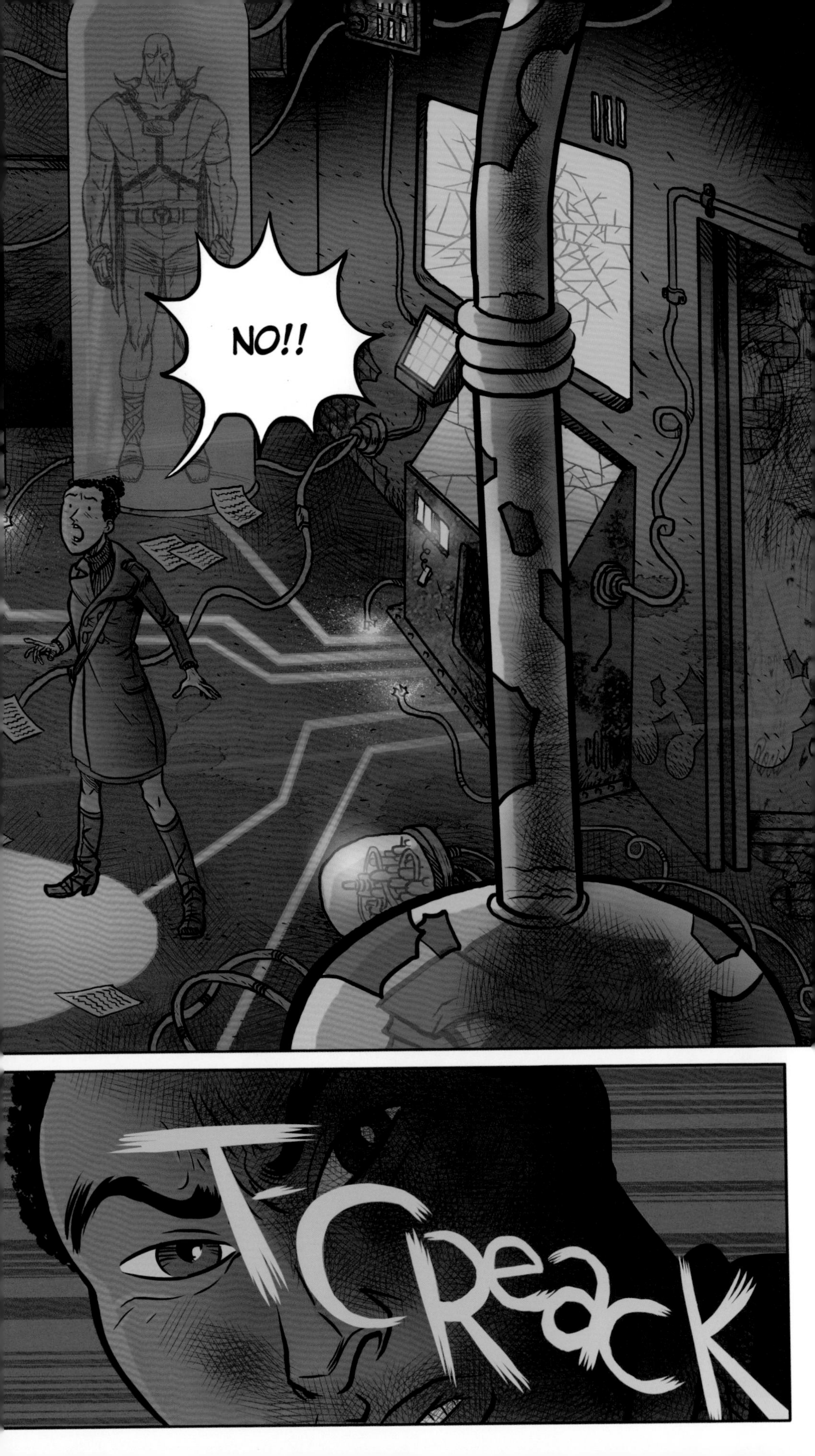
NO!!
T
CReack

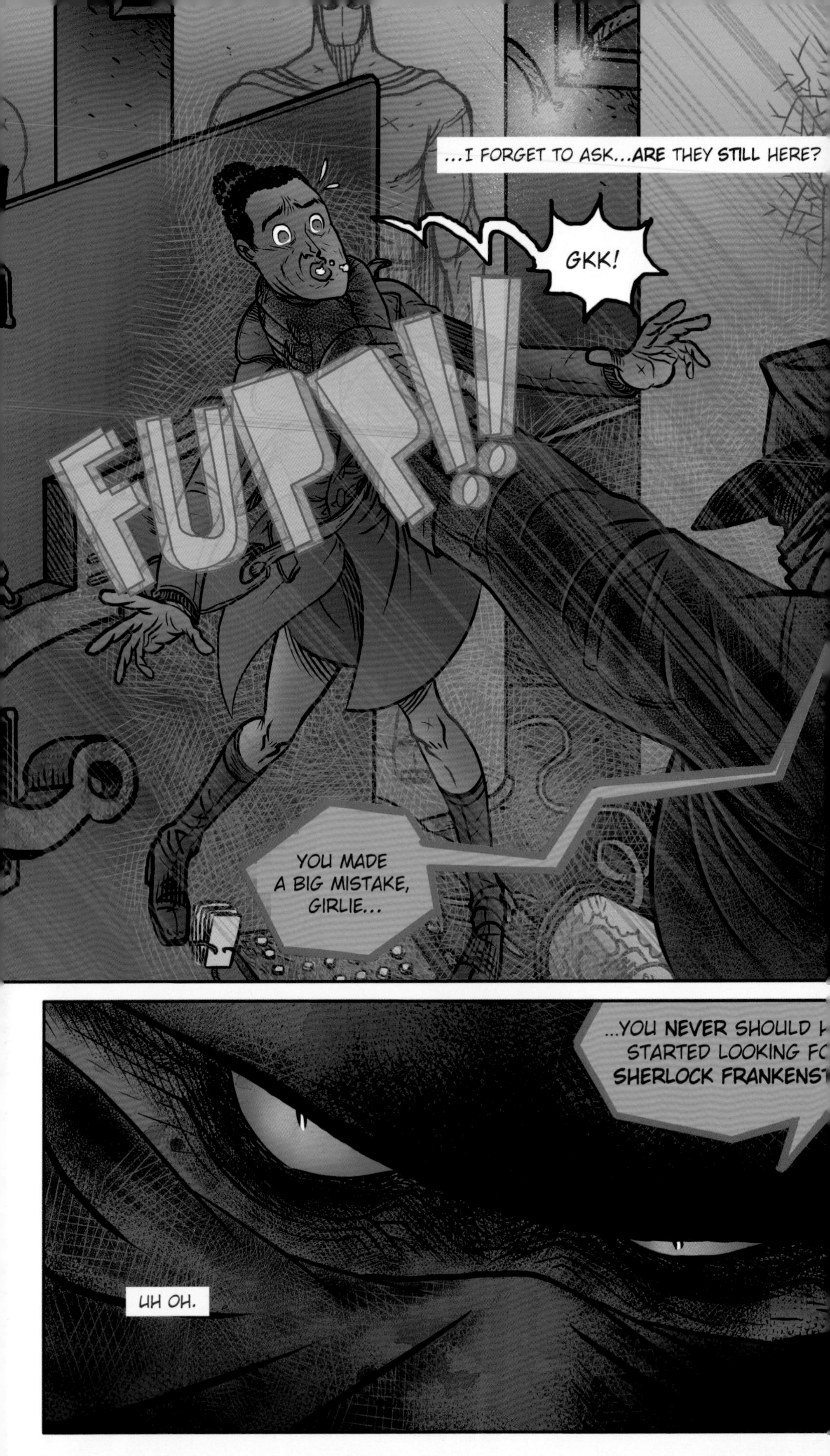
...I FORGET TO ASK...ARE THEY STILL HERE?
GKK!
FUPP!!
YOU MADE A BIG MISTAKE, GIRLIE...
...YOU NEVER SHOULD
STARTED LOOKING F
SHERLOCK FRANKENS
UH OH.

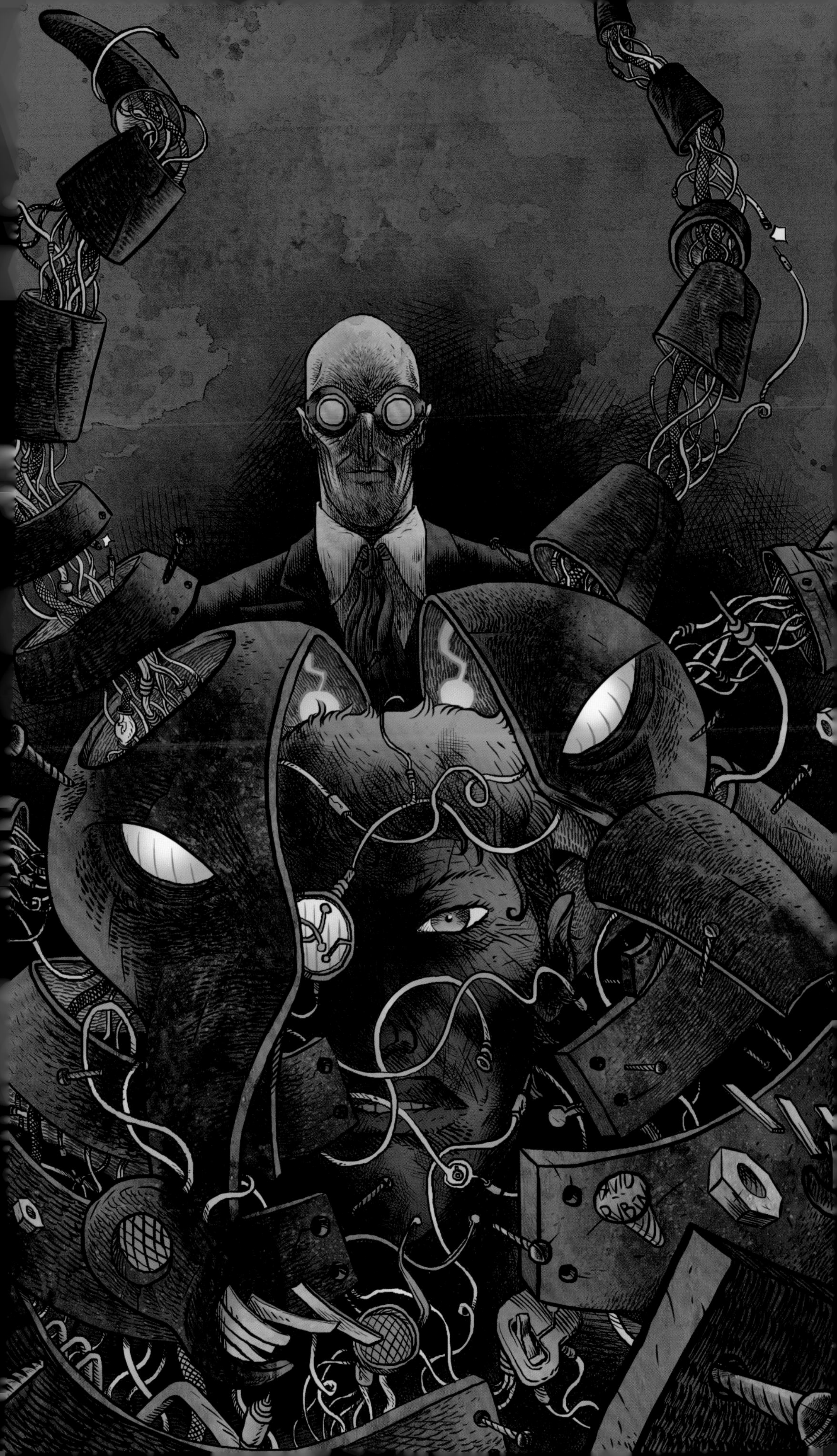

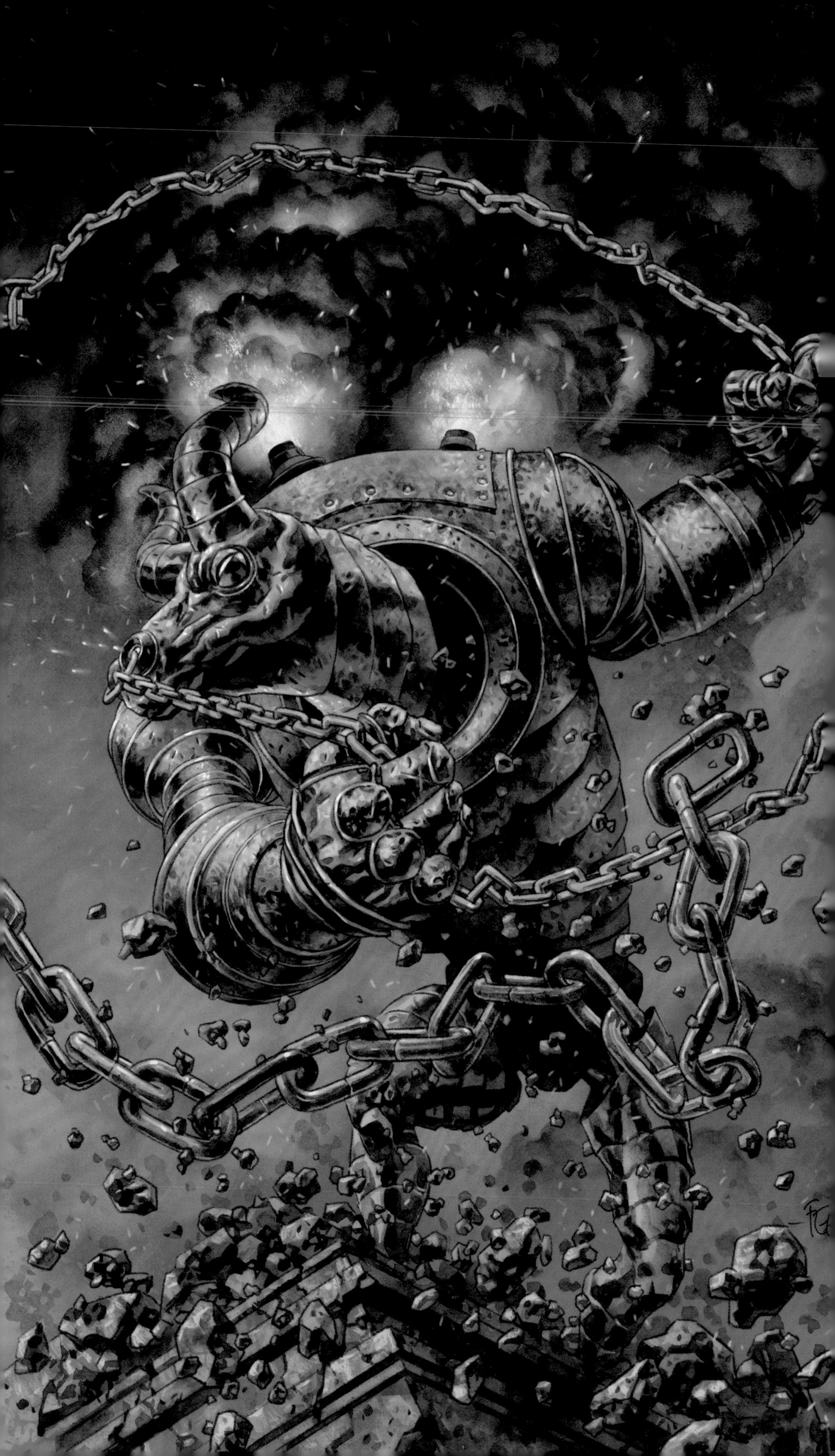

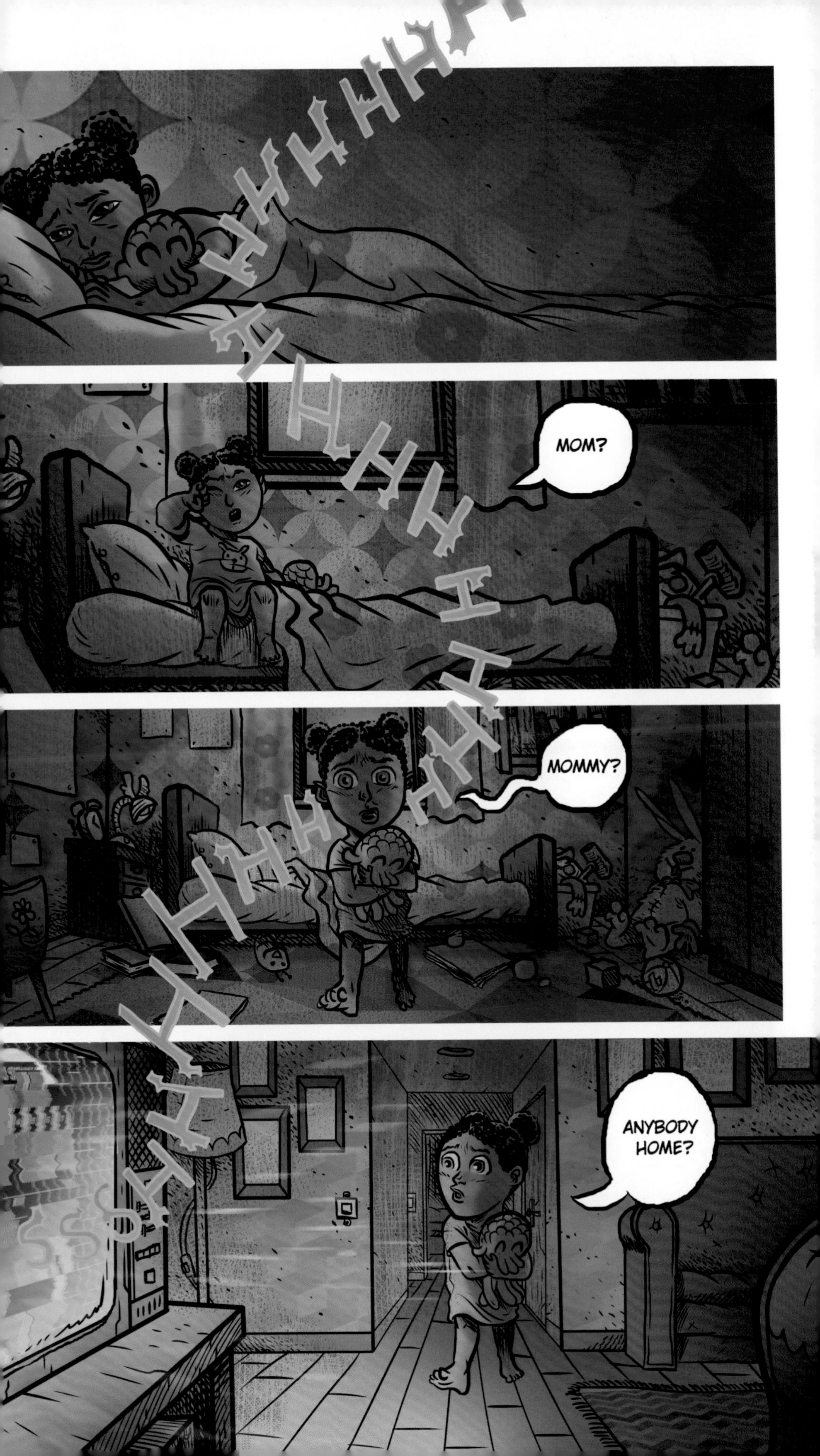
MOM?
MOMMY?
ANYBODY HOME?

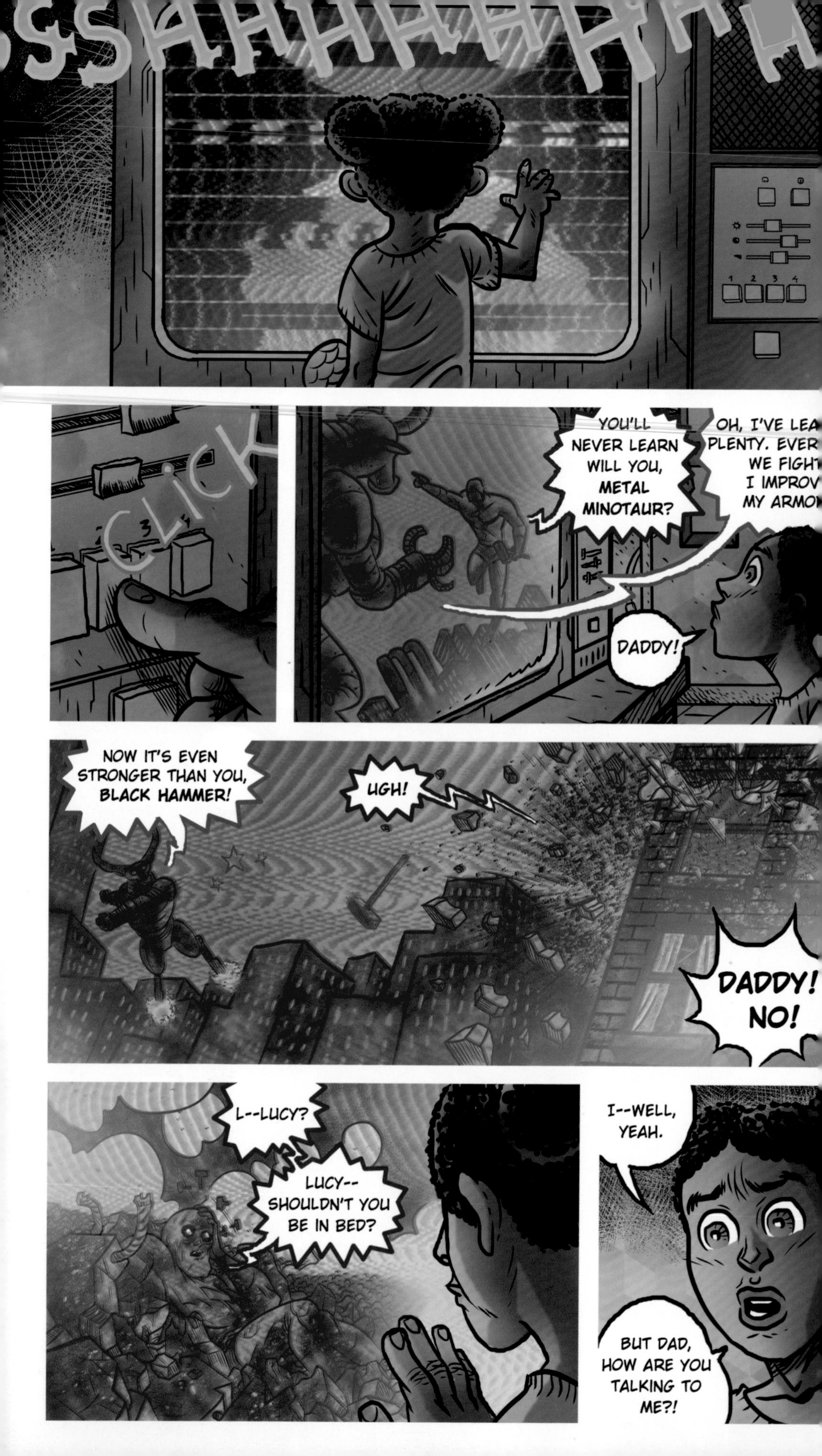
SSHHHHHHHHH
CLICK
YOU'LL NEVER LEARN WILL YOU, METAL MINOTAUR?
OH, I'VE LEA PLENTY. EVER WE FIGH I IMPROV MY ARMO
DADDY!
NOW IT'S EVEN STRONGER THAN YOU, BLACK HAMMER!
UGH!
DADDY! NO!
L--LUCY?
LUCY-- SHOULDN'T YOU BE IN BED?
I--WELL, YEAH.
BUT DAD, HOW ARE YOU TALKING TO ME?!

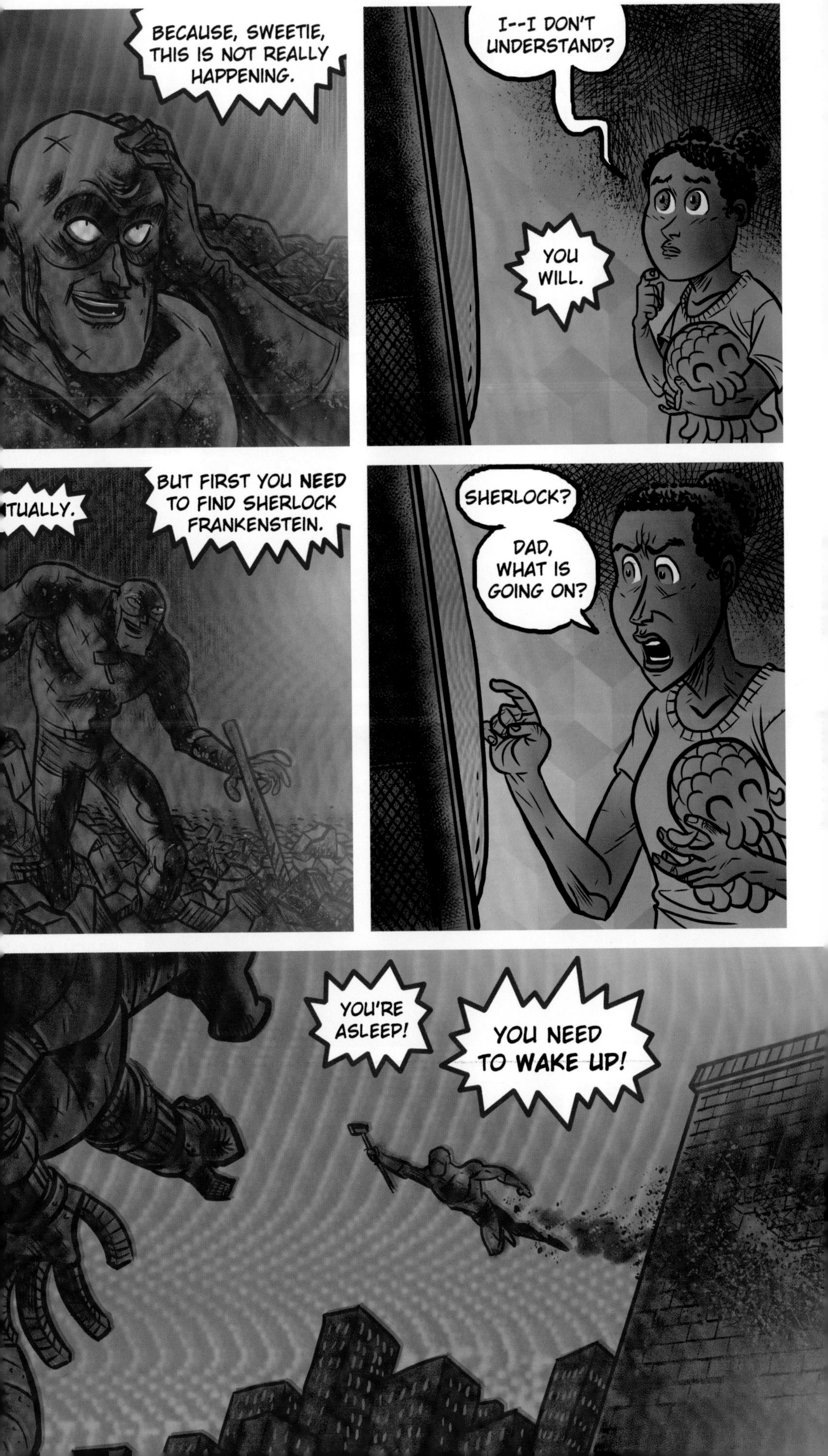
BECAUSE, SWEETIE, THIS IS NOT REALLY HAPPENING.
I--I DON'T UNDERSTAND?
YOU WILL.
TUALLY.
BUT FIRST YOU NEED TO FIND SHERLOCK FRANKENSTEIN.
SHERLOCK?
DAD, WHAT IS GOING ON?
YOU'RE ASLEEP!
YOU NEED TO WAKE UP!

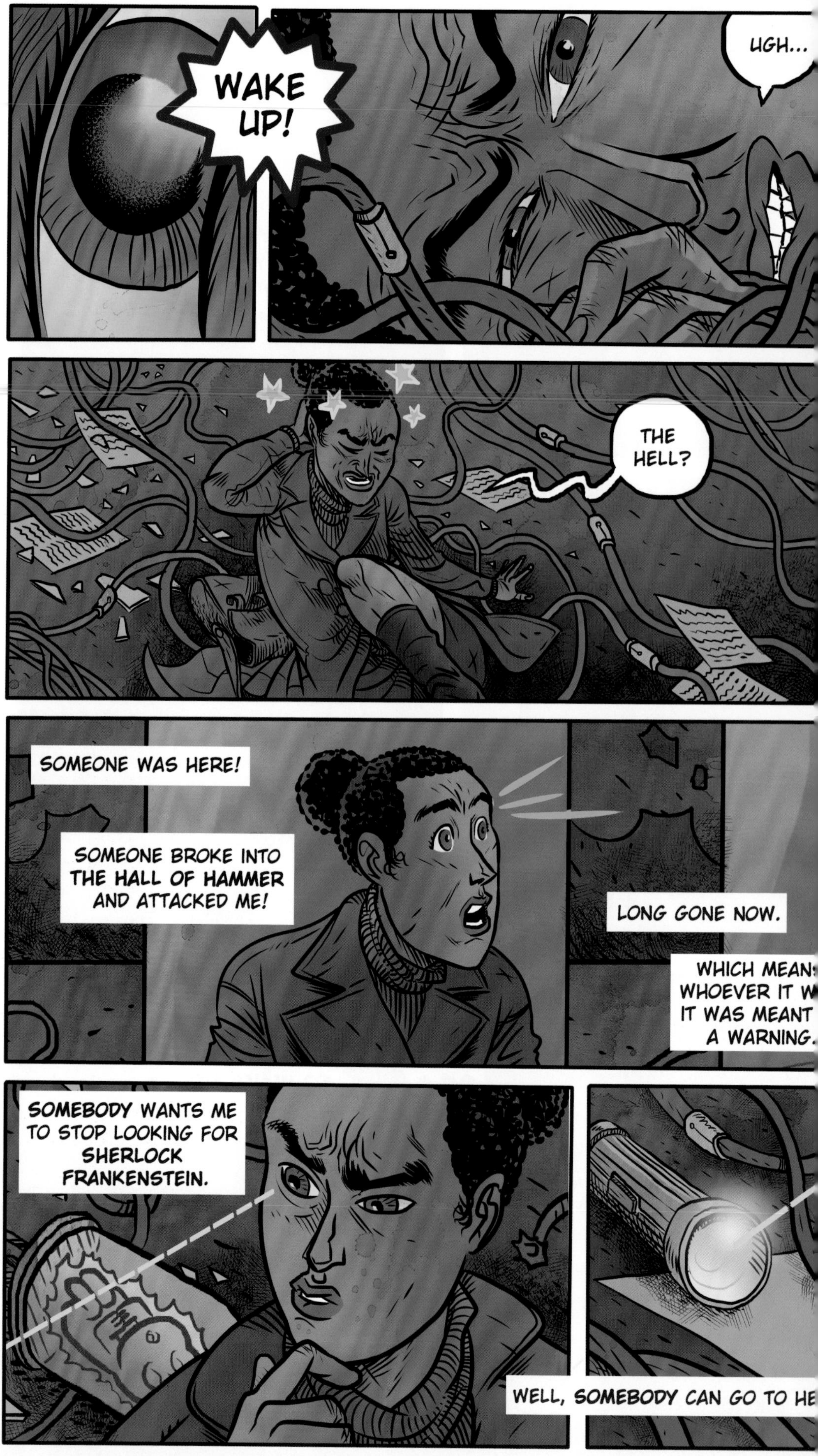

WAKE UP!
UGH...
THE HELL?
SOMEONE WAS HERE!
SOMEONE BROKE INTO THE HALL OF HAMMER AND ATTACKED ME!
LONG GONE NOW.
WHICH MEAN
WHOEVER IT W
IT WAS MEANT
A WARNING.
SOMEBODY WANTS ME TO STOP LOOKING FOR SHERLOCK FRANKENSTEIN.
WELL, SOMEBODY CAN GO TO HE

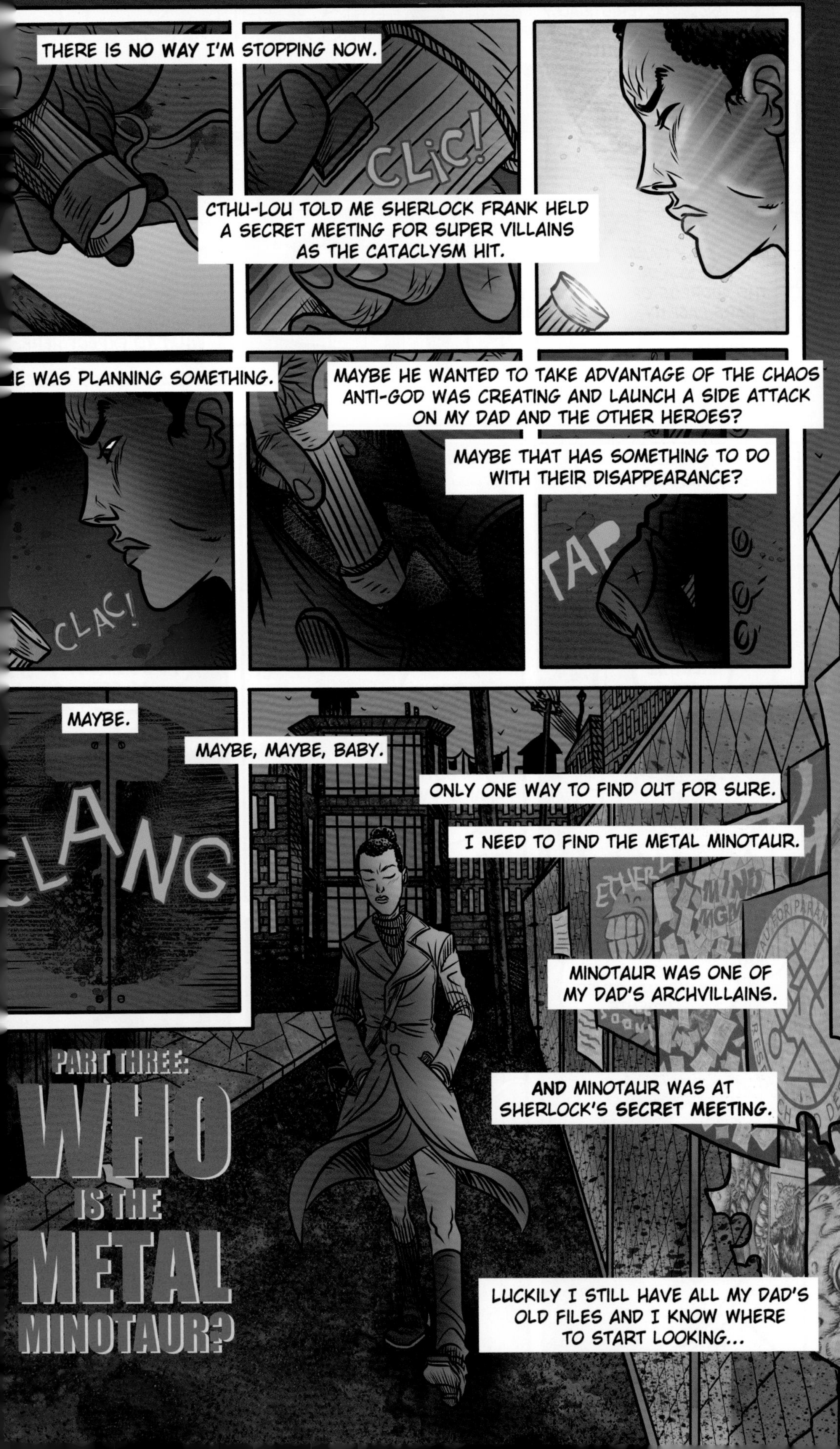

THERE IS NO WAY I'M STOPPING NOW.
CLIC!
CTHU-LOU TOLD ME SHERLOCK FRANK HELD A SECRET MEETING FOR SUPER VILLAINS AS THE CATACLYSM HIT.
E WAS PLANNING SOMETHING.
MAYBE HE WANTED TO TAKE ADVANTAGE OF THE CHAOS ANTI-GOD WAS CREATING AND LAUNCH A SIDE ATTACK ON MY DAD AND THE OTHER HEROES?
MAYBE THAT HAS SOMETHING TO DO WITH THEIR DISAPPEARANCE?
CLAC!
TAP
MAYBE.
MAYBE, MAYBE, BABY.
CLANG
ONLY ONE WAY TO FIND OUT FOR SURE.
I NEED TO FIND THE METAL MINOTAUR.
MINOTAUR WAS ONE OF MY DAD'S ARCHVILLAINS.
AND MINOTAUR WAS AT SHERLOCK'S SECRET MEETING.
PART THREE:
WHO IS THE METAL MINOTAUR?
LUCKILY I STILL HAVE ALL MY DAD'S OLD FILES AND I KNOW WHERE TO START LOOKING...

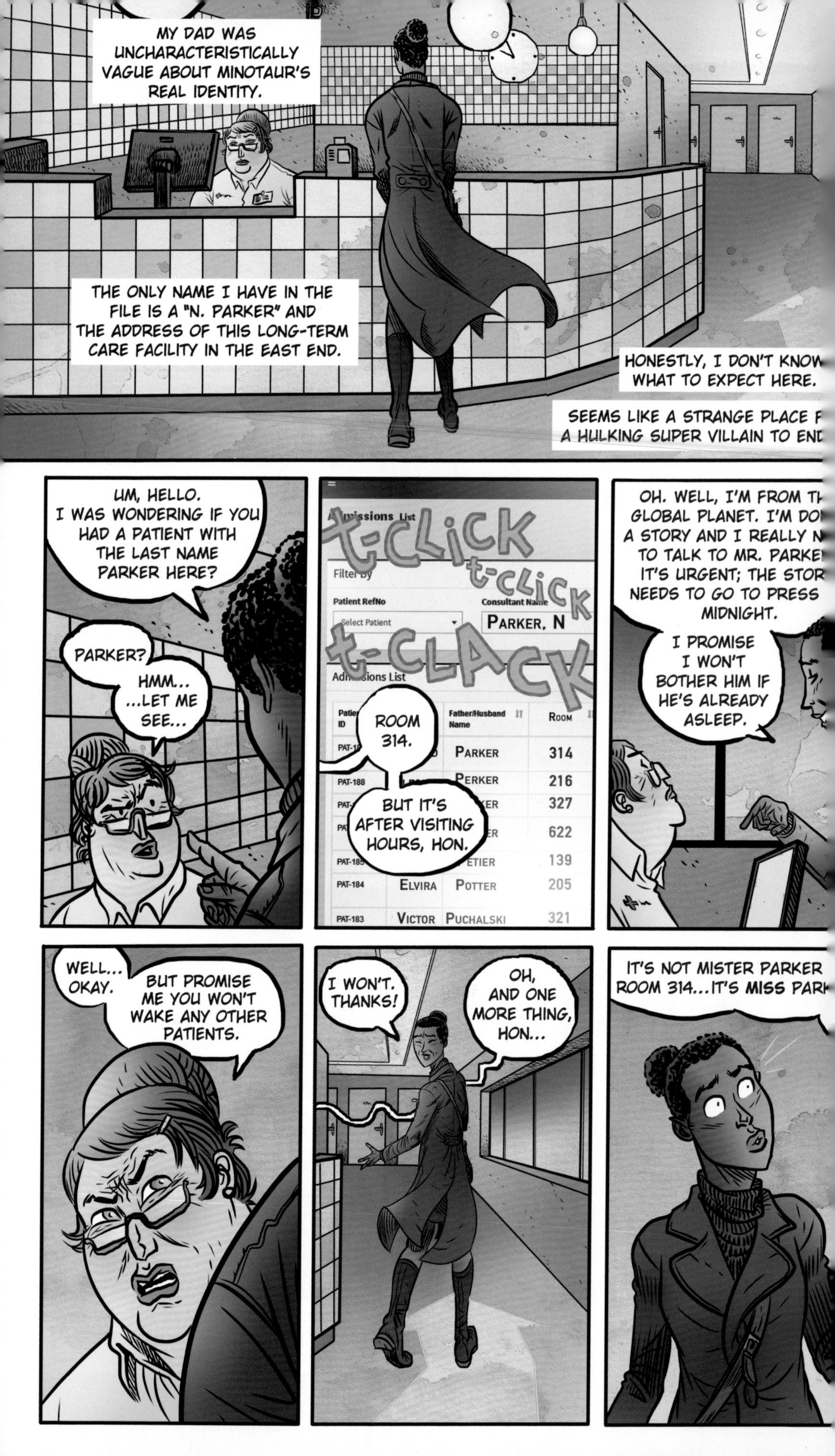

MY DAD WAS UNCHARACTERISTICALLY VAGUE ABOUT MINOTAUR'S REAL IDENTITY.
THE ONLY NAME I HAVE IN THE FILE IS A "N. PARKER" AND THE ADDRESS OF THIS LONG-TERM CARE FACILITY IN THE EAST END.
HONESTLY, I DON'T KNOW WHAT TO EXPECT HERE.
SEEMS LIKE A STRANGE PLACE F A HULKING SUPER VILLAIN TO END
UM, HELLO. I WAS WONDERING IF YOU HAD A PATIENT WITH THE LAST NAME PARKER HERE?
PARKER?
HMM... ...LET ME SEE...
T-CLICK T-CLICK T-CLACK
Filter By
Patient RefNo
Select Patient
Consultant Name
PARKER, N
Father/Husband Name
ROOM
PARKER 314
PAT-188 PERKER 216
327
622
PAT-185 139
PAT-184 ELVIRA POTTER 205
PAT-183 VICTOR PUCHALSKI 321
ROOM 314.
BUT IT'S AFTER VISITING HOURS, HON.
OH. WELL, I'M FROM TH GLOBAL PLANET. I'M DO A STORY AND I REALLY N TO TALK TO MR. PARKE IT'S URGENT; THE STOR NEEDS TO GO TO PRESS MIDNIGHT.
I PROMISE I WON'T BOTHER HIM IF HE'S ALREADY ASLEEP.
WELL... OKAY.
BUT PROMISE ME YOU WON'T WAKE ANY OTHER PATIENTS.
I WON'T. THANKS!
OH, AND ONE MORE THING, HON...
IT'S NOT MISTER PARKER ROOM 314...IT'S MISS PARK

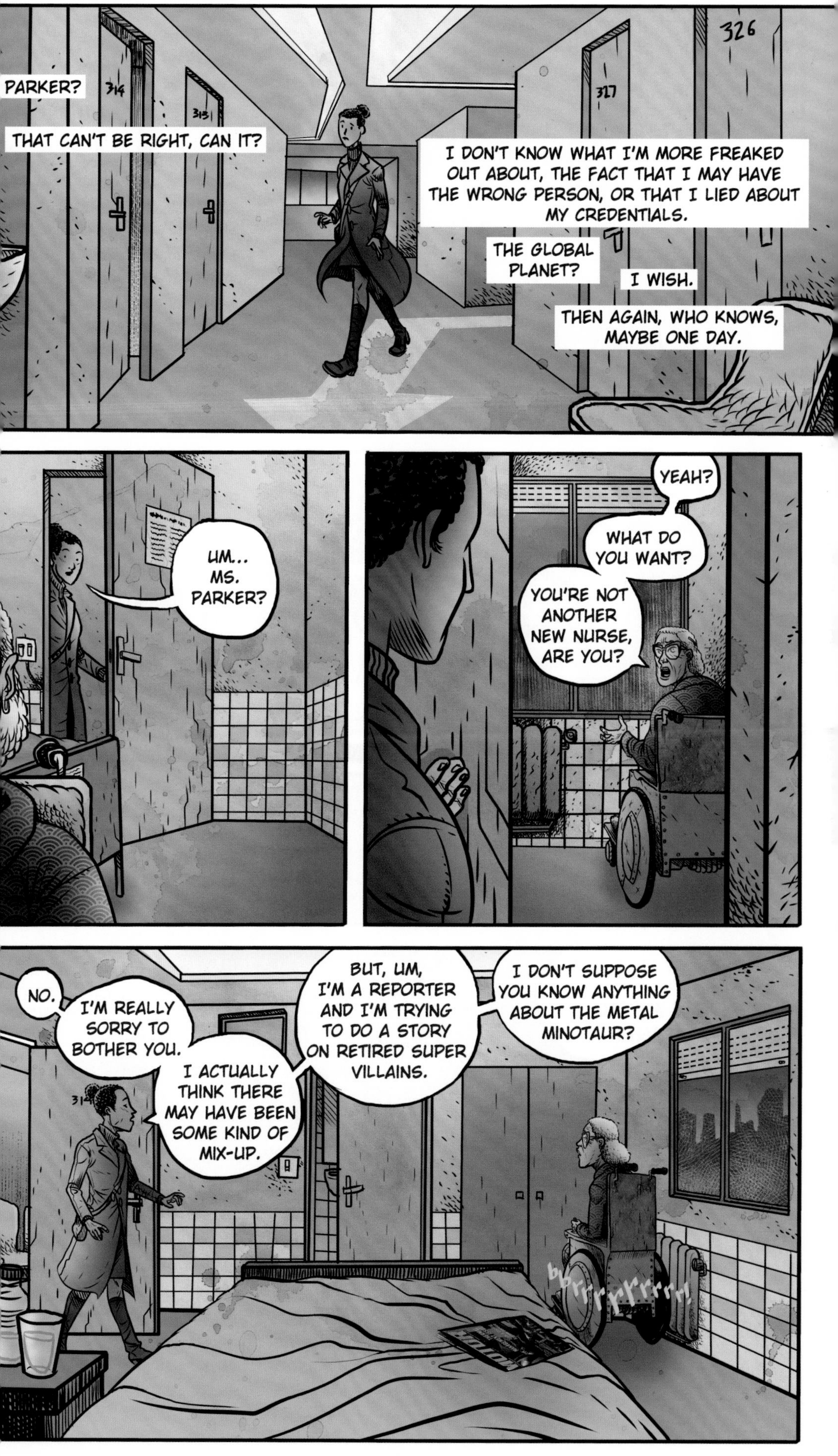
326
PARKER?
THAT CAN'T BE RIGHT, CAN IT?
I DON'T KNOW WHAT I'M MORE FREAKED OUT ABOUT, THE FACT THAT I MAY HAVE THE WRONG PERSON, OR THAT I LIED ABOUT MY CREDENTIALS.
THE GLOBAL PLANET?
I WISH.
THEN AGAIN, WHO KNOWS, MAYBE ONE DAY.
UM... MS. PARKER?
YEAH?
WHAT DO YOU WANT?
YOU'RE NOT ANOTHER NEW NURSE, ARE YOU?
NO.
I'M REALLY SORRY TO BOTHER YOU.
I ACTUALLY THINK THERE MAY HAVE BEEN SOME KIND OF MIX-UP.
BUT, UM, I'M A REPORTER AND I'M TRYING TO DO A STORY ON RETIRED SUPER VILLAINS.
I DON'T SUPPOSE YOU KNOW ANYTHING ABOUT THE METAL MINOTAUR?
bbrrrrrrrrr!

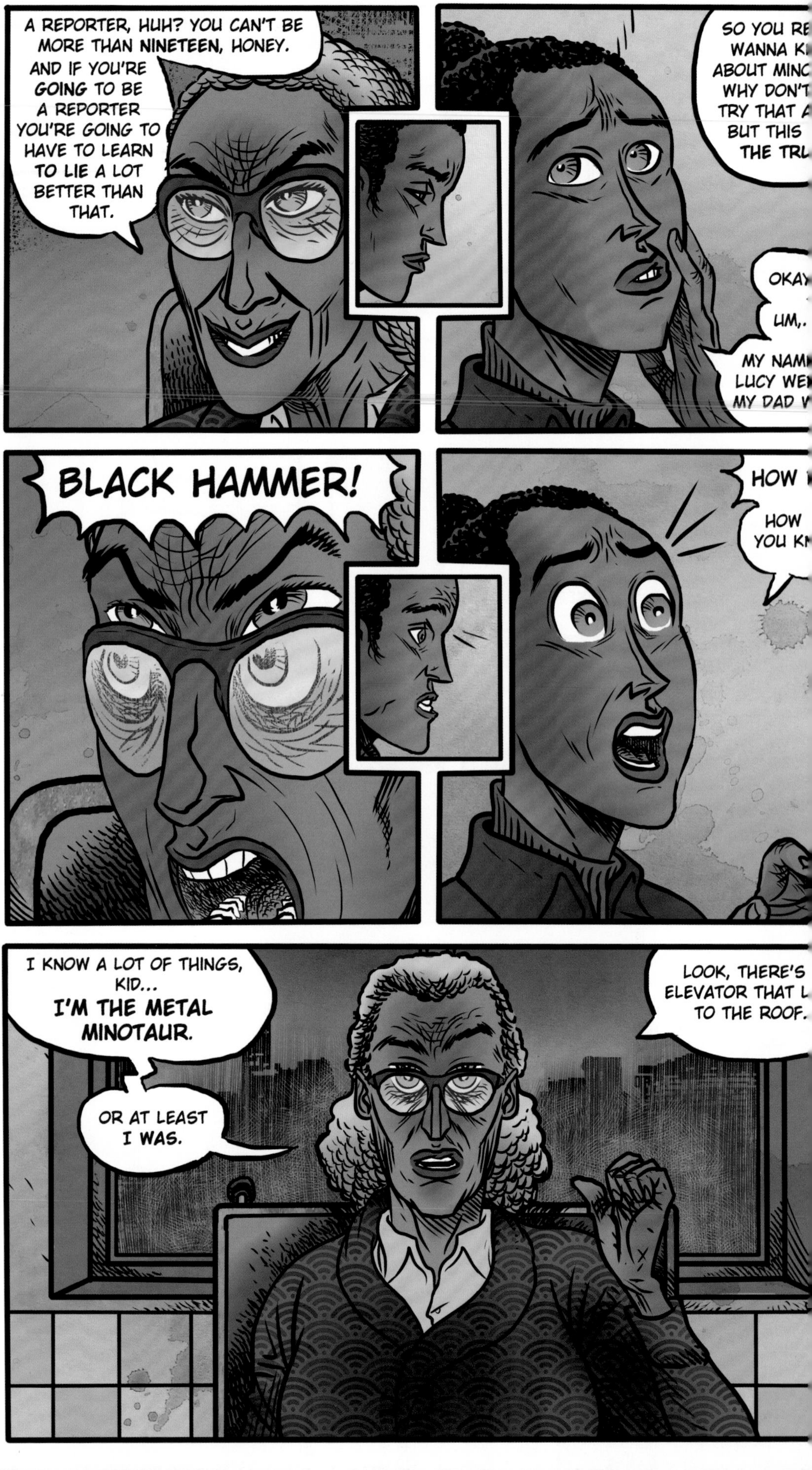
A REPORTER, HUH? YOU CAN'T BE MORE THAN NINETEEN, HONEY.
AND IF YOU'RE GOING TO BE A REPORTER YOU'RE GOING TO HAVE TO LEARN TO LIE A LOT BETTER THAN THAT.
SO YOU RE WANNA K ABOUT MINC WHY DON'T TRY THAT A BUT THIS THE TRU
OKAY
UM,.
MY NAM LUCY WE MY DAD
BLACK HAMMER!
HOW
HOW YOU K
I KNOW A LOT OF THINGS, KID... I'M THE METAL MINOTAUR.
OR AT LEAST I WAS.
LOOK, THERE'S ELEVATOR THAT TO THE ROOF.

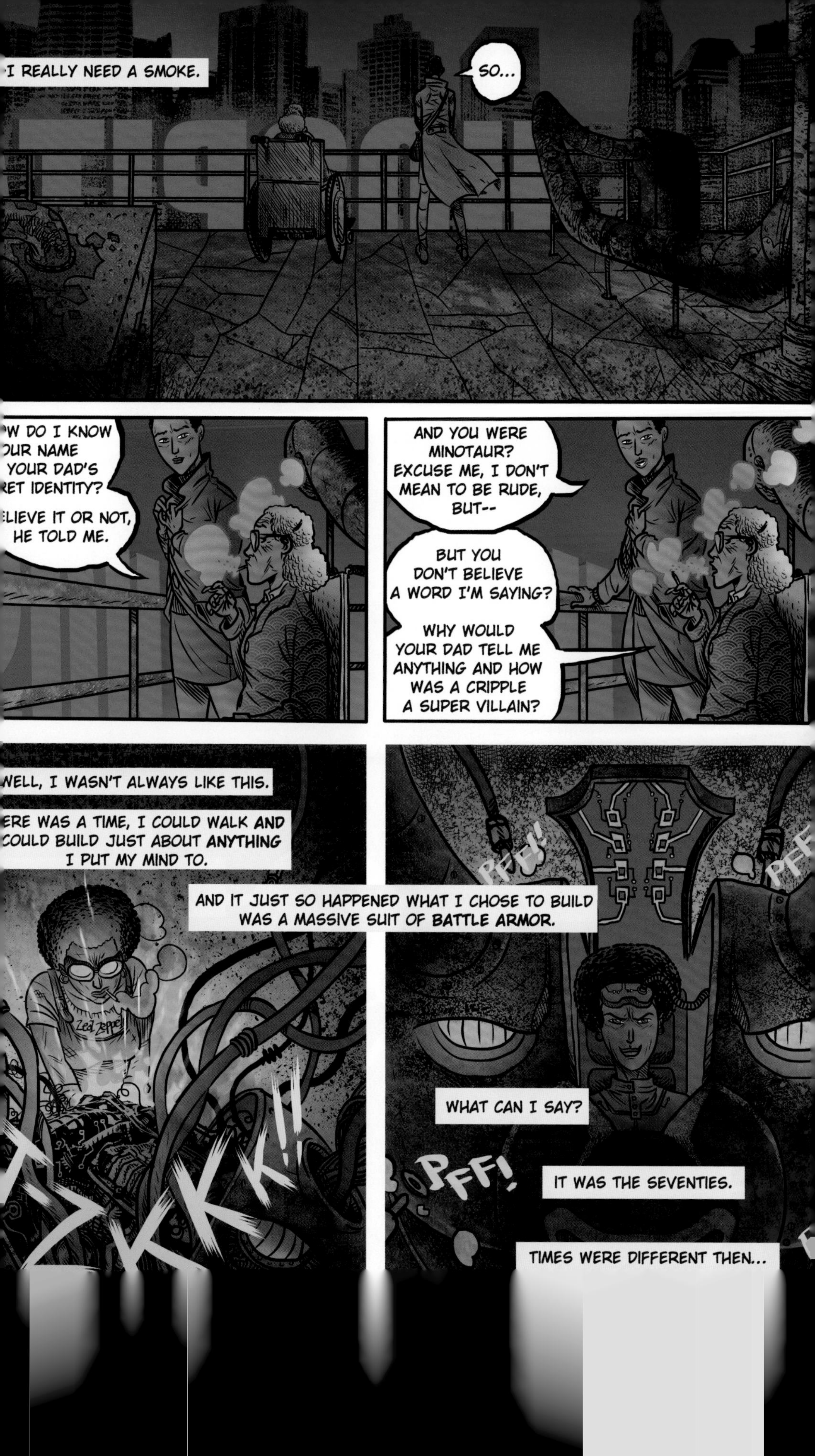
I REALLY NEED A SMOKE.
SO...
W DO I KNOW
UR NAME
YOUR DAD'S
ET IDENTITY?
LIEVE IT OR NOT,
HE TOLD ME.
AND YOU WERE MINOTAUR? EXCUSE ME, I DON'T MEAN TO BE RUDE, BUT--
BUT YOU DON'T BELIEVE A WORD I'M SAYING?
WHY WOULD YOUR DAD TELL ME ANYTHING AND HOW WAS A CRIPPLE A SUPER VILLAIN?
VELL, I WASN'T ALWAYS LIKE THIS.
ERE WAS A TIME, I COULD WALK AND COULD BUILD JUST ABOUT ANYTHING I PUT MY MIND TO.
AND IT JUST SO HAPPENED WHAT I CHOSE TO BUILD WAS A MASSIVE SUIT OF BATTLE ARMOR.
Zed Zeppelin
PFF!
WHAT CAN I SAY?
PFF!
IT WAS THE SEVENTIES.
TIMES WERE DIFFERENT THEN...

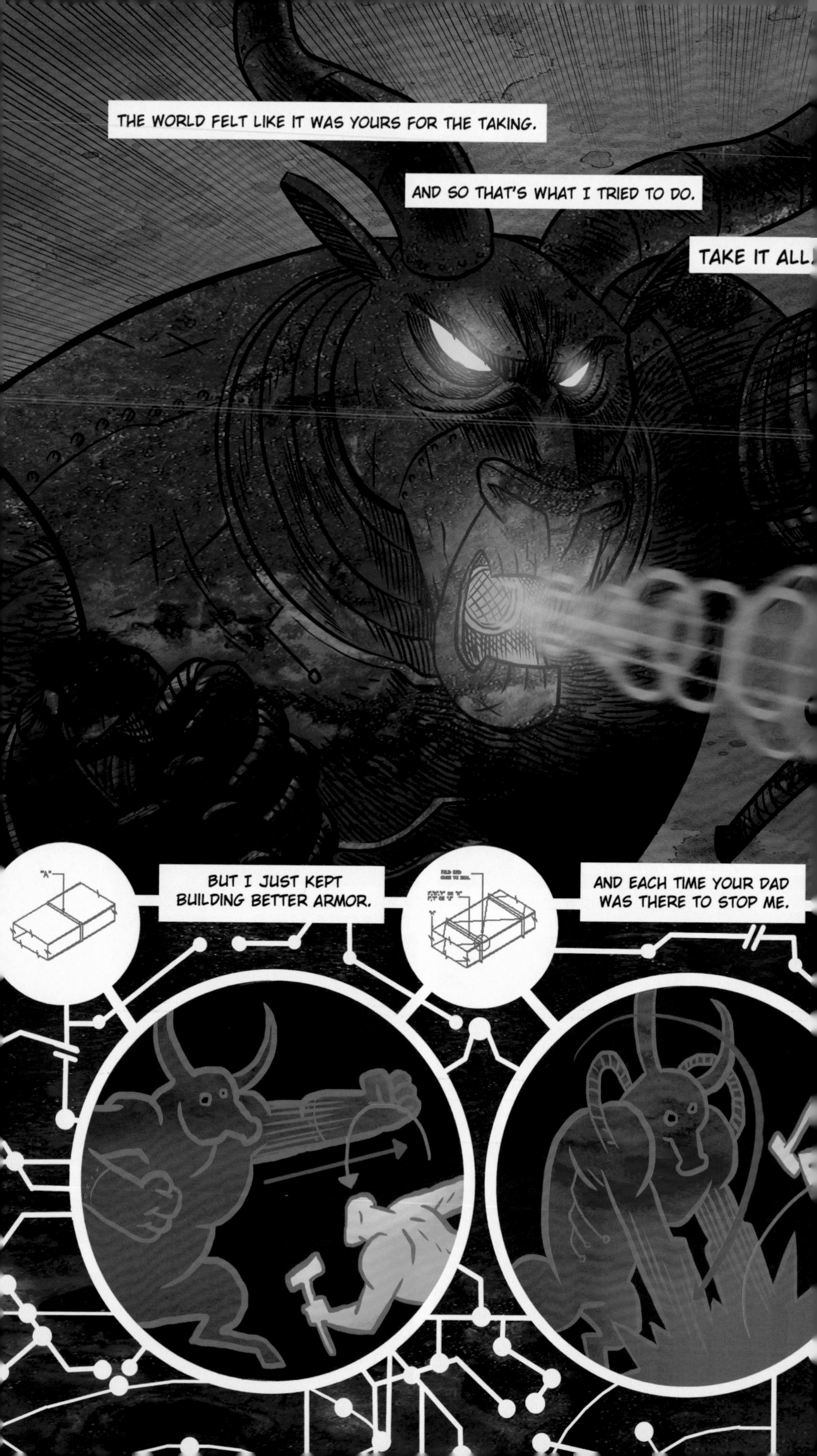
THE WORLD FELT LIKE IT WAS YOURS FOR THE TAKING.
AND SO THAT'S WHAT I TRIED TO DO.
TAKE IT ALL.
"A"
BUT I JUST KEPT BUILDING BETTER ARMOR.
AND EACH TIME YOUR DAD WAS THERE TO STOP ME.

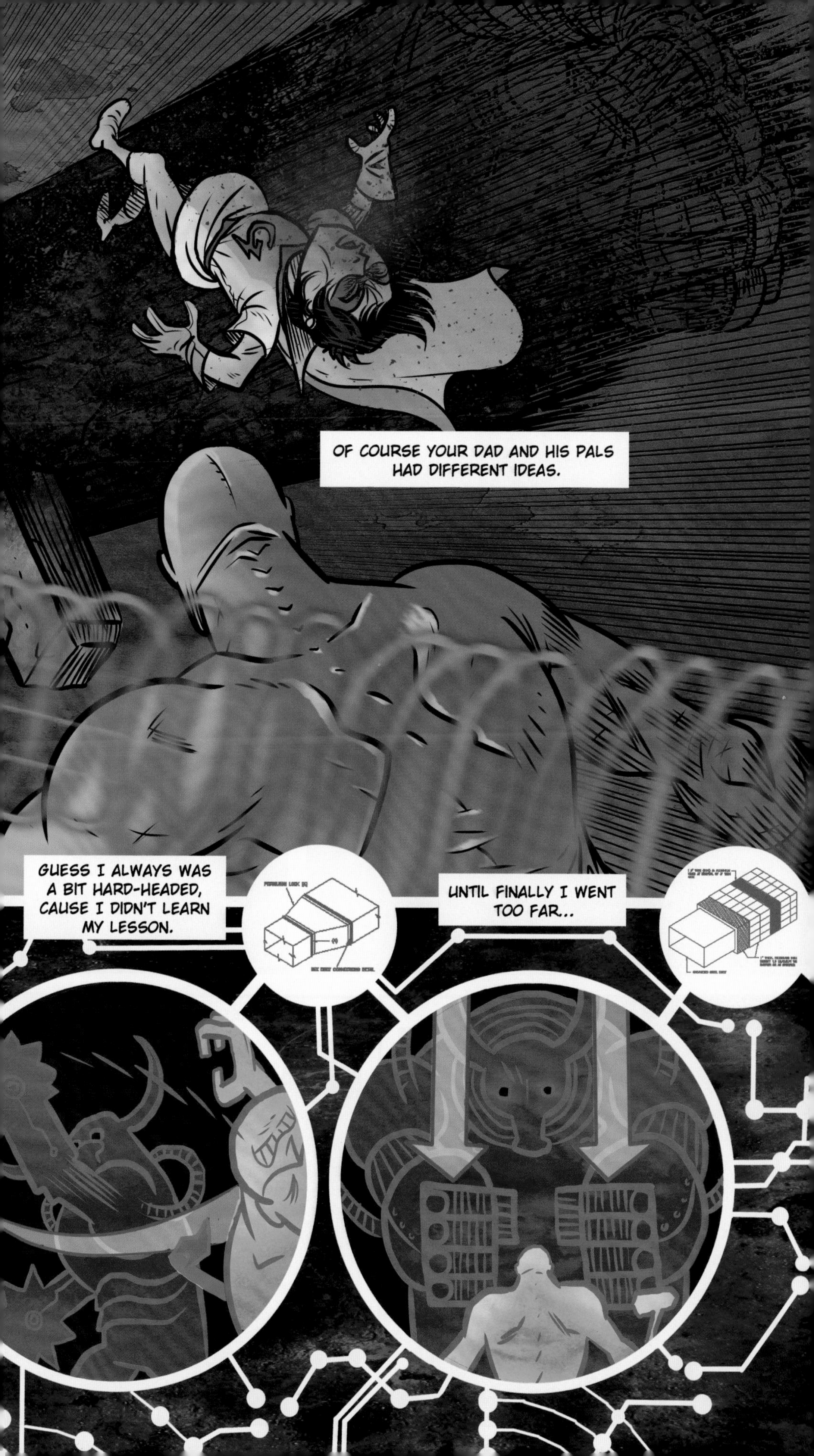
OF COURSE YOUR DAD AND HIS PALS HAD DIFFERENT IDEAS.
GUESS I ALWAYS WAS A BIT HARD-HEADED, CAUSE I DIDN'T LEARN MY LESSON.
UNTIL FINALLY I WENT TOO FAR...

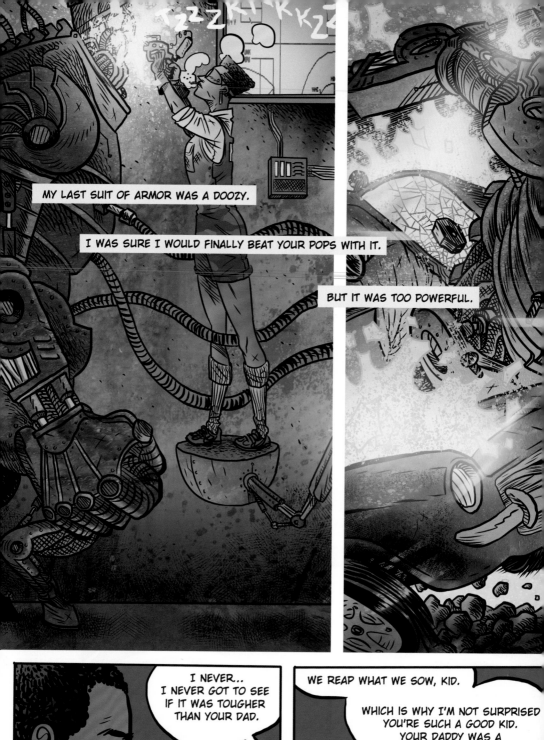

MY LAST SUIT OF ARMOR WAS A DOOZY.

I WAS SURE I WOULD FINALLY BEAT YOUR POPS WITH IT.

BUT IT WAS TOO POWERFUL.

I NEVER... I NEVER GOT TO SEE IF IT WAS TOUGHER THAN YOUR DAD.

OH GOD.

I'M-- I'M SO SORRY.

WE REAP WHAT WE SOW, KID.

WHICH IS WHY I'M NOT SURPRISED YOU'RE SUCH A GOOD KID. YOUR DADDY WAS A DAMN GOOD MAN.

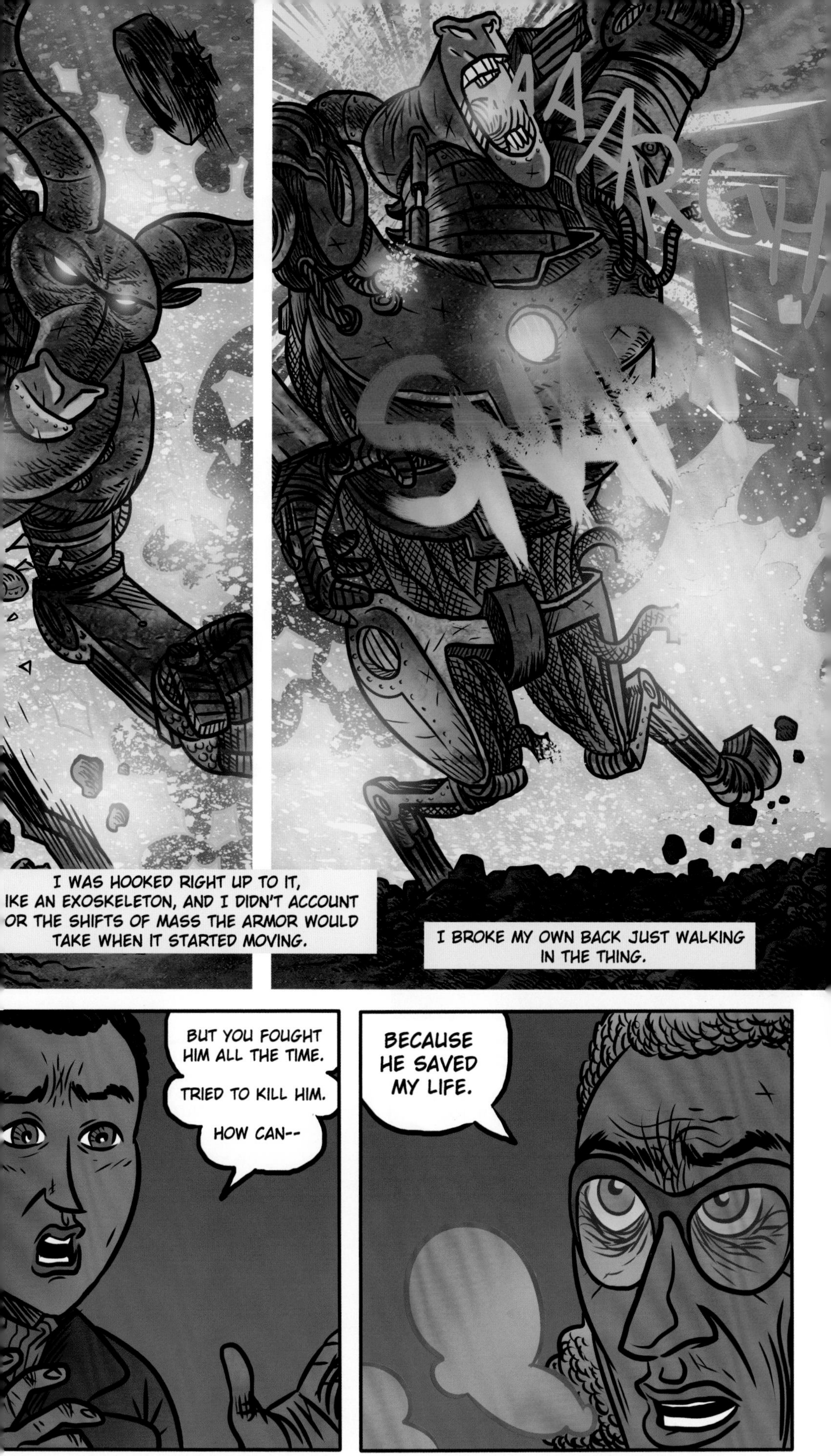
I WAS HOOKED RIGHT UP TO IT, IKE AN EXOSKELETON, AND I DIDN'T ACCOUNT OR THE SHIFTS OF MASS THE ARMOR WOULD TAKE WHEN IT STARTED MOVING.
I BROKE MY OWN BACK JUST WALKING IN THE THING.
BUT YOU FOUGHT HIM ALL THE TIME.
TRIED TO KILL HIM.
HOW CAN--
BECAUSE HE SAVED MY LIFE.

HOLD ON!

I-- HELP ME-- I--I CAN'T FEEL MY LEGS.

HE GOT ME OUT OF THAT THAT TIN CAN AN BROUGHT ME TO NEW WORLD, THAT PLANET WHERE HIS POWERS CAME FR AS FAST AS HE COULD.

HELP! I NEED HELP!

ME AND YOUR DAD WERE AT EACH OTHERS' THROATS DOZENS OF TIMES OVER THE YEARS, BUT I TELL YOU WHAT--AT THE END OF THE DAY, WE RESPECTED EACH OTHER, TOO.

WAIT A MINUTE. THERE'S ONE THING I DON'T UNDERSTAND.

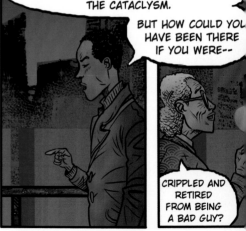

I JUST TALKED TO CTHU-LOU AND HE TOLD M YOU WERE AT A SECRET MEETING THAT SHERLOCK FRANKENSTEIN CALLED DURING THE CATACLYSM.

BUT HOW COULD YOU HAVE BEEN THERE IF YOU WERE--

CRIPPLED AND RETIRED FROM BEING A BAD GUY?

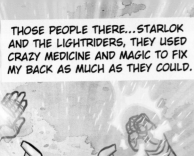

THOSE PEOPLE THERE...STARLOK AND THE LIGHTRIDERS, THEY USED CRAZY MEDICINE AND MAGIC TO FIX MY BACK AS MUCH AS THEY COULD.

I KNEW I'D NEVER WALK AGAIN, BUT IT COULD HAVE BEEN WORSE.

IF YOUR DAD HADN'T RUSHED ME AWAY I WOULD HAVE DIED.

THE WHOLE TIME I WAS THERE HE VISITED, KEPT ME COMPANY. HE TOLD ME ALL ABOUT YOU.

BOY, WAS HE PROUD OF YOU.

WELL... YEAH.

I COULD STILL WALK USING SOME OF MY OLDER ARMOR.

WHEN WE GOT WORD OF SHERLOCK'S MEETING I HAD MANACONDA HELP ME GET INTO IT.

ONE LAST MISSION.

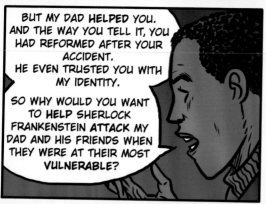

BUT MY DAD HELPED YOU. AND THE WAY YOU TELL IT, YOU HAD REFORMED AFTER YOUR ACCIDENT.
HE EVEN TRUSTED YOU WITH MY IDENTITY.

SO WHY WOULD YOU WANT TO HELP SHERLOCK FRANKENSTEIN ATTACK MY DAD AND HIS FRIENDS WHEN THEY WERE AT THEIR MOST VULNERABLE?

ATTACK THEM?!

IS-- IS THAT WHAT YO[U] THINK SHERLOCK WAS PLANNING AT THAT MEETING[?]

SHERLOCK DIDN'T CALL THAT MEETING TO PLAN AN ATTACK ON THE SUPERHEROES...

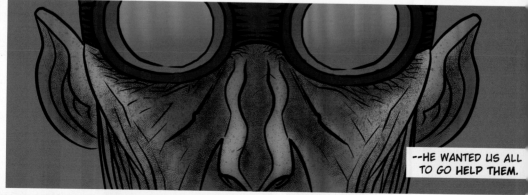

--HE WANTED US ALL TO GO HELP THEM.

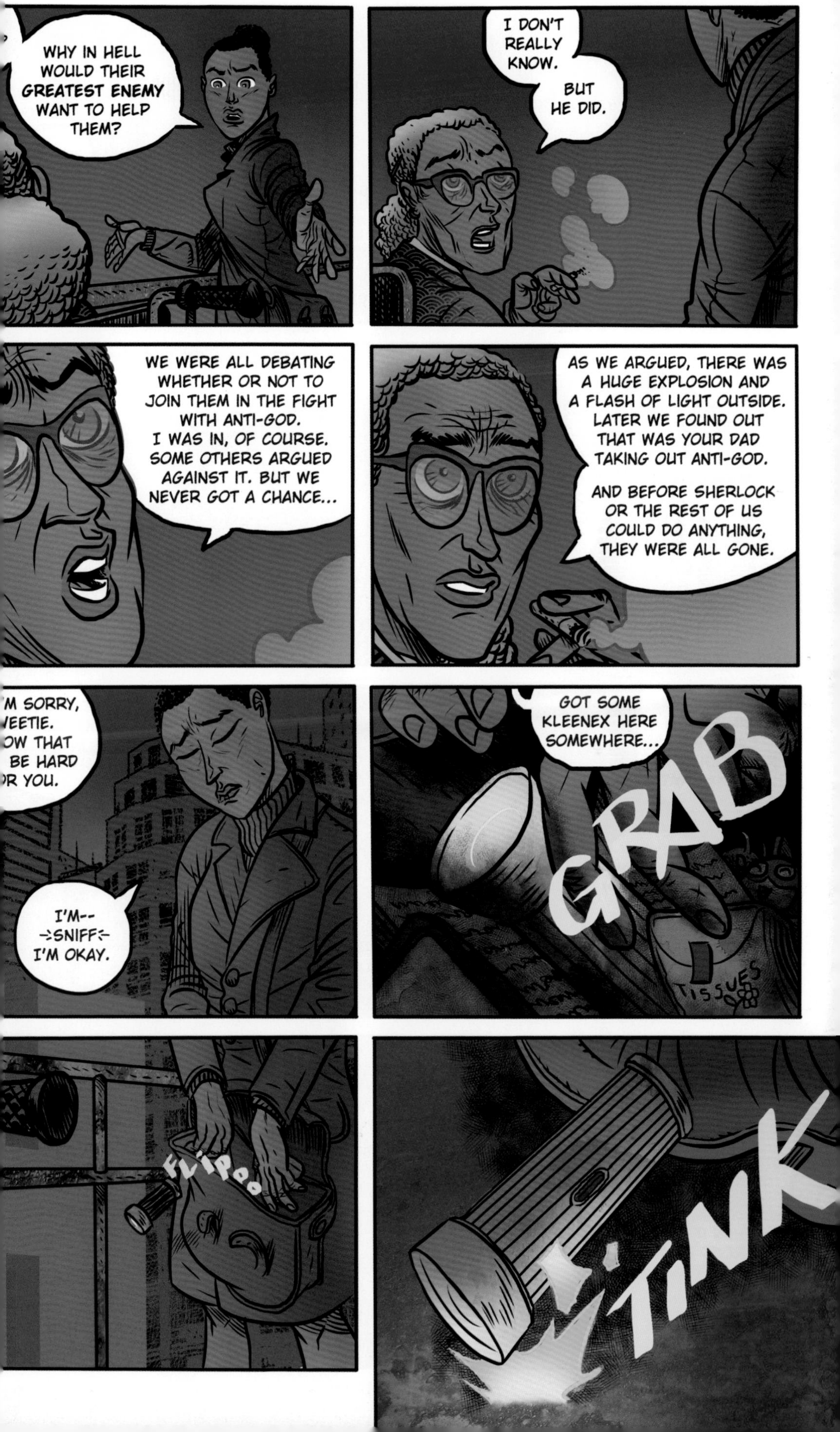
WHY IN HELL WOULD THEIR GREATEST ENEMY WANT TO HELP THEM?
I DON'T REALLY KNOW.
BUT HE DID.
WE WERE ALL DEBATING WHETHER OR NOT TO JOIN THEM IN THE FIGHT WITH ANTI-GOD. I WAS IN, OF COURSE. SOME OTHERS ARGUED AGAINST IT. BUT WE NEVER GOT A CHANCE...
AS WE ARGUED, THERE WAS A HUGE EXPLOSION AND A FLASH OF LIGHT OUTSIDE. LATER WE FOUND OUT THAT WAS YOUR DAD TAKING OUT ANTI-GOD.
AND BEFORE SHERLOCK OR THE REST OF US COULD DO ANYTHING, THEY WERE ALL GONE.
'M SORRY, EETIE. OW THAT BE HARD R YOU.
I'M-- SNIFF I'M OKAY.
GOT SOME KLEENEX HERE SOMEWHERE...
GRAB
TISSUES
FLIPOO
TINK

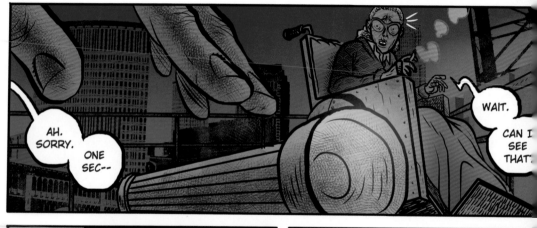

AH. SORRY. ONE SEC--

WAIT. CAN I SEE THAT.

WHERE DID YOU GET THIS?

OH, IT'S A LONG STORY.

SOMEONE TRASHED MY DAD'S HEADQUARTERS, I GUESS AS A WARNING TO ME, AND THEY LEFT THAT BEHIND.

WHY? DO YOU-- DO YOU KNOW IT?

KNOW IT? HONEY, I'D RECOGNIZE ONE OF TH ANYWHERE.

THE GUARDS AT SPIRAL ASYLUM CARRIED FLASHLIGHTS JUST LIKE THAT.

THE GUARDS AT SPIRAL?! ARE YOU SURE?

I SURE SPENT EN TIME LOCKED L IN THERE. I SHOULD KNO

THEN IT HITS ME. ALL THE PIECES START TO FIT TOGETHER AND I KNOW...

...I KNOW WHERE SHERLOC FRANKENSTEIN IS!

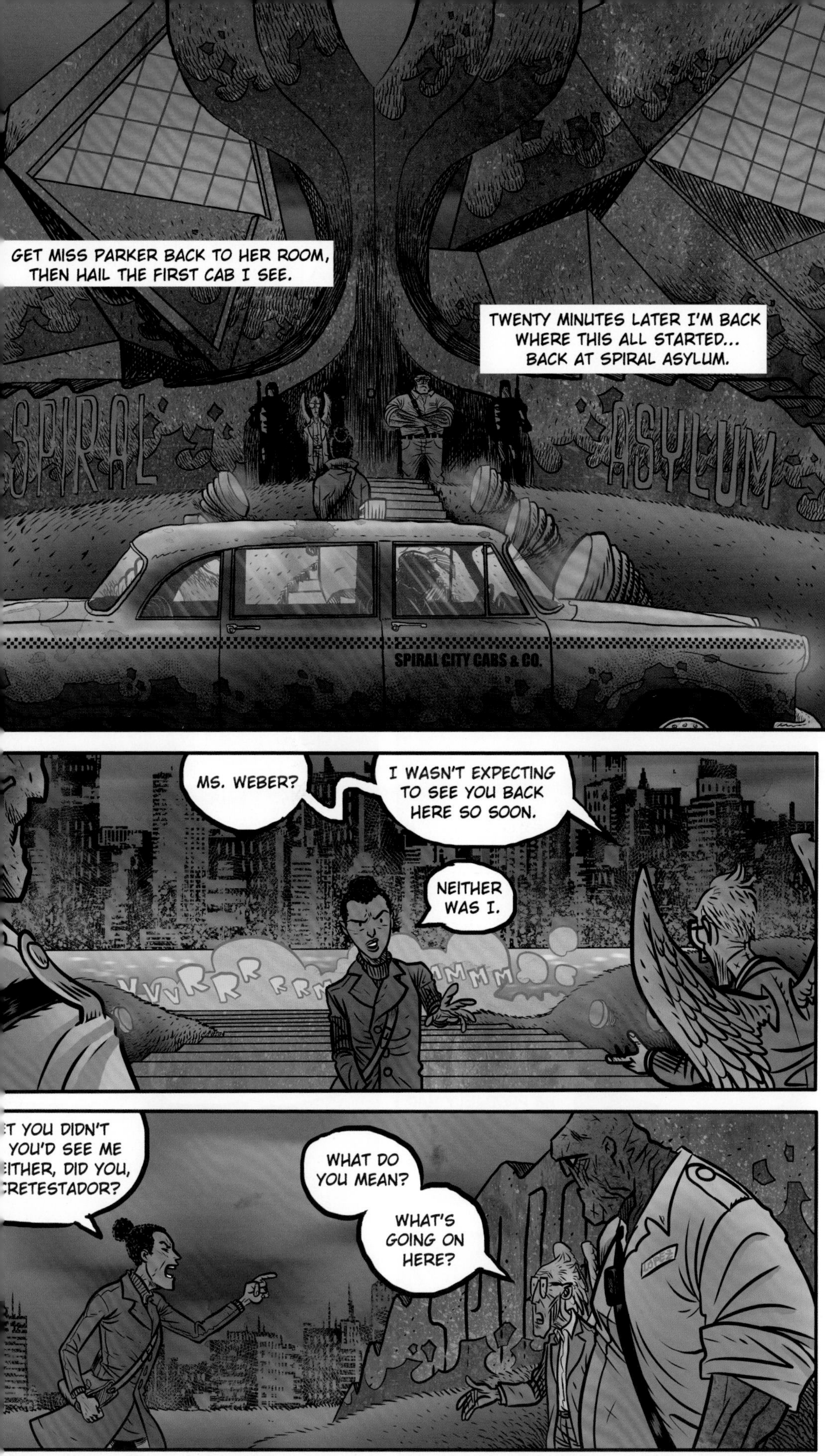

GET MISS PARKER BACK TO HER ROOM, THEN HAIL THE FIRST CAB I SEE.
TWENTY MINUTES LATER I'M BACK WHERE THIS ALL STARTED... BACK AT SPIRAL ASYLUM.
SPIRAL
ASYLUM
SPIRAL CITY CABS & CO.
MS. WEBER?
I WASN'T EXPECTING TO SEE YOU BACK HERE SO SOON.
NEITHER WAS I.
T YOU DIDN'T YOU'D SEE ME ITHER, DID YOU, RETESTADOR?
WHAT DO YOU MEAN?
WHAT'S GOING ON HERE?

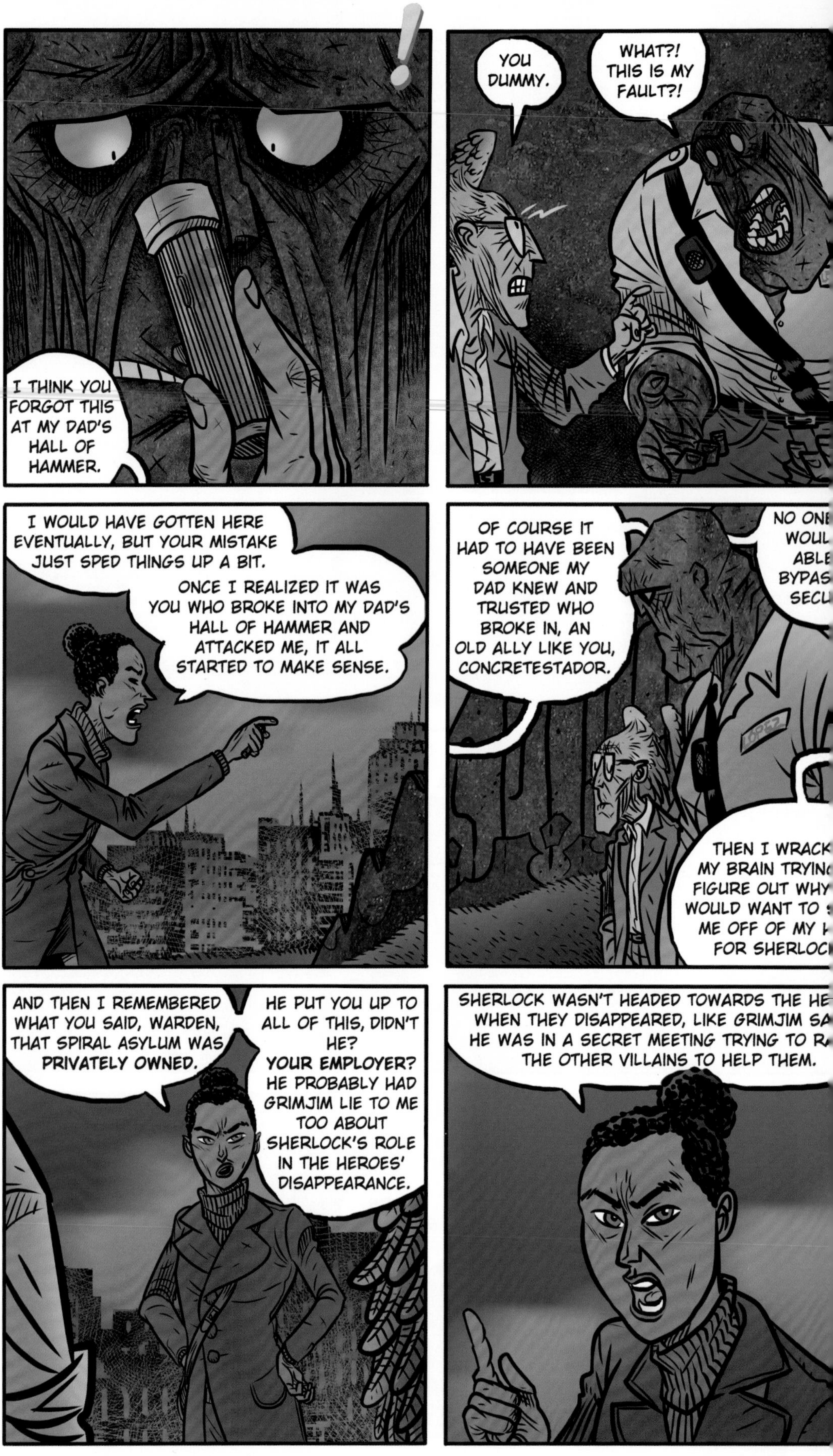
!
I THINK YOU FORGOT THIS AT MY DAD'S HALL OF HAMMER.
YOU DUMMY.
WHAT?! THIS IS MY FAULT?!
I WOULD HAVE GOTTEN HERE EVENTUALLY, BUT YOUR MISTAKE JUST SPED THINGS UP A BIT.
ONCE I REALIZED IT WAS YOU WHO BROKE INTO MY DAD'S HALL OF HAMMER AND ATTACKED ME, IT ALL STARTED TO MAKE SENSE.
OF COURSE IT HAD TO HAVE BEEN SOMEONE MY DAD KNEW AND TRUSTED WHO BROKE IN, AN OLD ALLY LIKE YOU, CONCRETESTADOR.
NO ONE WOUL ABLE BYPAS SECU
THEN I WRACK MY BRAIN TRYIN FIGURE OUT WHY WOULD WANT TO ME OFF OF MY FOR SHERLOC
AND THEN I REMEMBERED WHAT YOU SAID, WARDEN, THAT SPIRAL ASYLUM WAS PRIVATELY OWNED.
HE PUT YOU UP TO ALL OF THIS, DIDN'T HE? YOUR EMPLOYER? HE PROBABLY HAD GRIMJIM LIE TO ME TOO ABOUT SHERLOCK'S ROLE IN THE HEROES' DISAPPEARANCE.
SHERLOCK WASN'T HEADED TOWARDS THE HE WHEN THEY DISAPPEARED, LIKE GRIMJIM SA HE WAS IN A SECRET MEETING TRYING TO R THE OTHER VILLAINS TO HELP THEM.

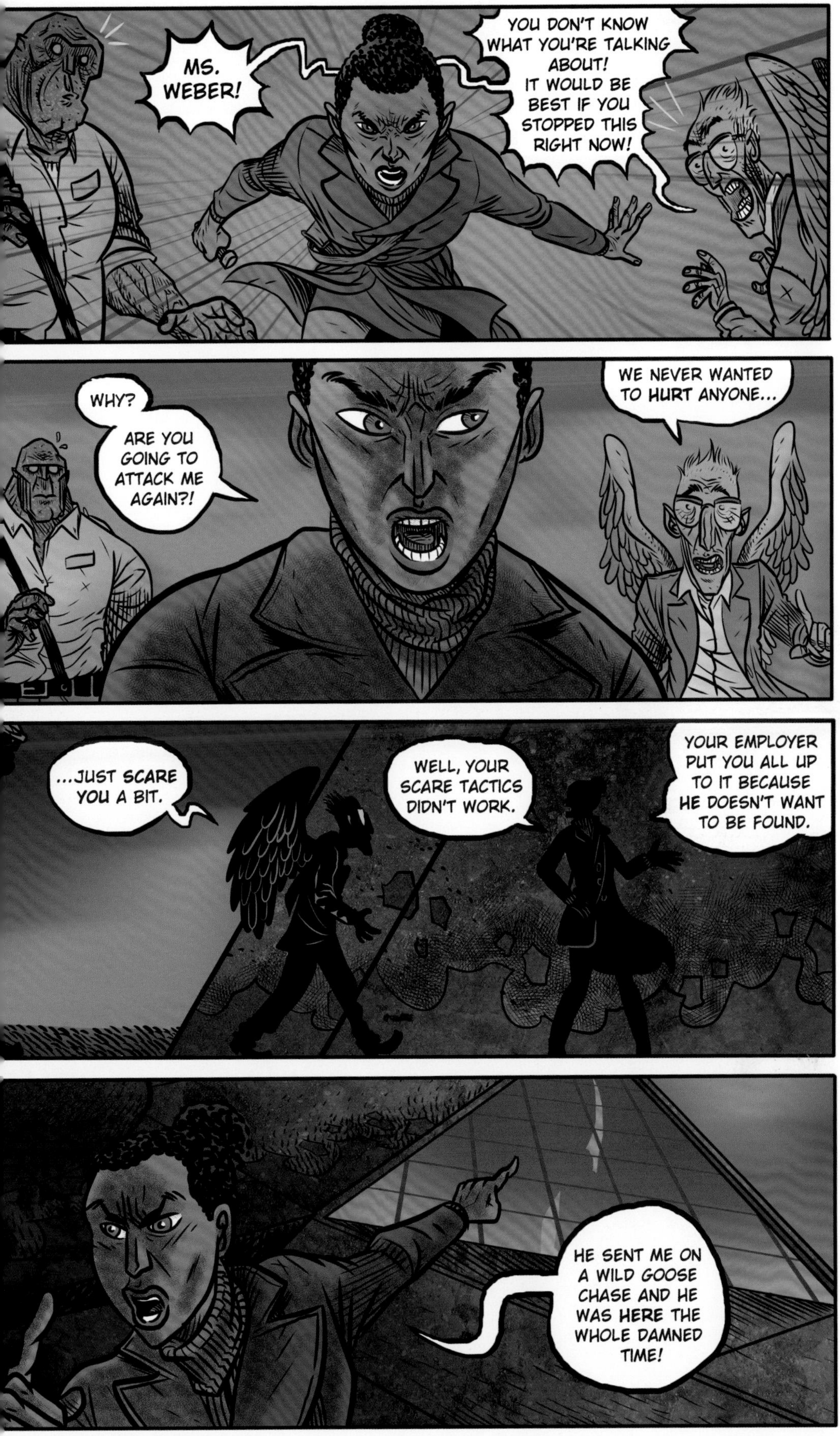
MS. WEBER!
YOU DON'T KNOW WHAT YOU'RE TALKING ABOUT! IT WOULD BE BEST IF YOU STOPPED THIS RIGHT NOW!
WHY? ARE YOU GOING TO ATTACK ME AGAIN?!
WE NEVER WANTED TO HURT ANYONE...
...JUST SCARE YOU A BIT.
WELL, YOUR SCARE TACTICS DIDN'T WORK.
YOUR EMPLOYER PUT YOU ALL UP TO IT BECAUSE HE DOESN'T WANT TO BE FOUND.
HE SENT ME ON A WILD GOOSE CHASE AND HE WAS HERE THE WHOLE DAMNED TIME!

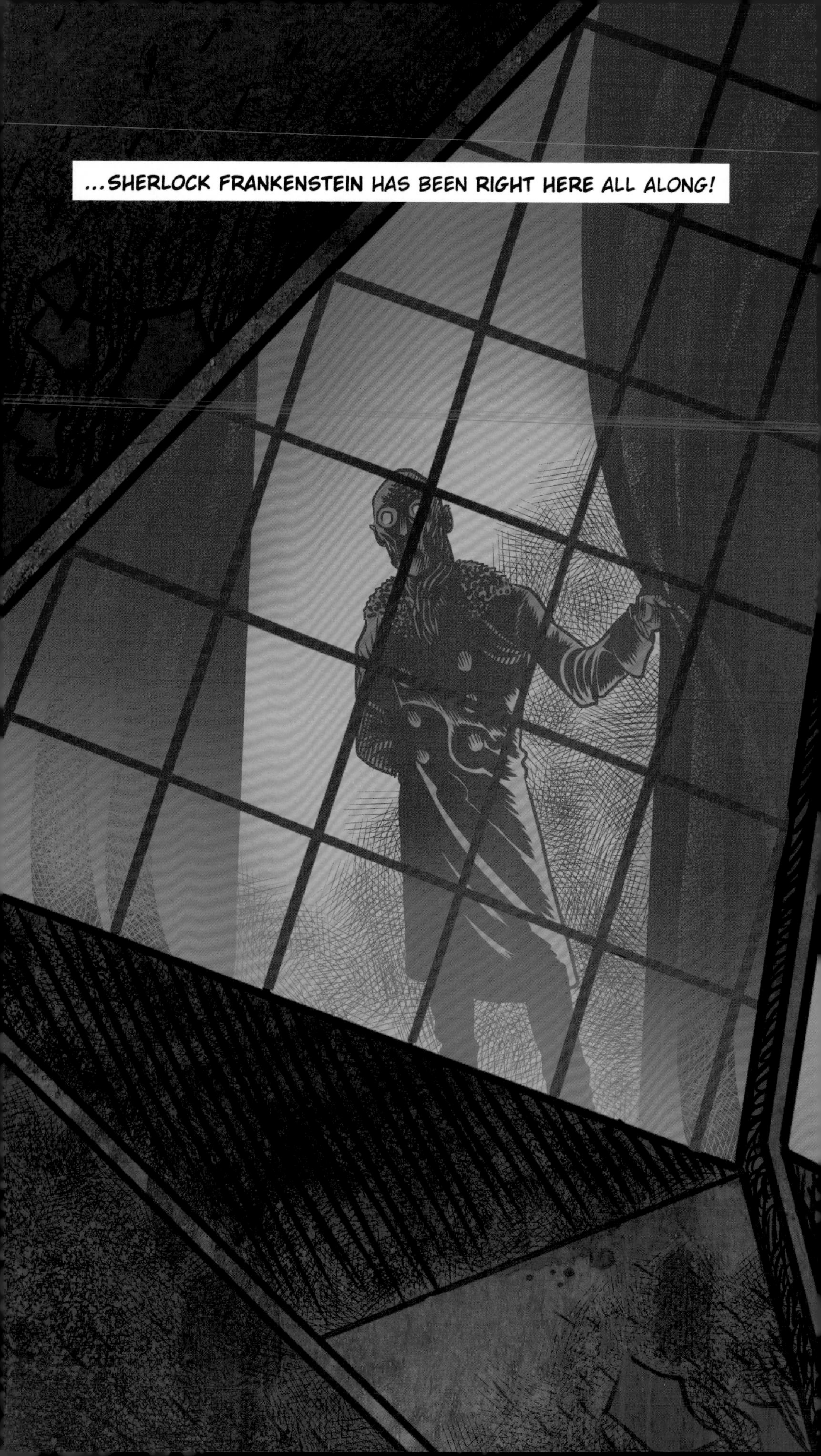
...SHERLOCK FRANKENSTEIN HAS BEEN RIGHT HERE ALL ALONG!

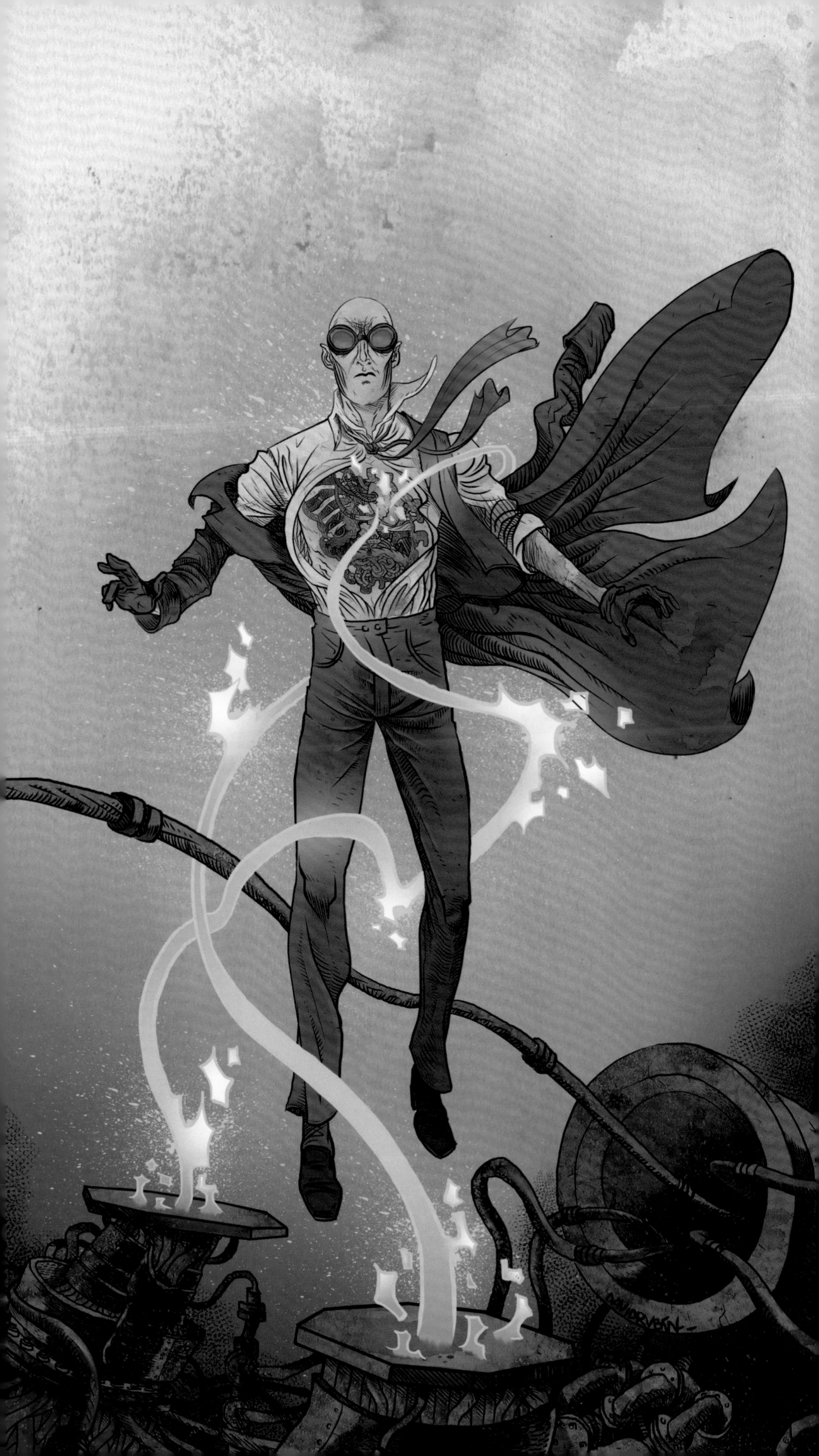

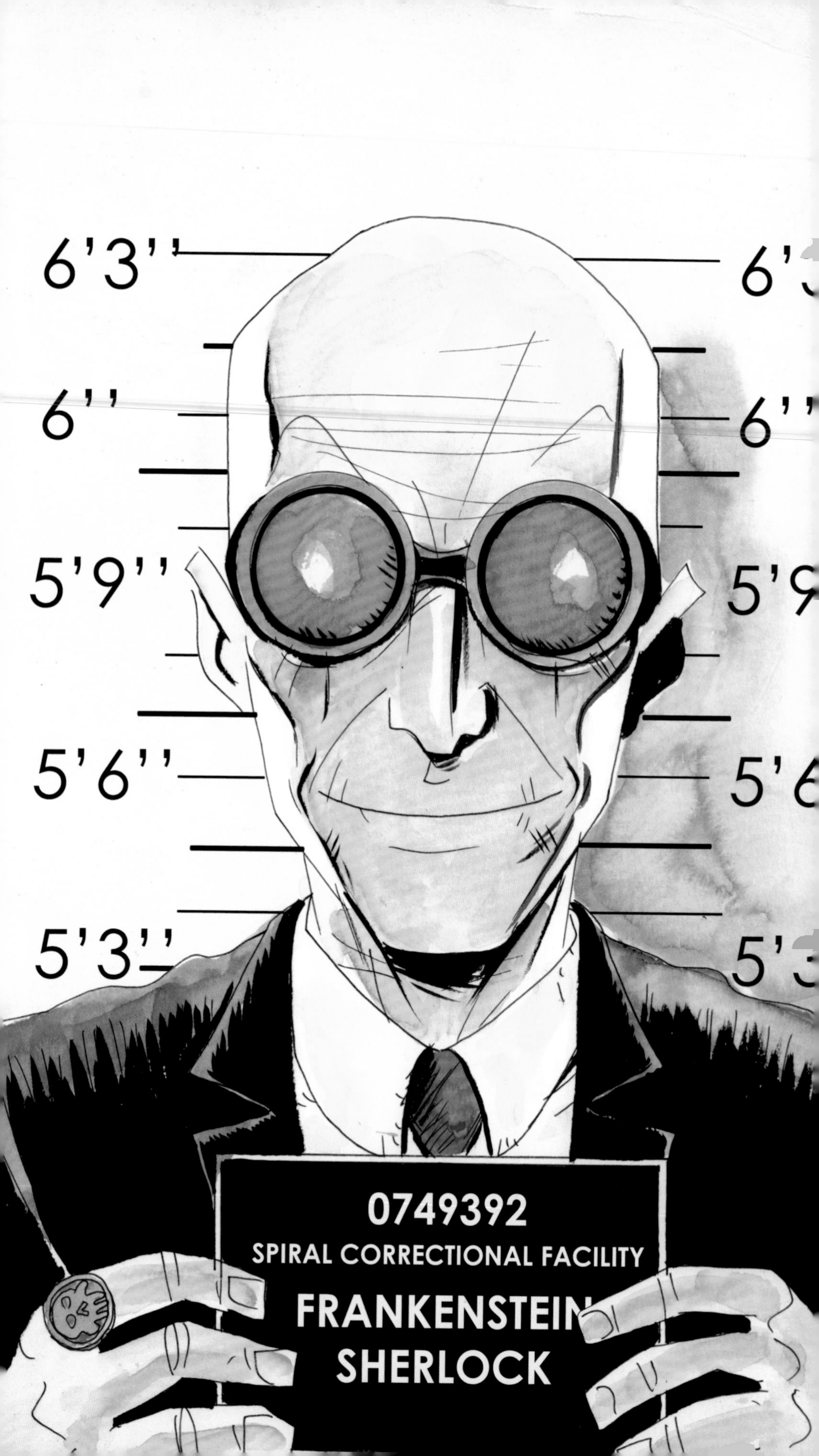
6'3''
6''
5'9''
5'6''
5'3''
0749392
SPIRAL CORRECTIONAL FACILITY
FRANKENSTEIN
SHERLOCK

LET ME TELL YOU A STORY...

AFTER ALL, THAT IS WHAT THIS IS ALL ABOUT, ISN'T IT?

STORIES.

WELL, THIS STORY STARTS A LONG TIME AGO, IN LONDON.

IT STARTS IN 1893 AND IT STARTS WITH A MAN...
A MAN WHO USED HIS MIND TO MAKE HIMSELF
MORE THAN A MAN.

HIS BODY WAS WEAK, FAILING HIM.

SOON HE WOULD BE DEAD.

AND WHILE HIS BODY WASTED AWAY THERE
WERE THOSE WHO SHOWED HIM KINDNESS.

E KNEW THAT HER MERCY
OULD NOT SAVE HIM.

THERE,
THERE.

IT WILL BE
OVER SOON.
GOD WILL HAVE
MERCY ON
YOU.

ONLY HIS MIND COULD DO THAT.

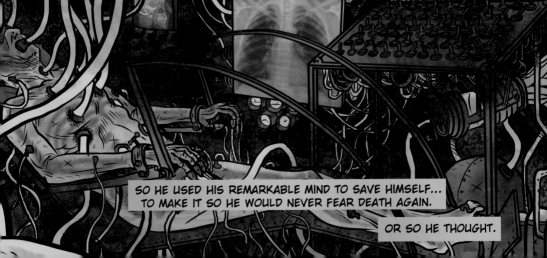

SO HE USED HIS REMARKABLE MIND TO SAVE HIMSELF...
TO MAKE IT SO HE WOULD NEVER FEAR DEATH AGAIN.

OR SO HE THOUGHT.

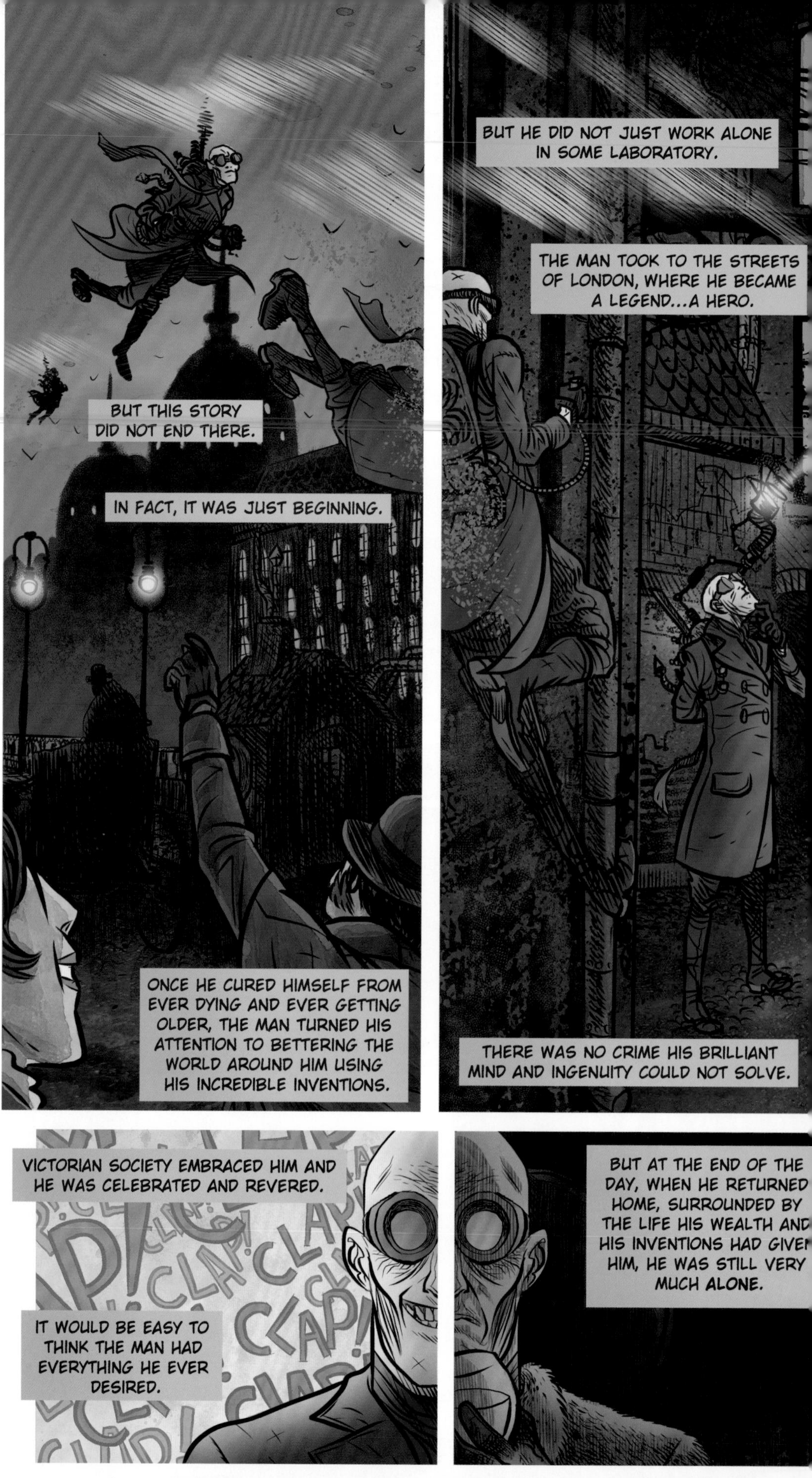
BUT THIS STORY DID NOT END THERE.
IN FACT, IT WAS JUST BEGINNING.
ONCE HE CURED HIMSELF FROM EVER DYING AND EVER GETTING OLDER, THE MAN TURNED HIS ATTENTION TO BETTERING THE WORLD AROUND HIM USING HIS INCREDIBLE INVENTIONS.
BUT HE DID NOT JUST WORK ALONE IN SOME LABORATORY.
THE MAN TOOK TO THE STREETS OF LONDON, WHERE HE BECAME A LEGEND...A HERO.
THERE WAS NO CRIME HIS BRILLIANT MIND AND INGENUITY COULD NOT SOLVE.
VICTORIAN SOCIETY EMBRACED HIM AND HE WAS CELEBRATED AND REVERED.
CLAP!
CLAP!
CLAP!
IT WOULD BE EASY TO THINK THE MAN HAD EVERYTHING HE EVER DESIRED.
BUT AT THE END OF THE DAY, WHEN HE RETURNED HOME, SURROUNDED BY THE LIFE HIS WEALTH AND HIS INVENTIONS HAD GIVE HIM, HE WAS STILL VERY MUCH ALONE.

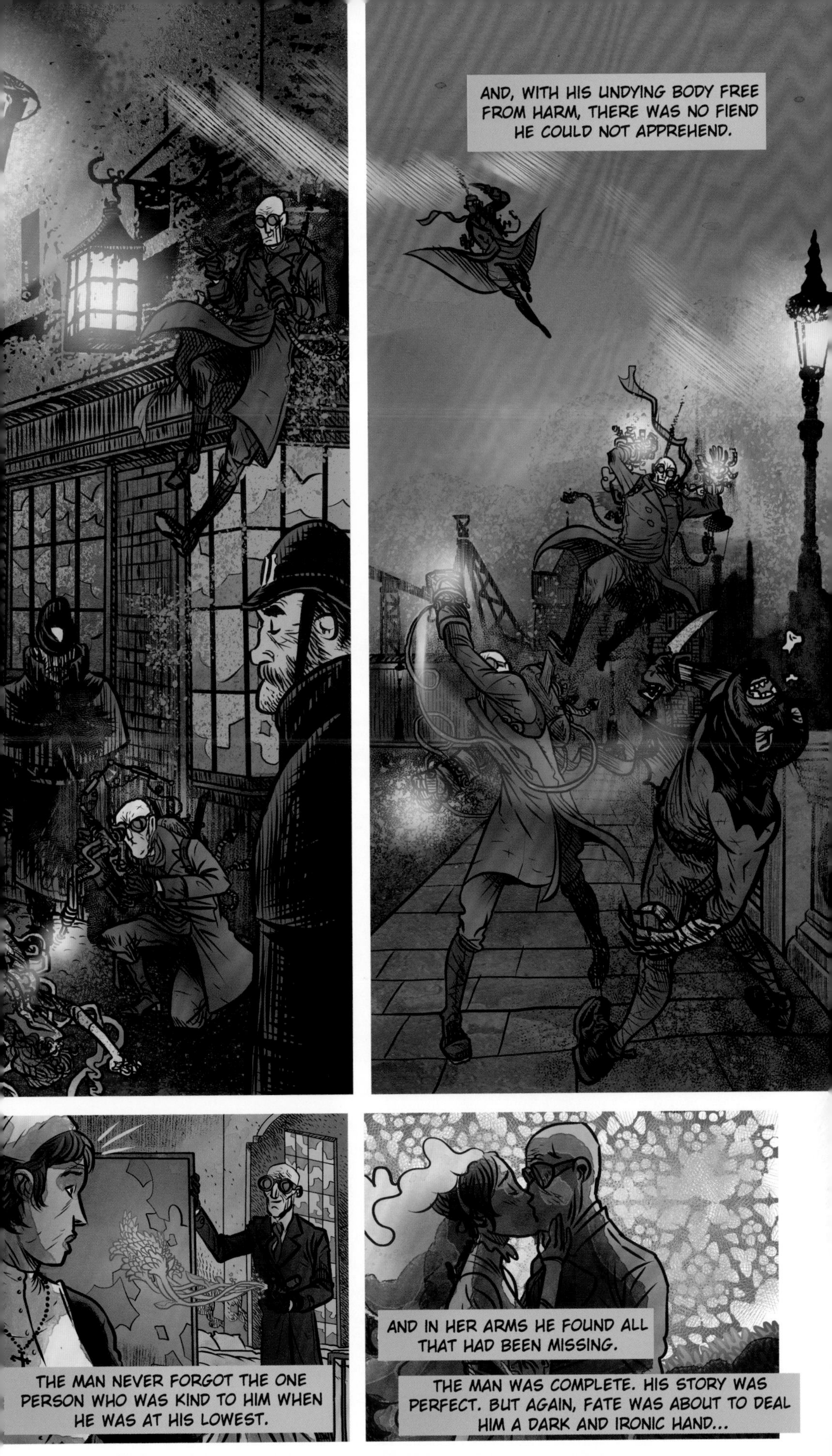
AND, WITH HIS UNDYING BODY FREE FROM HARM, THERE WAS NO FIEND HE COULD NOT APPREHEND.
THE MAN NEVER FORGOT THE ONE PERSON WHO WAS KIND TO HIM WHEN HE WAS AT HIS LOWEST.
AND IN HER ARMS HE FOUND ALL THAT HAD BEEN MISSING.
THE MAN WAS COMPLETE. HIS STORY WAS PERFECT. BUT AGAIN, FATE WAS ABOUT TO DEAL HIM A DARK AND IRONIC HAND...

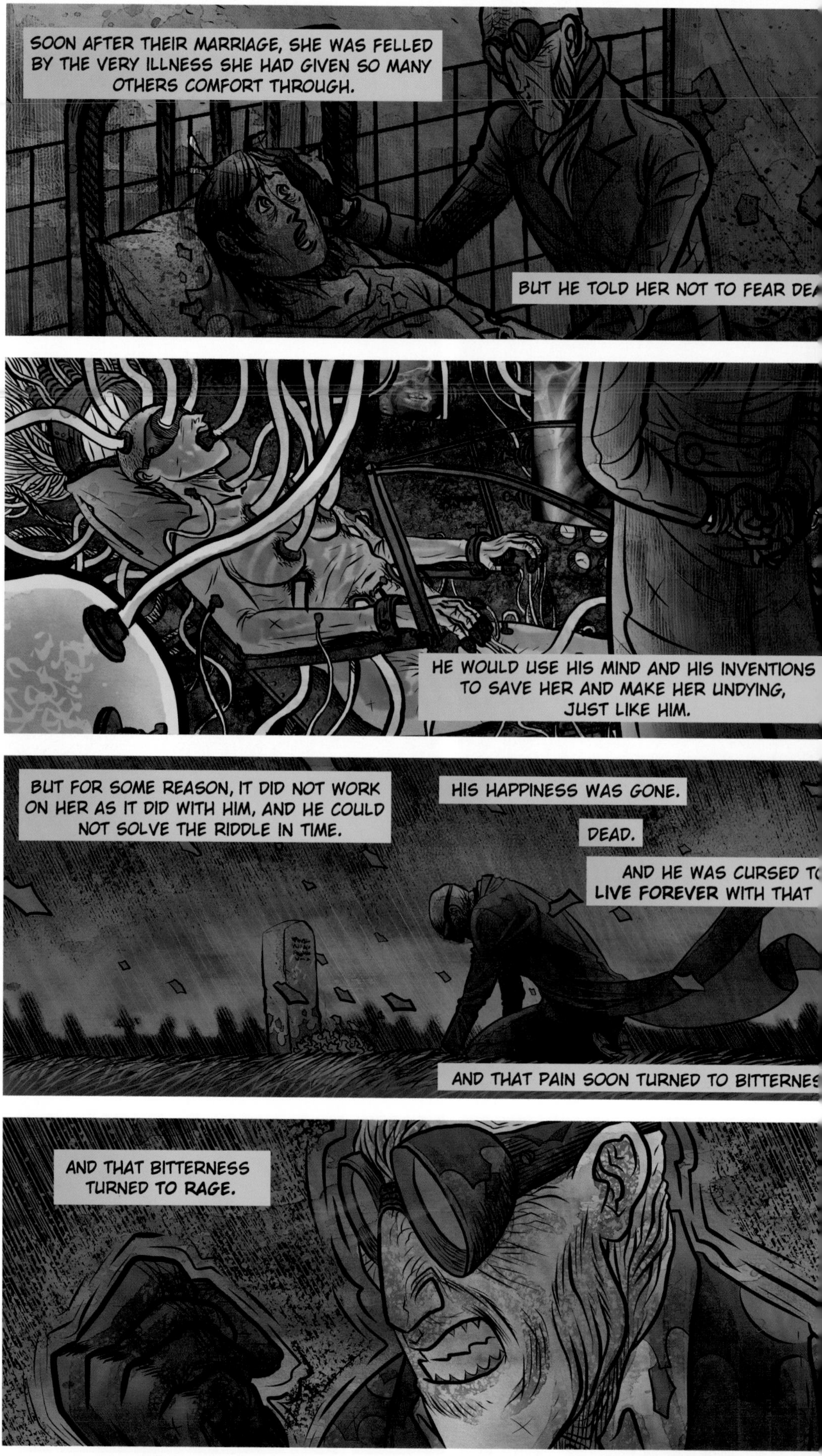

SOON AFTER THEIR MARRIAGE, SHE WAS FELLED BY THE VERY ILLNESS SHE HAD GIVEN SO MANY OTHERS COMFORT THROUGH.
BUT HE TOLD HER NOT TO FEAR DEA
HE WOULD USE HIS MIND AND HIS INVENTIONS TO SAVE HER AND MAKE HER UNDYING, JUST LIKE HIM.
BUT FOR SOME REASON, IT DID NOT WORK ON HER AS IT DID WITH HIM, AND HE COULD NOT SOLVE THE RIDDLE IN TIME.
HIS HAPPINESS WAS GONE.
DEAD.
AND HE WAS CURSED T
LIVE FOREVER WITH THAT
AND THAT PAIN SOON TURNED TO BITTERNES
AND THAT BITTERNESS TURNED TO RAGE.

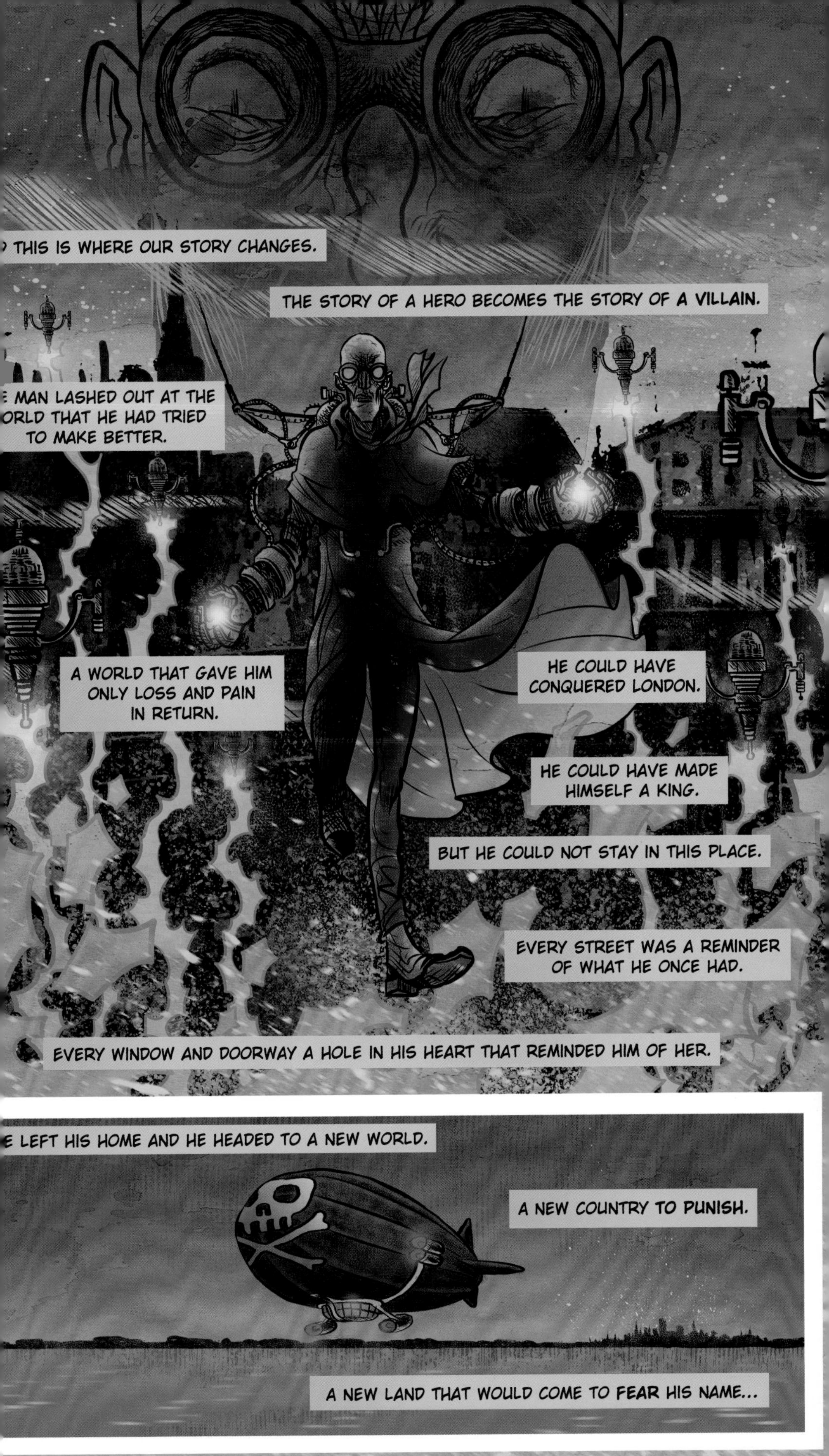
THIS IS WHERE OUR STORY CHANGES.
THE STORY OF A HERO BECOMES THE STORY OF A VILLAIN.
E MAN LASHED OUT AT THE ORLD THAT HE HAD TRIED TO MAKE BETTER.
A WORLD THAT GAVE HIM ONLY LOSS AND PAIN IN RETURN.
HE COULD HAVE CONQUERED LONDON.
HE COULD HAVE MADE HIMSELF A KING.
BUT HE COULD NOT STAY IN THIS PLACE.
EVERY STREET WAS A REMINDER OF WHAT HE ONCE HAD.
EVERY WINDOW AND DOORWAY A HOLE IN HIS HEART THAT REMINDED HIM OF HER.
E LEFT HIS HOME AND HE HEADED TO A NEW WORLD.
A NEW COUNTRY TO PUNISH.
A NEW LAND THAT WOULD COME TO FEAR HIS NAME...

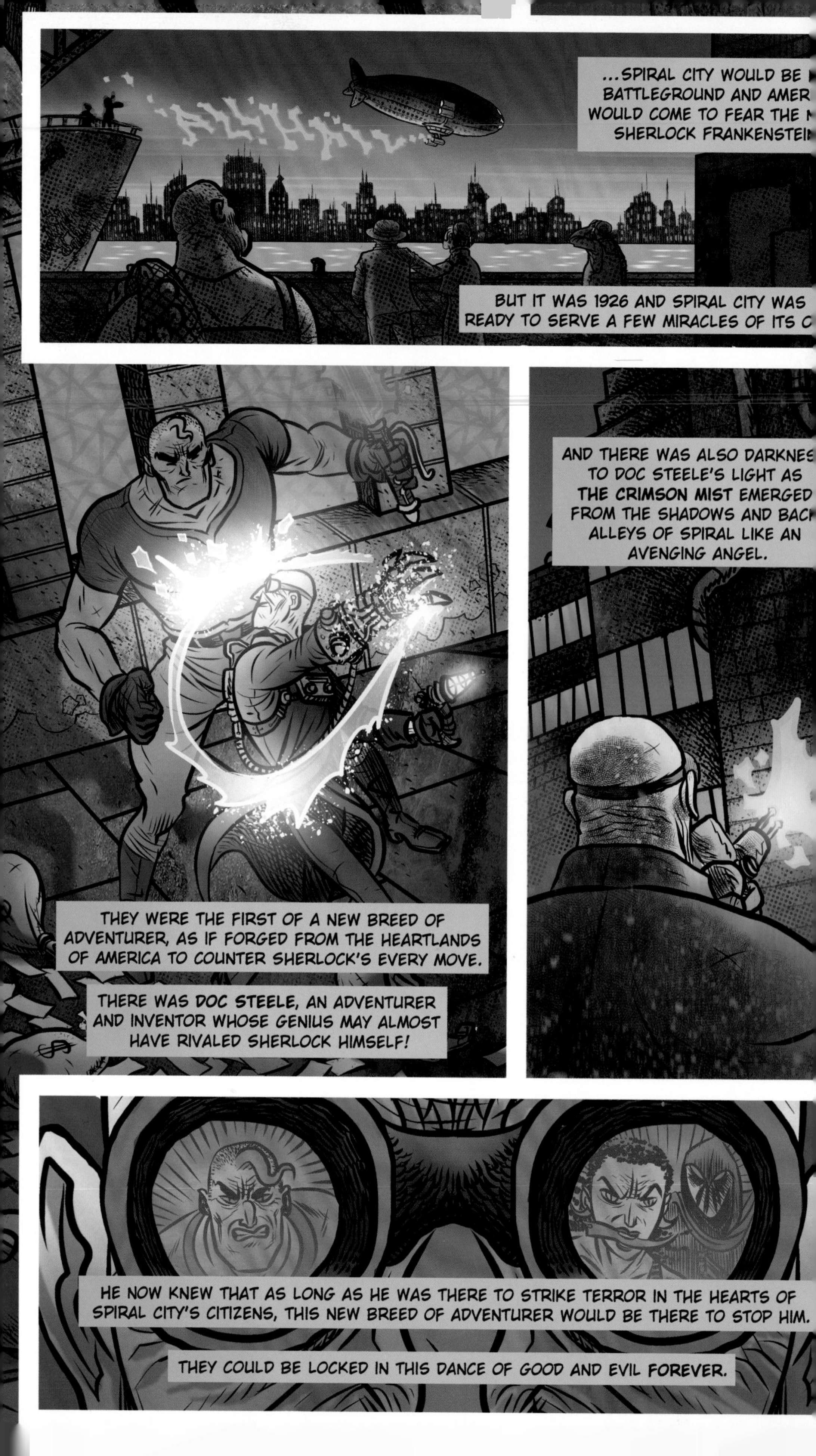

...SPIRAL CITY WOULD BE
BATTLEGROUND AND AMER
WOULD COME TO FEAR THE
SHERLOCK FRANKENSTEI
BUT IT WAS 1926 AND SPIRAL CITY WAS
READY TO SERVE A FEW MIRACLES OF ITS
THEY WERE THE FIRST OF A NEW BREED OF ADVENTURER, AS IF FORGED FROM THE HEARTLANDS OF AMERICA TO COUNTER SHERLOCK'S EVERY MOVE.
THERE WAS DOC STEELE, AN ADVENTURER AND INVENTOR WHOSE GENIUS MAY ALMOST HAVE RIVALED SHERLOCK HIMSELF!
AND THERE WAS ALSO DARKNES
TO DOC STEELE'S LIGHT AS
THE CRIMSON MIST EMERGED
FROM THE SHADOWS AND BAC
ALLEYS OF SPIRAL LIKE AN
AVENGING ANGEL.
HE NOW KNEW THAT AS LONG AS HE WAS THERE TO STRIKE TERROR IN THE HEARTS OF SPIRAL CITY'S CITIZENS, THIS NEW BREED OF ADVENTURER WOULD BE THERE TO STOP HIM.
THEY COULD BE LOCKED IN THIS DANCE OF GOOD AND EVIL FOREVER.

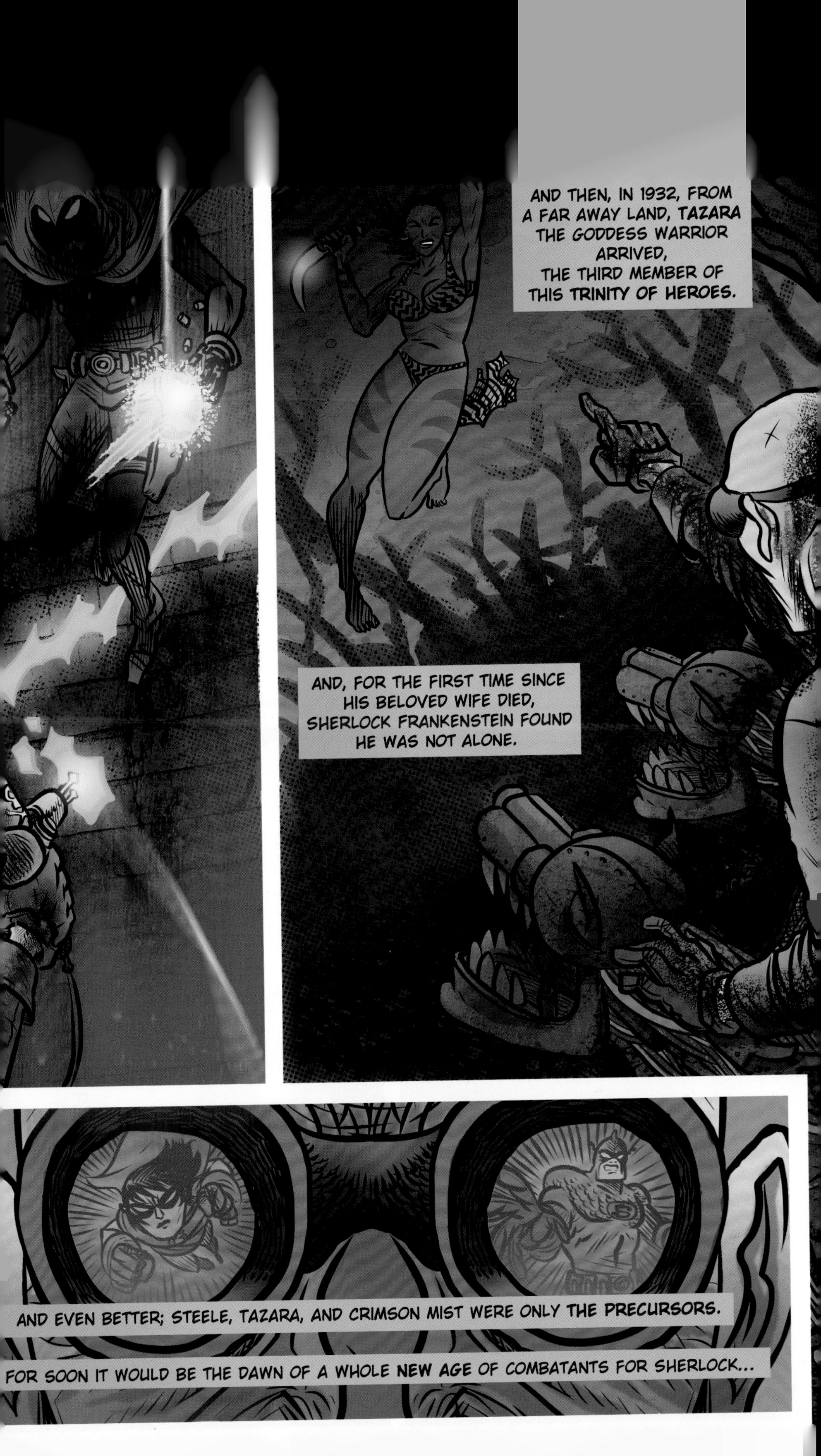
AND THEN, IN 1932, FROM A FAR AWAY LAND, TAZARA THE GODDESS WARRIOR ARRIVED, THE THIRD MEMBER OF THIS TRINITY OF HEROES.
AND, FOR THE FIRST TIME SINCE HIS BELOVED WIFE DIED, SHERLOCK FRANKENSTEIN FOUND HE WAS NOT ALONE.
AND EVEN BETTER; STEELE, TAZARA, AND CRIMSON MIST WERE ONLY THE PRECURSORS.
FOR SOON IT WOULD BE THE DAWN OF A WHOLE NEW AGE OF COMBATANTS FOR SHERLOCK...

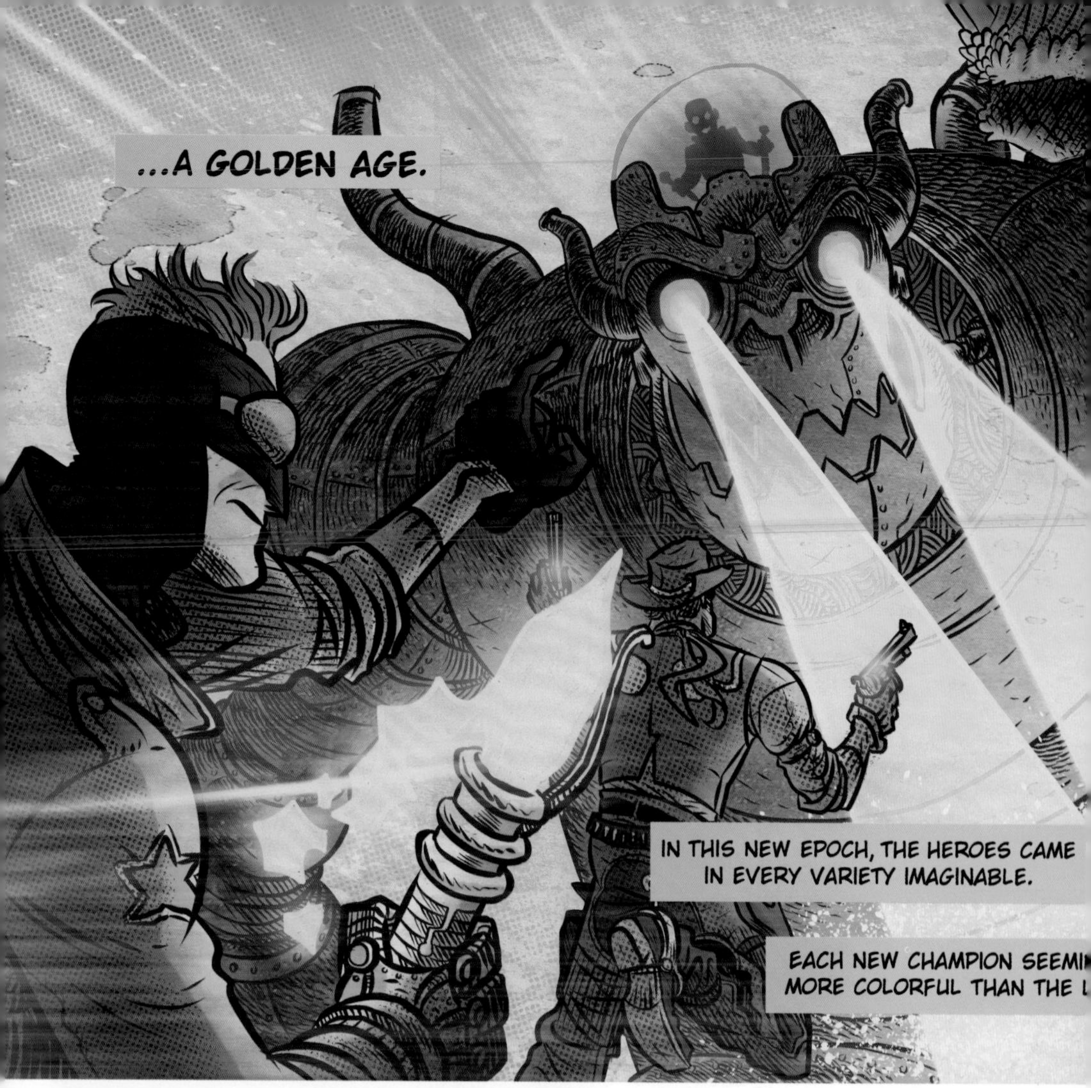
...A GOLDEN AGE.
IN THIS NEW EPOCH, THE HEROES CAME IN EVERY VARIETY IMAGINABLE.
EACH NEW CHAMPION SEEMI
MORE COLORFUL THAN THE L

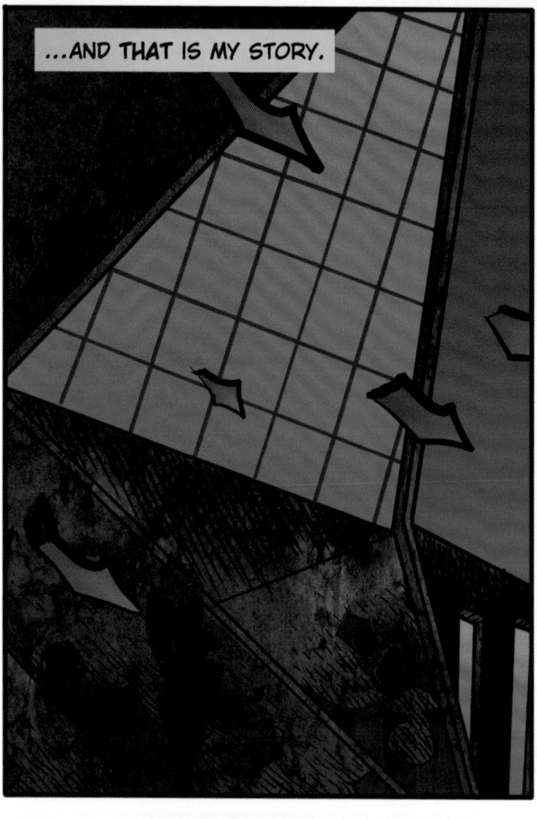
...AND THAT IS MY STORY.

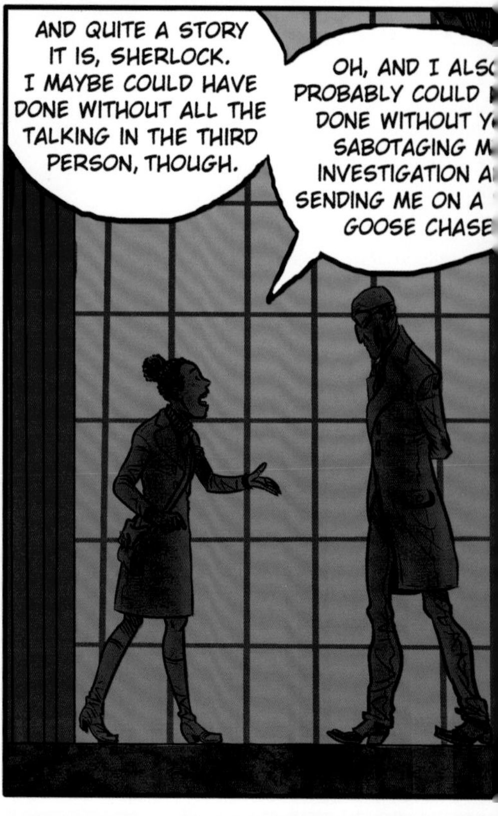
AND QUITE A STORY IT IS, SHERLOCK. I MAYBE COULD HAVE DONE WITHOUT ALL THE TALKING IN THE THIRD PERSON, THOUGH.
OH, AND I ALS
PROBABLY COULD
DONE WITHOUT Y
SABOTAGING M
INVESTIGATION A
SENDING ME ON A
GOOSE CHASE

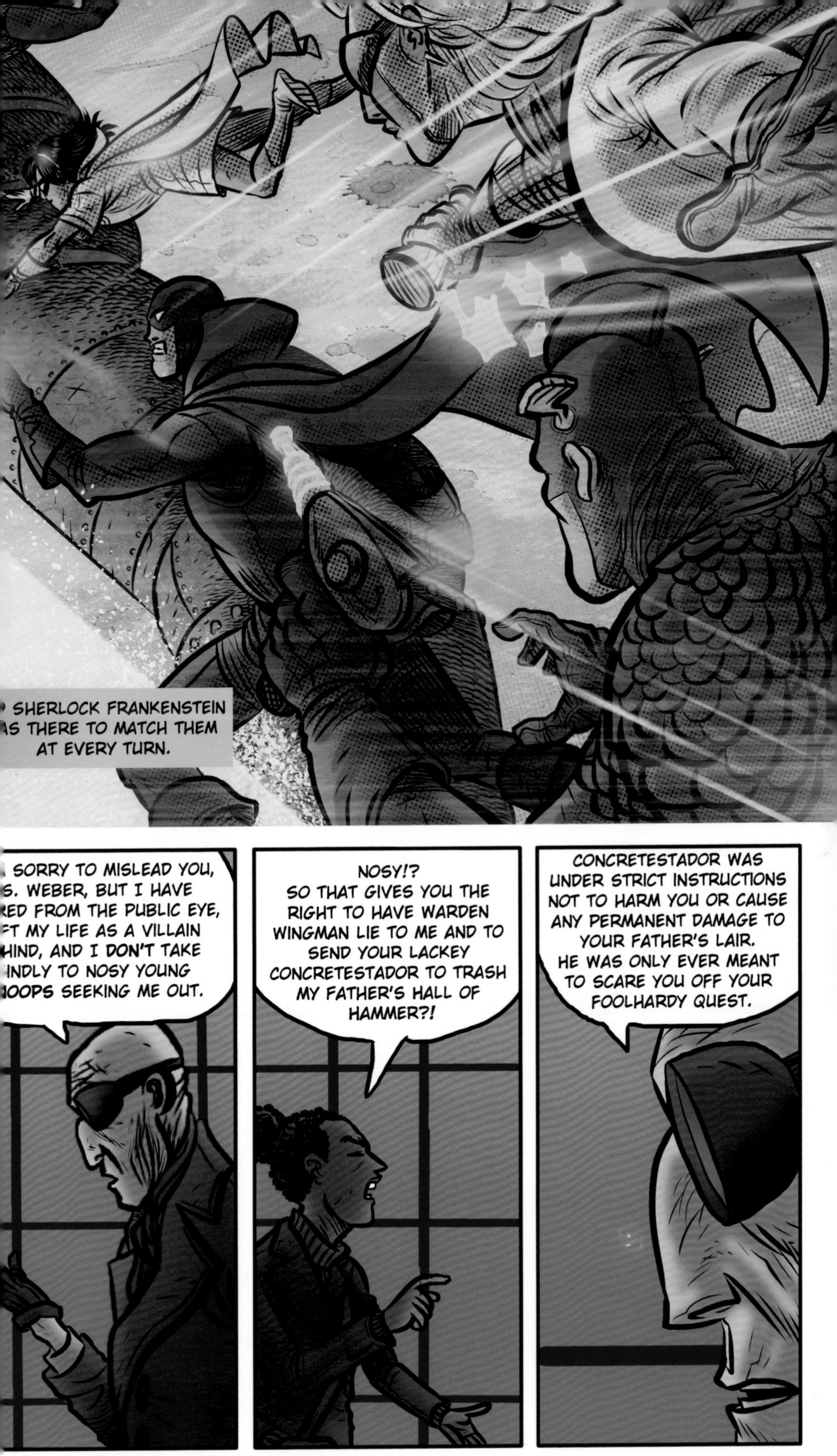

SHERLOCK FRANKENSTEIN AS THERE TO MATCH THEM AT EVERY TURN.
SORRY TO MISLEAD YOU, S. WEBER, BUT I HAVE RED FROM THE PUBLIC EYE, T MY LIFE AS A VILLAIN HIND, AND I DON'T TAKE INDLY TO NOSY YOUNG OOPS SEEKING ME OUT.
NOSY!? SO THAT GIVES YOU THE RIGHT TO HAVE WARDEN WINGMAN LIE TO ME AND TO SEND YOUR LACKEY CONCRETESTADOR TO TRASH MY FATHER'S HALL OF HAMMER?!
CONCRETESTADOR WAS UNDER STRICT INSTRUCTIONS NOT TO HARM YOU OR CAUSE ANY PERMANENT DAMAGE TO YOUR FATHER'S LAIR. HE WAS ONLY EVER MEANT TO SCARE YOU OFF YOUR FOOLHARDY QUEST.

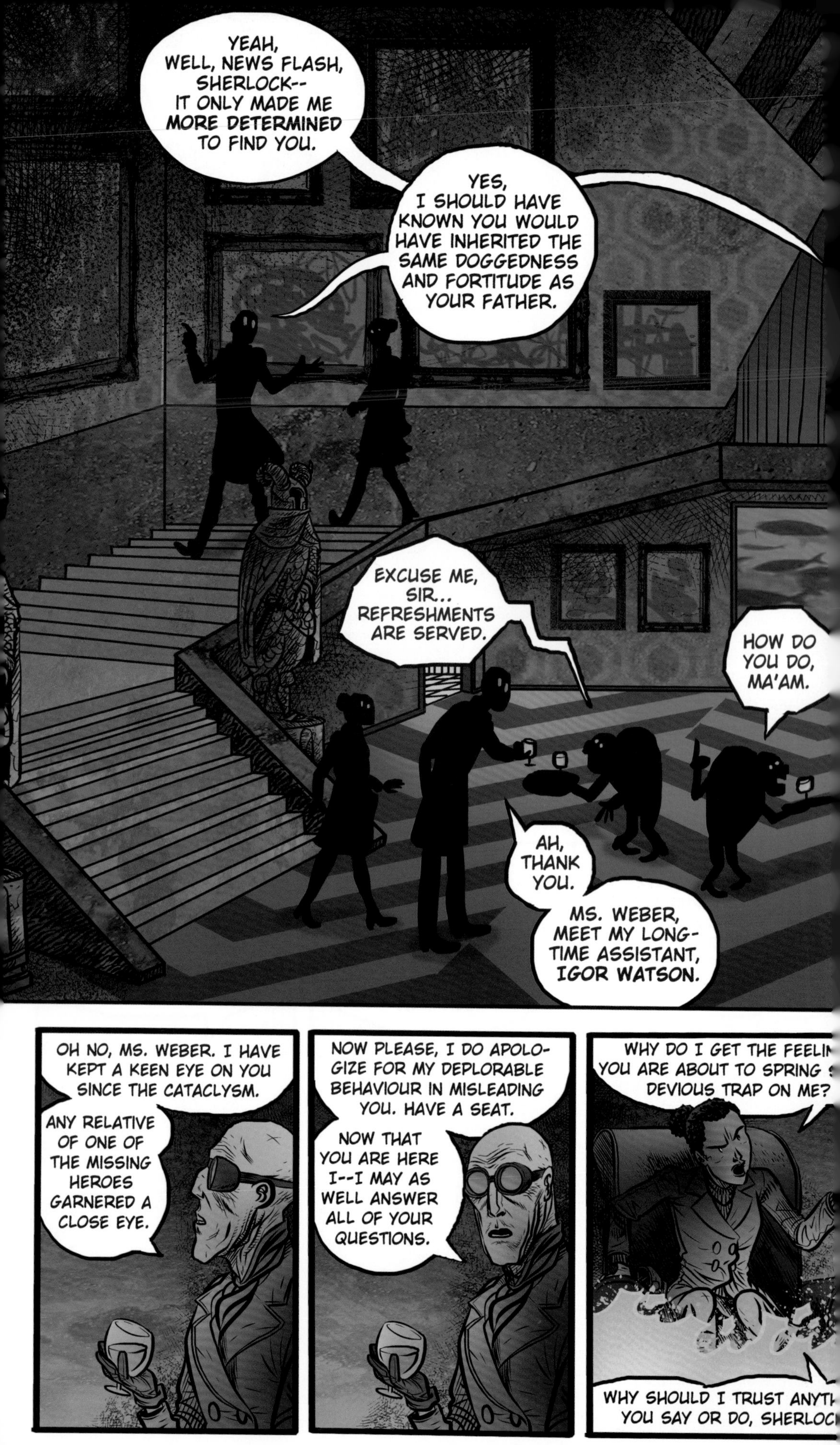
YEAH, WELL, NEWS FLASH, SHERLOCK-- IT ONLY MADE ME MORE DETERMINED TO FIND YOU.
YES, I SHOULD HAVE KNOWN YOU WOULD HAVE INHERITED THE SAME DOGGEDNESS AND FORTITUDE AS YOUR FATHER.
EXCUSE ME, SIR... REFRESHMENTS ARE SERVED.
HOW DO YOU DO, MA'AM.
AH, THANK YOU.
MS. WEBER, MEET MY LONG-TIME ASSISTANT, IGOR WATSON.
OH NO, MS. WEBER. I HAVE KEPT A KEEN EYE ON YOU SINCE THE CATACLYSM.
ANY RELATIVE OF ONE OF THE MISSING HEROES GARNERED A CLOSE EYE.
NOW PLEASE, I DO APOLOGIZE FOR MY DEPLORABLE BEHAVIOUR IN MISLEADING YOU. HAVE A SEAT.
NOW THAT YOU ARE HERE I--I MAY AS WELL ANSWER ALL OF YOUR QUESTIONS.
WHY DO I GET THE FEELI
YOU ARE ABOUT TO SPRING
DEVIOUS TRAP ON ME?
WHY SHOULD I TRUST ANYT
YOU SAY OR DO, SHERLOC

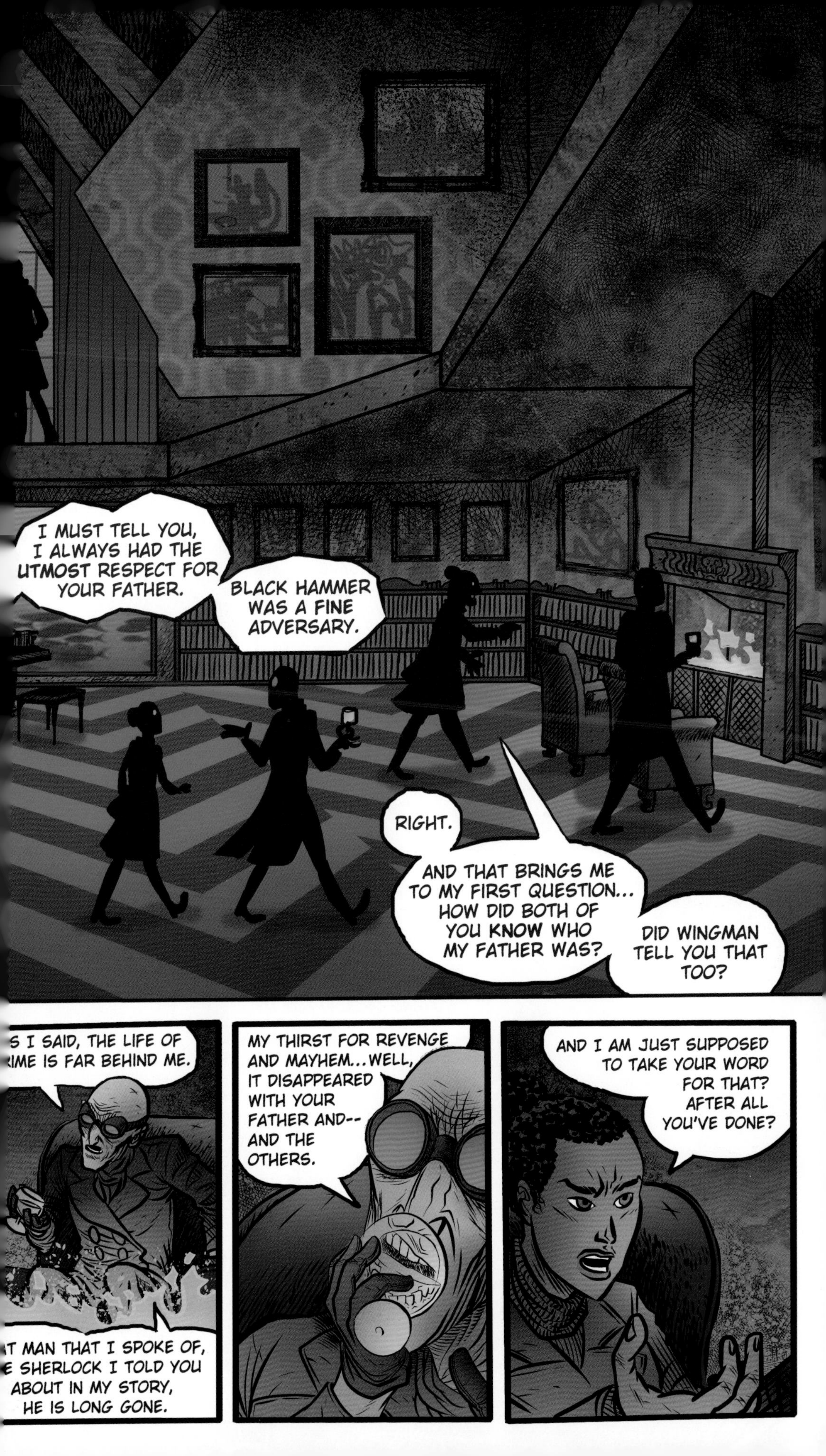
I MUST TELL YOU, I ALWAYS HAD THE UTMOST RESPECT FOR YOUR FATHER.
BLACK HAMMER WAS A FINE ADVERSARY.
RIGHT.
AND THAT BRINGS ME TO MY FIRST QUESTION... HOW DID BOTH OF YOU KNOW WHO MY FATHER WAS?
DID WINGMAN TELL YOU THAT TOO?
S I SAID, THE LIFE OF RIME IS FAR BEHIND ME.
T MAN THAT I SPOKE OF, E SHERLOCK I TOLD YOU ABOUT IN MY STORY, HE IS LONG GONE.
MY THIRST FOR REVENGE AND MAYHEM...WELL, IT DISAPPEARED WITH YOUR FATHER AND-- AND THE OTHERS.
AND I AM JUST SUPPOSED TO TAKE YOUR WORD FOR THAT? AFTER ALL YOU'VE DONE?

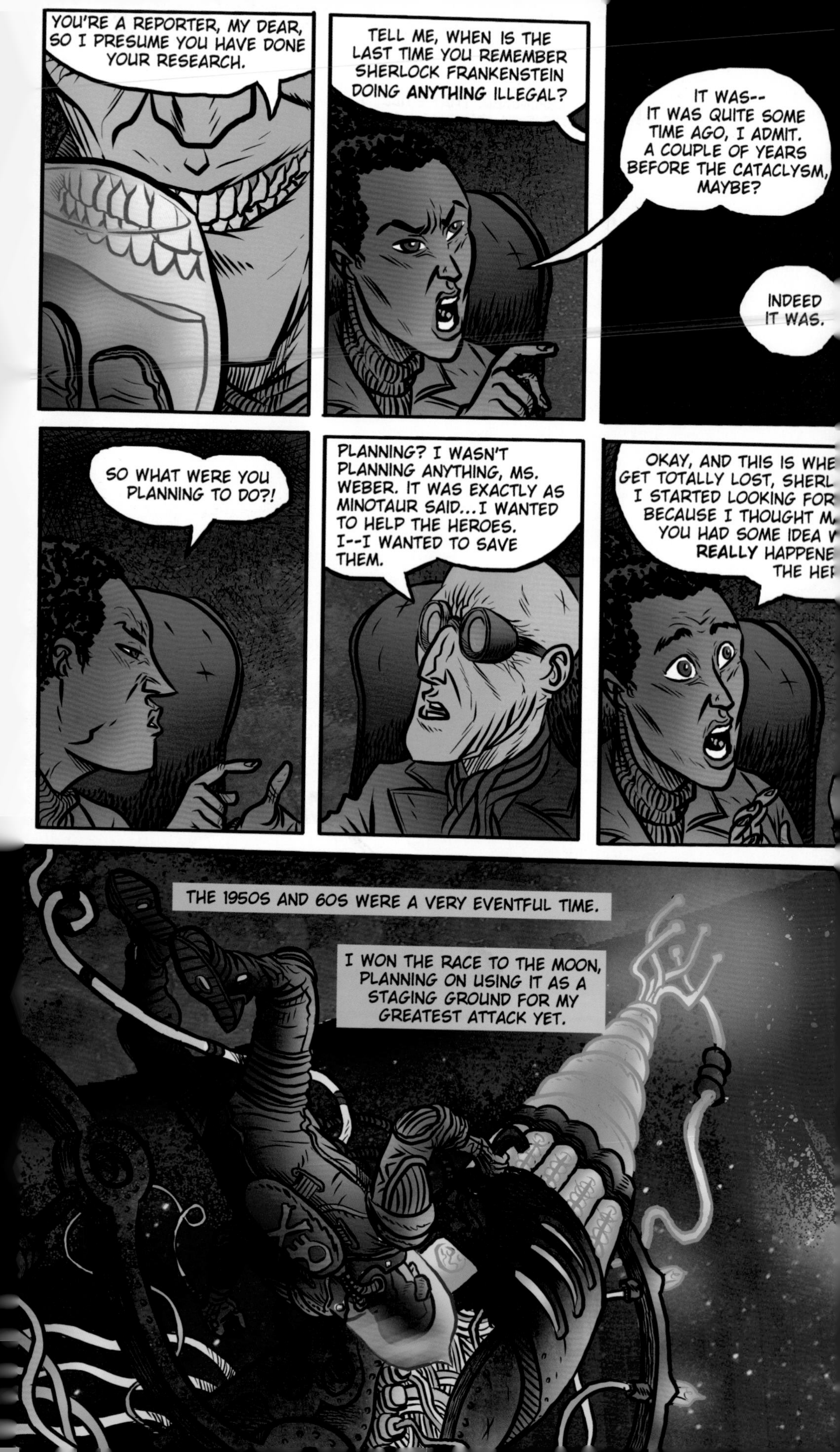
YOU'RE A REPORTER, MY DEAR, SO I PRESUME YOU HAVE DONE YOUR RESEARCH.
TELL ME, WHEN IS THE LAST TIME YOU REMEMBER SHERLOCK FRANKENSTEIN DOING ANYTHING ILLEGAL?
IT WAS-- IT WAS QUITE SOME TIME AGO, I ADMIT. A COUPLE OF YEARS BEFORE THE CATACLYSM, MAYBE?
INDEED IT WAS.
SO WHAT WERE YOU PLANNING TO DO?!
PLANNING? I WASN'T PLANNING ANYTHING, MS. WEBER. IT WAS EXACTLY AS MINOTAUR SAID... I WANTED TO HELP THE HEROES. I--I WANTED TO SAVE THEM.
OKAY, AND THIS IS WHE GET TOTALLY LOST, SHERL I STARTED LOOKING FOR BECAUSE I THOUGHT M YOU HAD SOME IDEA W REALLY HAPPENE THE HE
THE 1950S AND 60S WERE A VERY EVENTFUL TIME.
I WON THE RACE TO THE MOON, PLANNING ON USING IT AS A STAGING GROUND FOR MY GREATEST ATTACK YET.

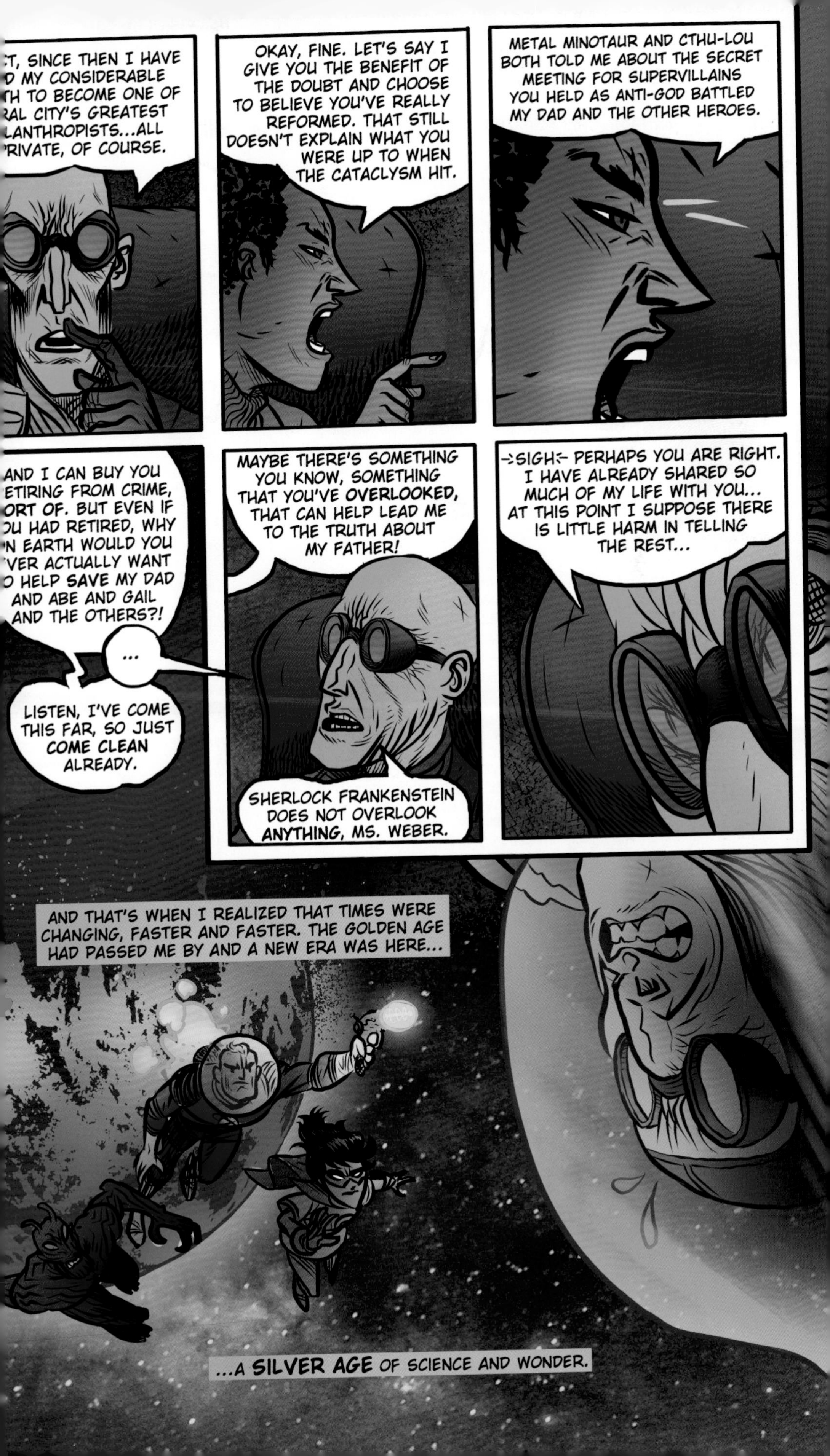

...T, SINCE THEN I HAVE ...D MY CONSIDERABLE ...TH TO BECOME ONE OF ...RAL CITY'S GREATEST ...LANTHROPISTS...ALL ...PRIVATE, OF COURSE.
OKAY, FINE. LET'S SAY I GIVE YOU THE BENEFIT OF THE DOUBT AND CHOOSE TO BELIEVE YOU'VE REALLY REFORMED. THAT STILL DOESN'T EXPLAIN WHAT YOU WERE UP TO WHEN THE CATACLYSM HIT.
METAL MINOTAUR AND CTHU-LOU BOTH TOLD ME ABOUT THE SECRET MEETING FOR SUPERVILLAINS YOU HELD AS ANTI-GOD BATTLED MY DAD AND THE OTHER HEROES.
AND I CAN BUY YOU ...ETIRING FROM CRIME, ...ORT OF. BUT EVEN IF ...OU HAD RETIRED, WHY ...N EARTH WOULD YOU ...VER ACTUALLY WANT ...O HELP SAVE MY DAD AND ABE AND GAIL AND THE OTHERS?!
...
LISTEN, I'VE COME THIS FAR, SO JUST COME CLEAN ALREADY.
MAYBE THERE'S SOMETHING YOU KNOW, SOMETHING THAT YOU'VE OVERLOOKED, THAT CAN HELP LEAD ME TO THE TRUTH ABOUT MY FATHER!
SHERLOCK FRANKENSTEIN DOES NOT OVERLOOK ANYTHING, MS. WEBER.
⇢SIGH⇠ PERHAPS YOU ARE RIGHT. I HAVE ALREADY SHARED SO MUCH OF MY LIFE WITH YOU... AT THIS POINT I SUPPOSE THERE IS LITTLE HARM IN TELLING THE REST...
AND THAT'S WHEN I REALIZED THAT TIMES WERE CHANGING, FASTER AND FASTER. THE GOLDEN AGE HAD PASSED ME BY AND A NEW ERA WAS HERE...
...A SILVER AGE OF SCIENCE AND WONDER.

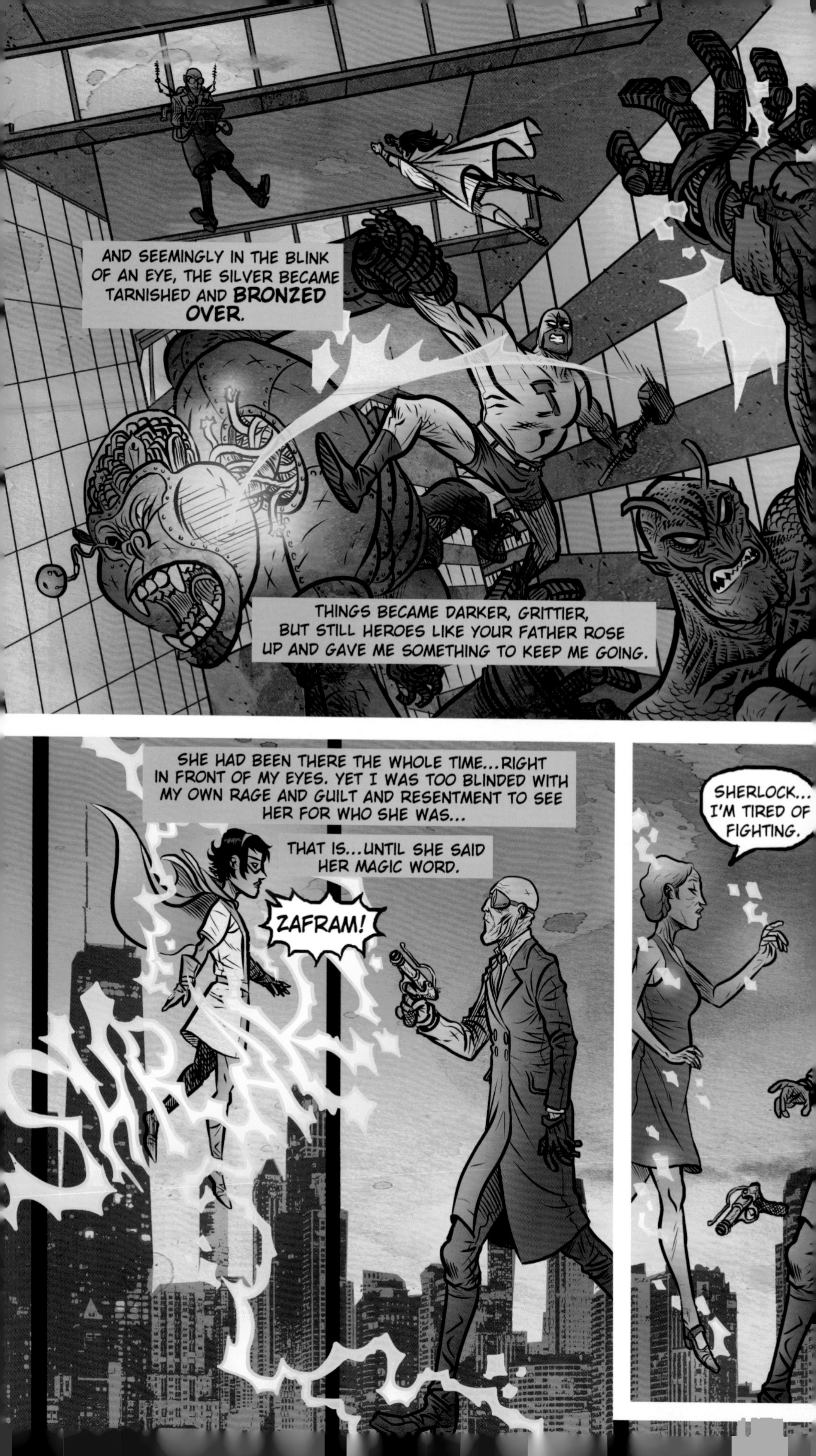
AND SEEMINGLY IN THE BLINK OF AN EYE, THE SILVER BECAME TARNISHED AND BRONZED OVER.
THINGS BECAME DARKER, GRITTIER, BUT STILL HEROES LIKE YOUR FATHER ROSE UP AND GAVE ME SOMETHING TO KEEP ME GOING.
SHE HAD BEEN THERE THE WHOLE TIME...RIGHT IN FRONT OF MY EYES. YET I WAS TOO BLINDED WITH MY OWN RAGE AND GUILT AND RESENTMENT TO SEE HER FOR WHO SHE WAS...
THAT IS...UNTIL SHE SAID HER MAGIC WORD.
ZAFRAM!
SHERLOCK... I'M TIRED OF FIGHTING.

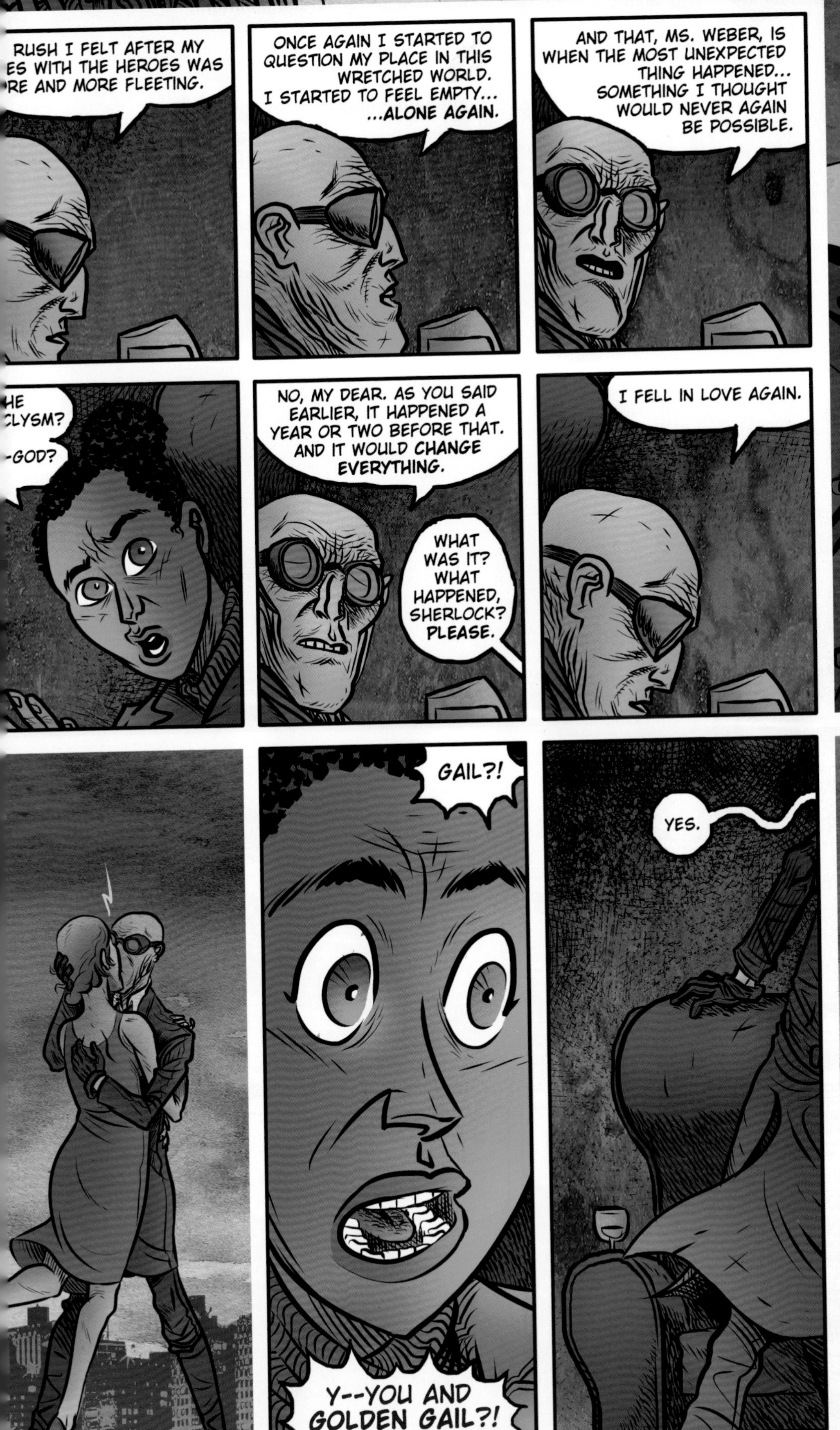
RUSH I FELT AFTER MY
ES WITH THE HEROES WAS
RE AND MORE FLEETING.
ONCE AGAIN I STARTED TO QUESTION MY PLACE IN THIS WRETCHED WORLD. I STARTED TO FEEL EMPTY... ...ALONE AGAIN.
AND THAT, MS. WEBER, IS WHEN THE MOST UNEXPECTED THING HAPPENED... SOMETHING I THOUGHT WOULD NEVER AGAIN BE POSSIBLE.
HE
CLYSM?
-GOD?
NO, MY DEAR. AS YOU SAID EARLIER, IT HAPPENED A YEAR OR TWO BEFORE THAT. AND IT WOULD CHANGE EVERYTHING.
WHAT WAS IT? WHAT HAPPENED, SHERLOCK? PLEASE.
I FELL IN LOVE AGAIN.
GAIL?!
Y--YOU AND GOLDEN GAIL?!
YES.

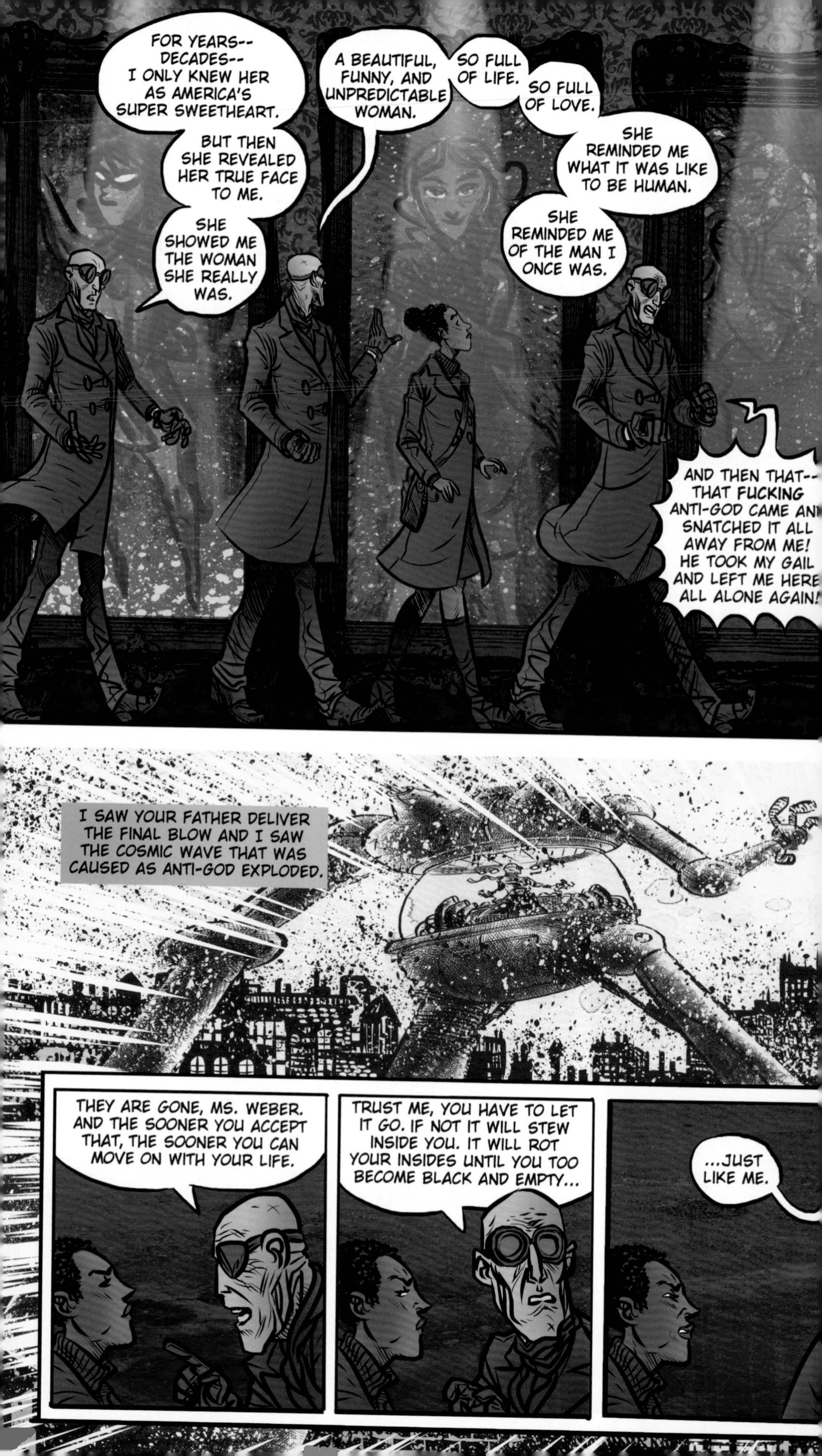
FOR YEARS-- DECADES-- I ONLY KNEW HER AS AMERICA'S SUPER SWEETHEART.
BUT THEN SHE REVEALED HER TRUE FACE TO ME.
SHE SHOWED ME THE WOMAN SHE REALLY WAS.
A BEAUTIFUL, FUNNY, AND UNPREDICTABLE WOMAN.
SO FULL OF LIFE.
SO FULL OF LOVE.
SHE REMINDED ME WHAT IT WAS LIKE TO BE HUMAN.
SHE REMINDED ME OF THE MAN I ONCE WAS.
AND THEN THAT-- THAT FUCKING ANTI-GOD CAME AN SNATCHED IT ALL AWAY FROM ME! HE TOOK MY GAIL AND LEFT ME HERE ALL ALONE AGAIN!
I SAW YOUR FATHER DELIVER THE FINAL BLOW AND I SAW THE COSMIC WAVE THAT WAS CAUSED AS ANTI-GOD EXPLODED.
THEY ARE GONE, MS. WEBER. AND THE SOONER YOU ACCEPT THAT, THE SOONER YOU CAN MOVE ON WITH YOUR LIFE.
TRUST ME, YOU HAVE TO LET IT GO. IF NOT IT WILL STEW INSIDE YOU. IT WILL ROT YOUR INSIDES UNTIL YOU TOO BECOME BLACK AND EMPTY...
...JUST LIKE ME.

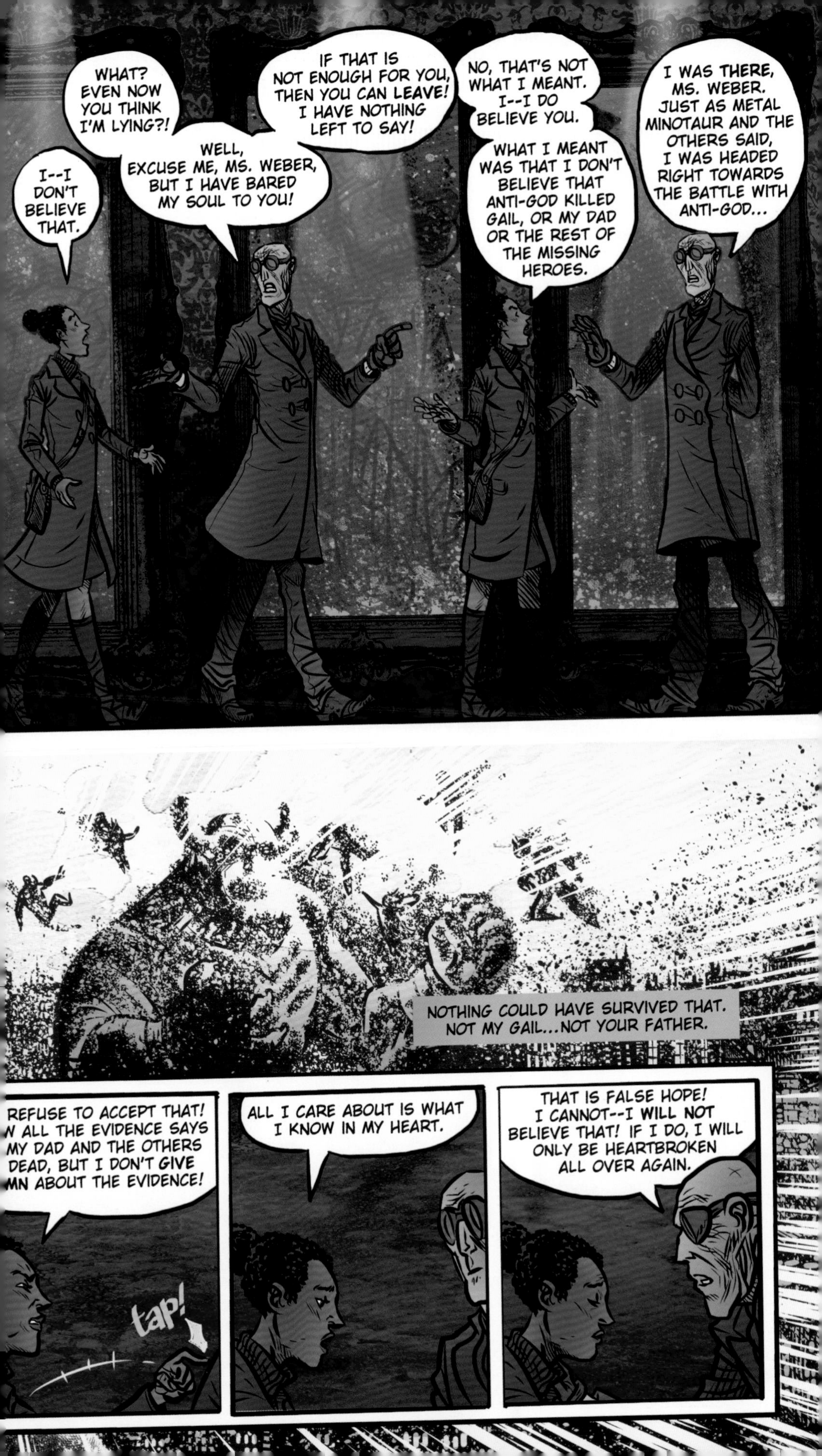
I--I DON'T BELIEVE THAT.
WHAT? EVEN NOW YOU THINK I'M LYING?!
WELL, EXCUSE ME, MS. WEBER, BUT I HAVE BARED MY SOUL TO YOU!
IF THAT IS NOT ENOUGH FOR YOU, THEN YOU CAN LEAVE! I HAVE NOTHING LEFT TO SAY!
NO, THAT'S NOT WHAT I MEANT. I--I DO BELIEVE YOU.
WHAT I MEANT WAS THAT I DON'T BELIEVE THAT ANTI-GOD KILLED GAIL, OR MY DAD OR THE REST OF THE MISSING HEROES.
I WAS THERE, MS. WEBER. JUST AS METAL MINOTAUR AND THE OTHERS SAID, I WAS HEADED RIGHT TOWARDS THE BATTLE WITH ANTI-GOD...
NOTHING COULD HAVE SURVIVED THAT. NOT MY GAIL...NOT YOUR FATHER.
REFUSE TO ACCEPT THAT! N ALL THE EVIDENCE SAYS MY DAD AND THE OTHERS DEAD, BUT I DON'T GIVE MN ABOUT THE EVIDENCE!
tap!
ALL I CARE ABOUT IS WHAT I KNOW IN MY HEART.
THAT IS FALSE HOPE! I CANNOT--I WILL NOT BELIEVE THAT! IF I DO, I WILL ONLY BE HEARTBROKEN ALL OVER AGAIN.

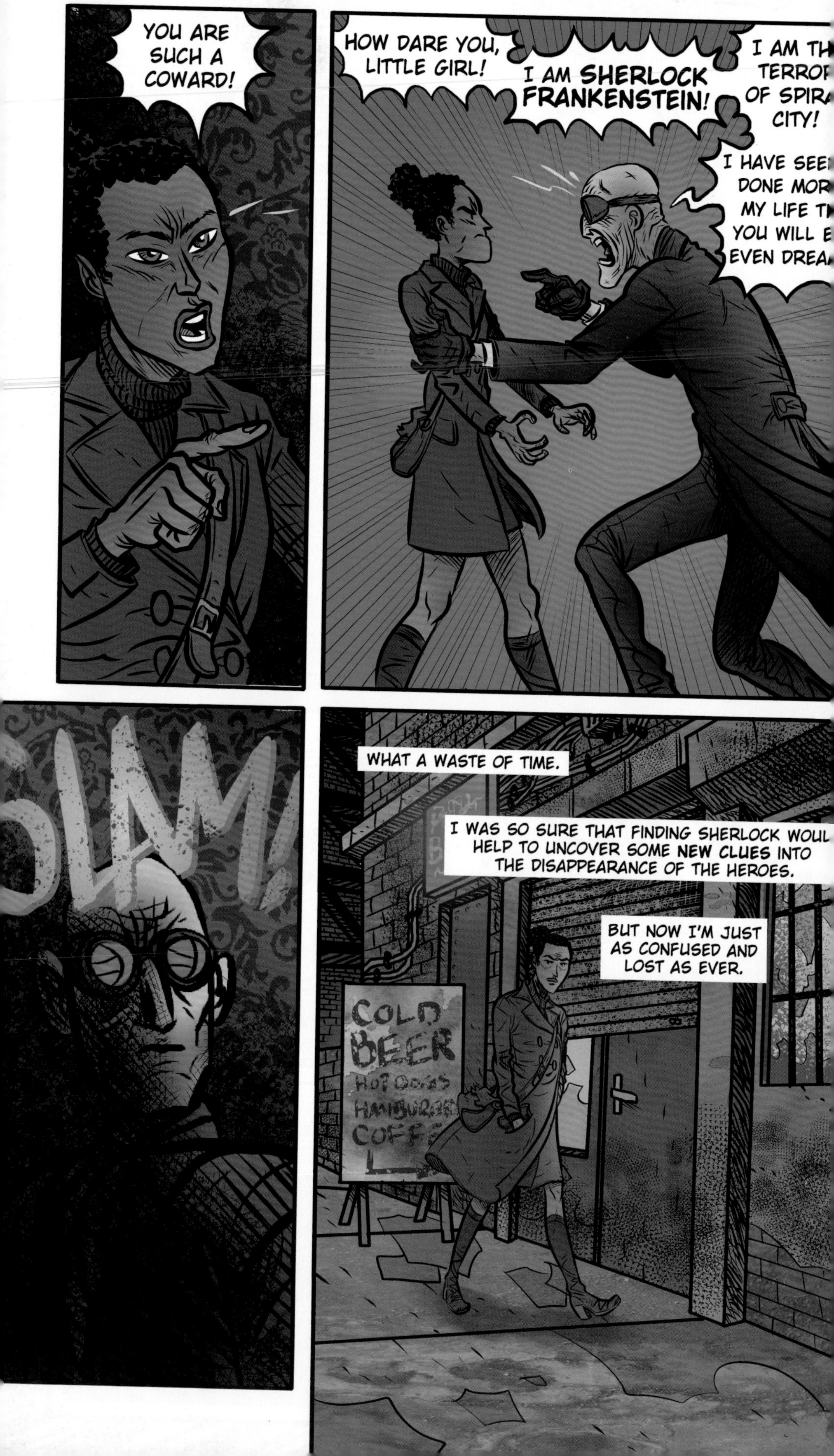

YOU ARE SUCH A COWARD!
HOW DARE YOU, LITTLE GIRL!
I AM SHERLOCK FRANKENSTEIN!
I AM TH TERROR OF SPIRA CITY!
I HAVE SEE DONE MOR MY LIFE T YOU WILL E EVEN DREA
SLAM!
WHAT A WASTE OF TIME.
I WAS SO SURE THAT FINDING SHERLOCK WOUL HELP TO UNCOVER SOME NEW CLUES INTO THE DISAPPEARANCE OF THE HEROES.
BUT NOW I'M JUST AS CONFUSED AND LOST AS EVER.
COLD BEER

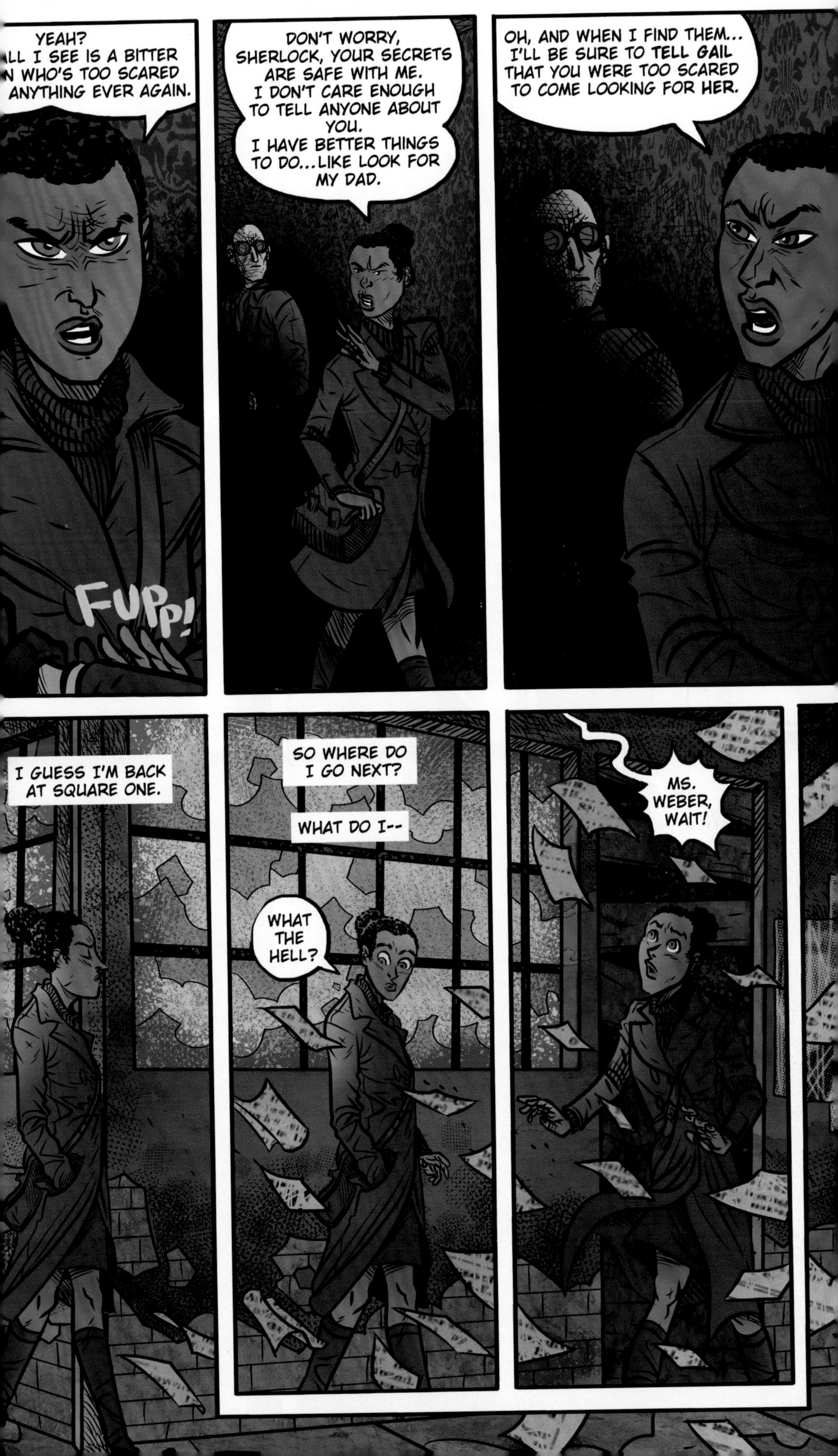

YEAH?
LL I SEE IS A BITTER
N WHO'S TOO SCARED
ANYTHING EVER AGAIN.
FUPP!
DON'T WORRY, SHERLOCK, YOUR SECRETS ARE SAFE WITH ME. I DON'T CARE ENOUGH TO TELL ANYONE ABOUT YOU. I HAVE BETTER THINGS TO DO...LIKE LOOK FOR MY DAD.
OH, AND WHEN I FIND THEM... I'LL BE SURE TO TELL GAIL THAT YOU WERE TOO SCARED TO COME LOOKING FOR HER.
I GUESS I'M BACK AT SQUARE ONE.
SO WHERE DO I GO NEXT?
WHAT DO I--
WHAT THE HELL?
MS. WEBER, WAIT!

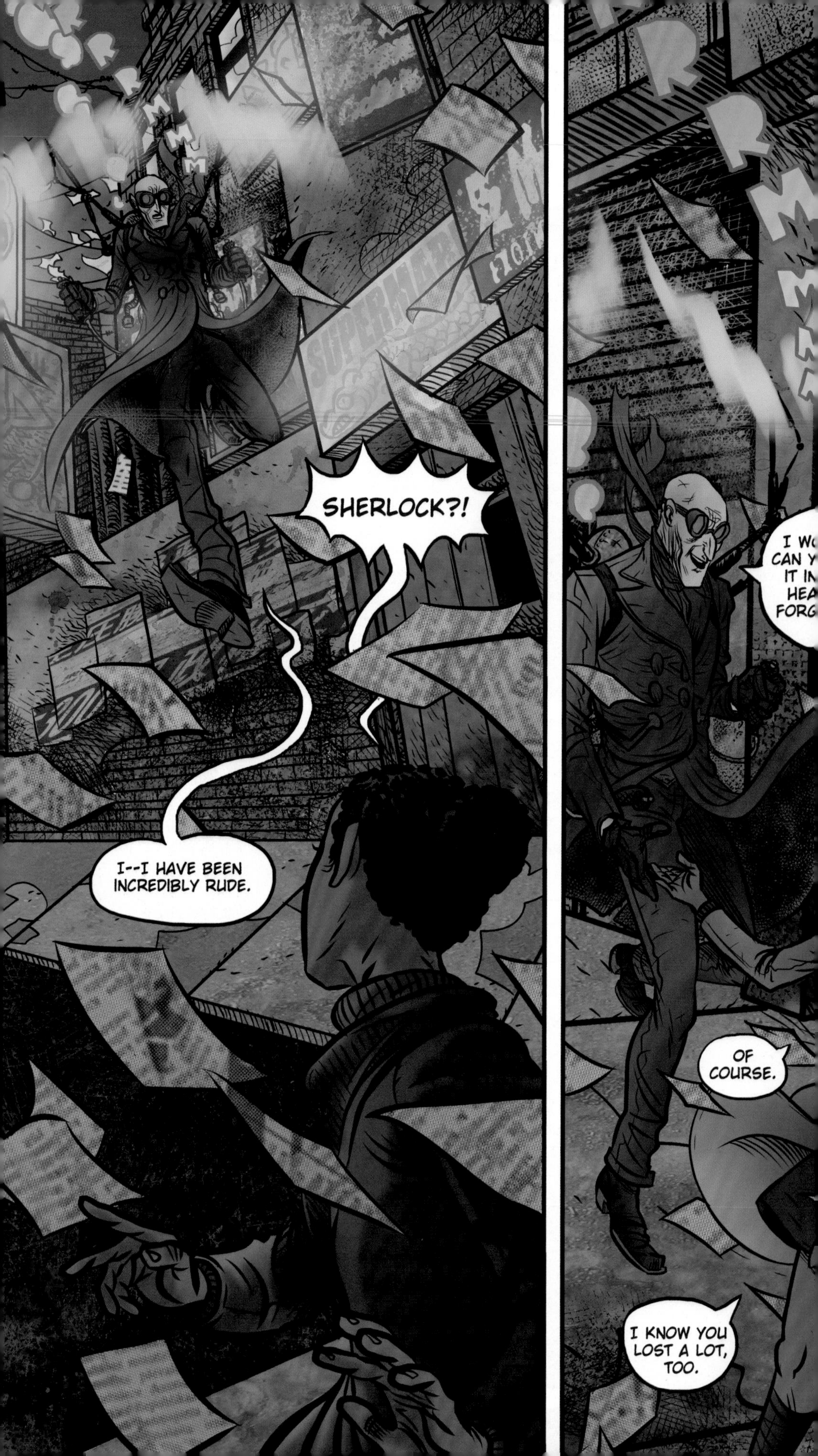
SHERLOCK?!
I--I HAVE BEEN INCREDIBLY RUDE.
OF COURSE.
I KNOW YOU LOST A LOT, TOO.

ALL I DID WAS HIDE E THE WORLD FINALLY RTED TO PASS ME BY.

DOES THIS MEAN YOU BELIEVE ME? DO YOU THINK GAIL AND MY DAD AND THE REST ARE STILL ALIVE SOMEWHERE?

I BELIEVE THAT YOU BELIEVE THAT. AND--DESPITE MY BEST EFFORTS--SEEING YOUR FAITH SEEMS TO HAVE REKINDLED SOMETHING IN ME AS WELL.

SO I WILL PROMISE YOU THIS. AS LONG AS YOU BELIEVE... AS LONG AS YOU WANT TO KEEP LOOKING, I WILL PROVIDE YOU WITH ANY AND EVERY RESOURCE YOU MAY NEED.

MY WEALTH IS RIVALED ONLY BY MY GENIUS, MS. WEBER. AND IT IS NOW AT YOUR DISPOSAL.

-WOW. N'T KNOW T TO SAY.

HOW ABOUT YOU SAVE YOUR WORDS FOR GAIL, SHOULD YOU FIND HER...

CLIC!!

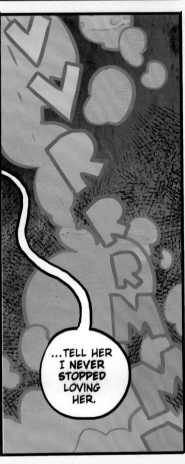

...TELL HER I NEVER STOPPED LOVING HER.

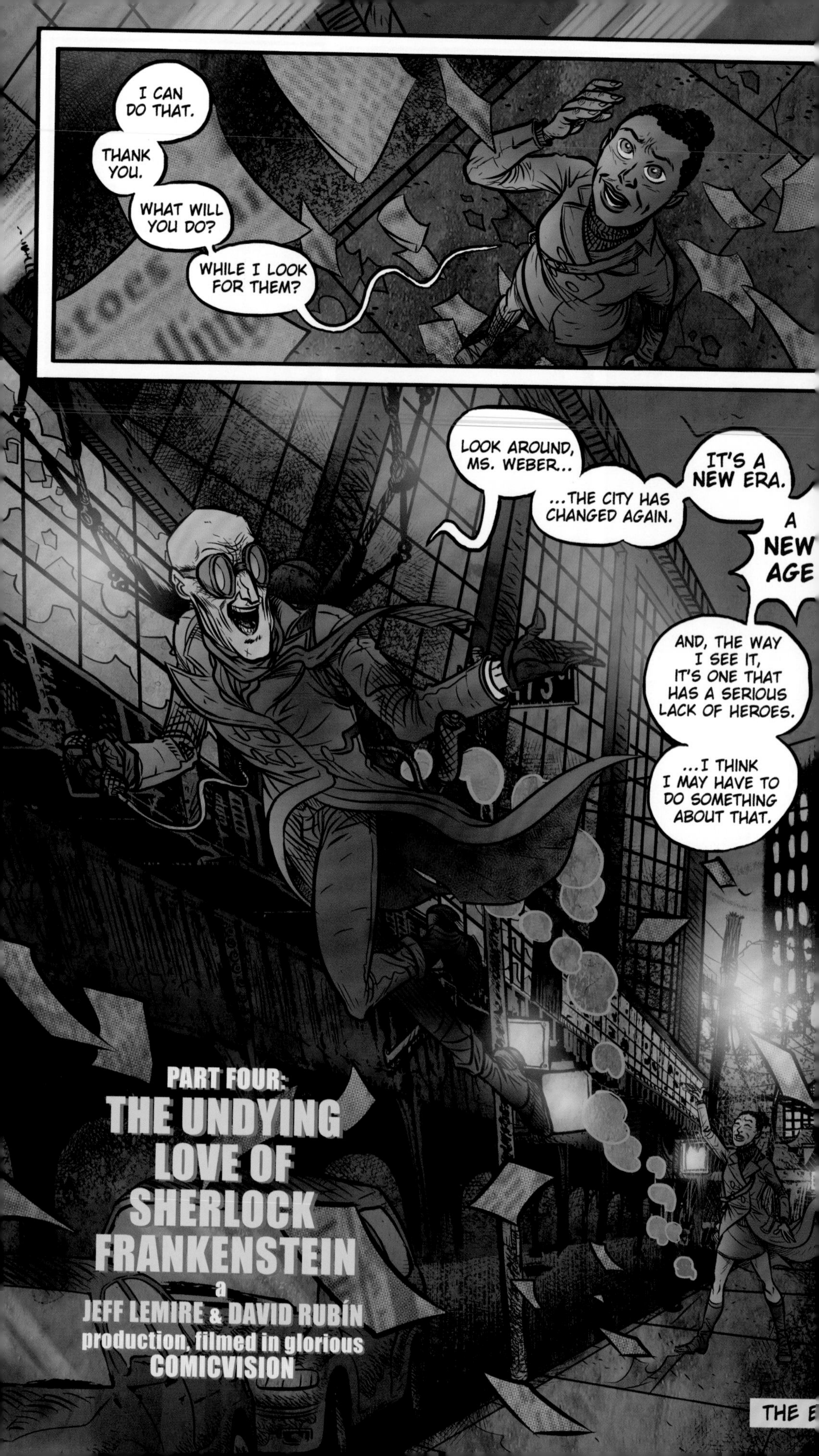
I CAN DO THAT.
THANK YOU.
WHAT WILL YOU DO?
WHILE I LOOK FOR THEM?
LOOK AROUND, MS. WEBER...
...THE CITY HAS CHANGED AGAIN.
IT'S A NEW ERA.
A NEW AGE
AND, THE WAY I SEE IT, IT'S ONE THAT HAS A SERIOUS LACK OF HEROES.
...I THINK I MAY HAVE TO DO SOMETHING ABOUT THAT.
PART FOUR:
THE UNDYING LOVE OF SHERLOCK FRANKENSTEIN
a
JEFF LEMIRE & DAVID RUBÍN
production, filmed in glorious
COMICVISION

JEFF LEMIRE
DAVID RUBÍN

SHERLOCK FRANKENSTEIN™

SKETCHBOOK

Notes by Jeff Lemire and David Rubín

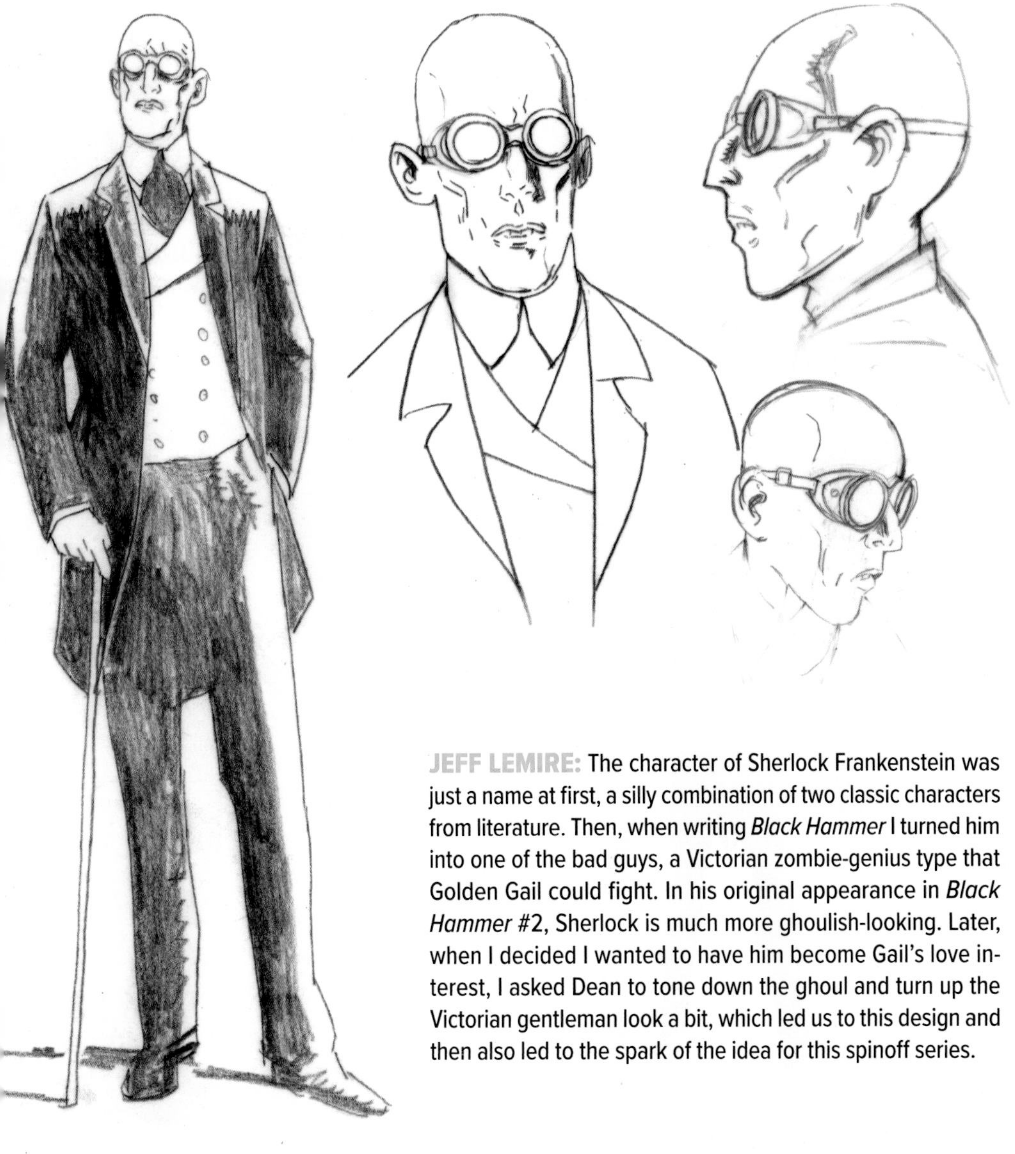

JEFF LEMIRE: The character of Sherlock Frankenstein was just a name at first, a silly combination of two classic characters from literature. Then, when writing *Black Hammer* I turned him into one of the bad guys, a Victorian zombie-genius type that Golden Gail could fight. In his original appearance in *Black Hammer* #2, Sherlock is much more ghoulish-looking. Later, when I decided I wanted to have him become Gail's love interest, I asked Dean to tone down the ghoul and turn up the Victorian gentleman look a bit, which led us to this design and then also led to the spark of the idea for this spinoff series.

JL: One of the great joys of *Black Hammer*, aside from my love of the core characters themselves, is the world building I get to do. I have eighty years of comic book and superhero history to draw from, so there is just so much raw material to inspire me. I really wanted to start to color in the world of *Black Hammer* here and really start to lay down its history. There can't be a superhero universe without a World War II-era super team. It's a classic element of superhero history that harkens back to *The Invaders* at Marvel and *The Justice Society* at DC. So I set out to build my own version with The Liberty Squadron.

Some of these characters popped up pretty quickly like the husband and wife team of Captain Night and Doctor Day. While others I've been kicking around in sketchbooks and notebooks for over a decade, like "the haunted spectre of the prairies": The Horseless Rider. But none of these characters came to life until David designed them. David is a genius and he instantly imbued my ideas with life and energy.

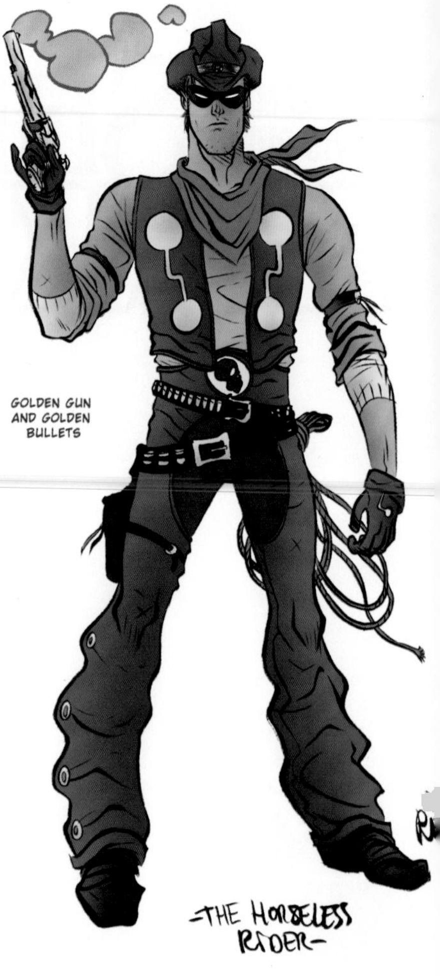
GOLDEN GUN
AND GOLDEN
BULLETS
-THE HORSELESS
RIDER-

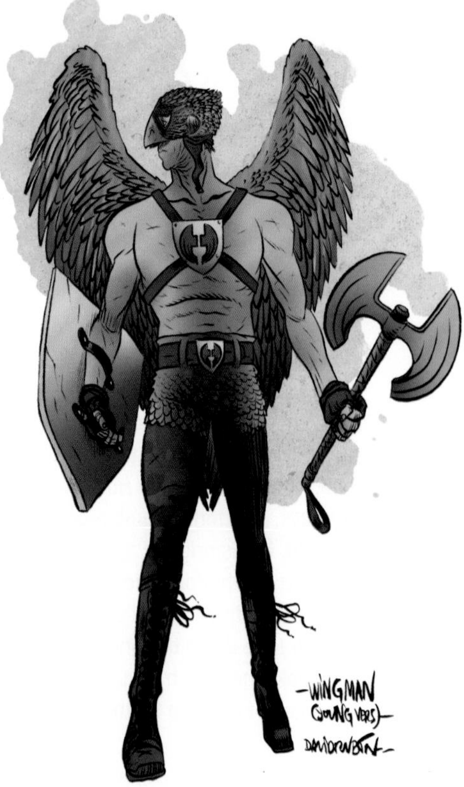
-WINGMAN
(YOUNG VERS)-

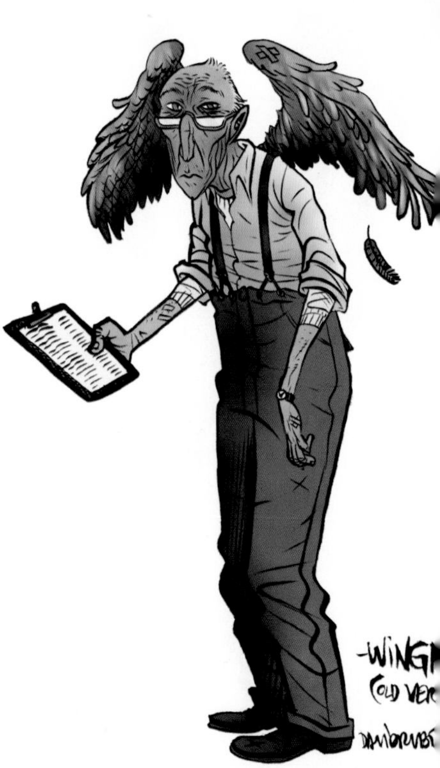
-WING
(OLD VER

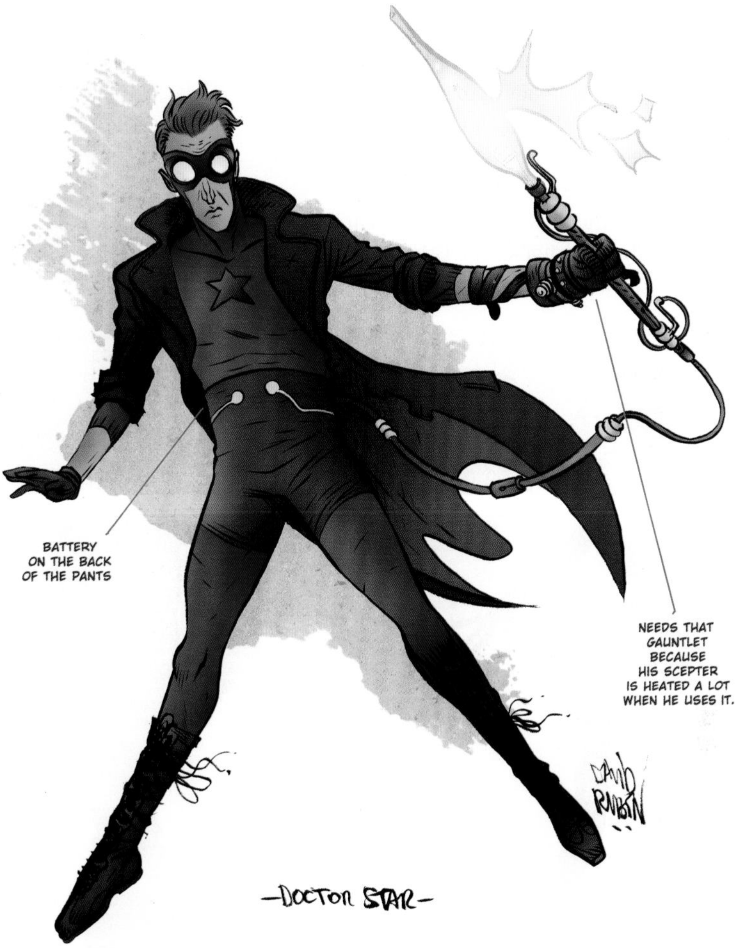

BATTERY ON THE BACK OF THE PANTS
NEEDS THAT GAUNTLET BECAUSE HIS SCEPTER IS HEATED A LOT WHEN HE USES IT.
DAVID RUBIN
-DOCTOR STAR-

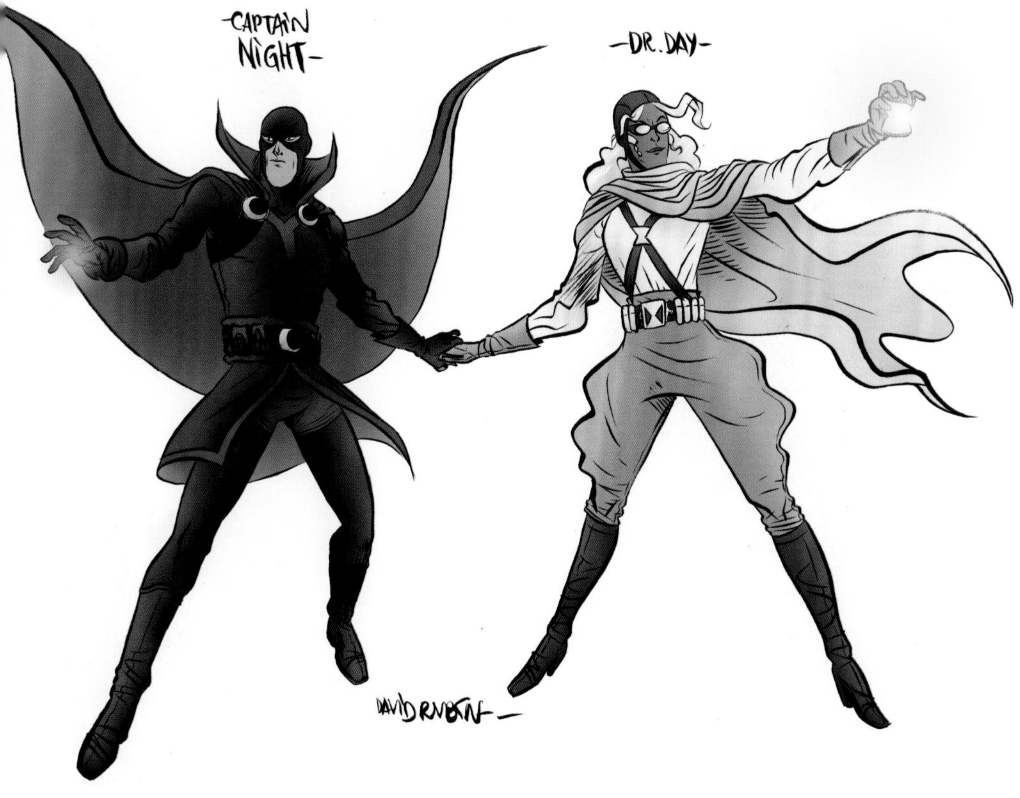

-CAPTAIN NIGHT-
-DR. DAY-
DAVID RUBIN

JL: You can't have a book about a bad guy without some other bad guys. I had a few that already appeared in *Black Hammer*, like Metal Minotaur and Cthu-Lou, but I needed more. I literally just started writing down funny or evocative names, picked the best three or four and sent them off to David without any instruction. The rest is all him. I love these guys, especially Tenterhooks and GrimJim and expect to use them all again.

-BLACK STALLION

TENTER HOOKS-

SADOMASOCHISTIC, LOVES PAIN

SPIKES ON THE INTERIOR OF THE CORSET.

HER FACE IS MARKED BY A BURN, BUT SHE'S STILL VERY BEAUTIFUL.

-SULTRIX-
x DAVID RUBIN-

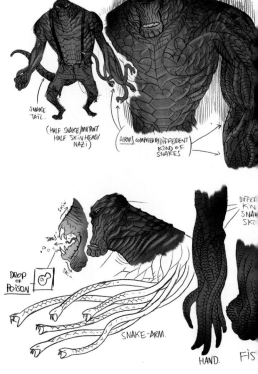

MANACONDA x DAVID RUBIN -

SNAKE TAIL.

(HALF SNAKE/MUTANT HALF SKIN HEAD/ NAZI)

ARMS COMPOSED BY DIFFERENT KIND OF SNAKES

DIFFE KIN SNAK SKI

SKIN

JAW

SKIN

DROP OF POISON

SNAKE-ARM.

HAND.

FIS

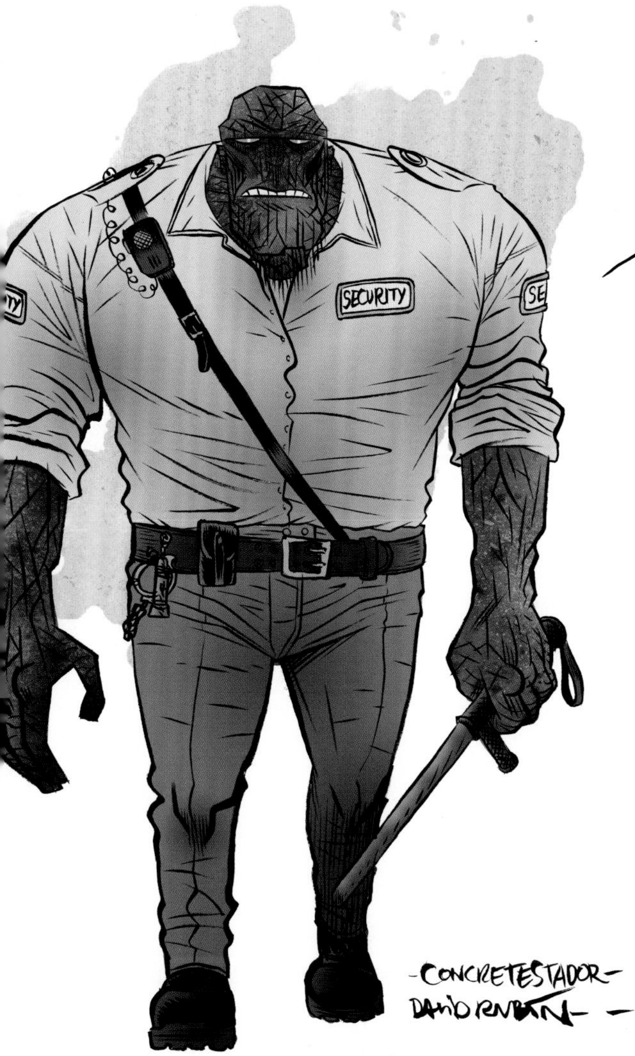
SECURITY
-CONCRETESTADOR-

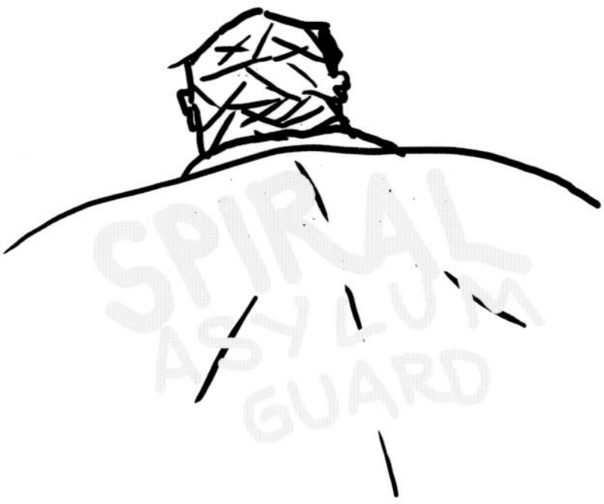
SPIRAL
ASYLUM
GUARD

JL: Concretestador was a name that Canadian comedian Brett Butt threw out to me on Twitter one day. So he is to blame for that one. My son Gus came up with the name Metal Minotaur.

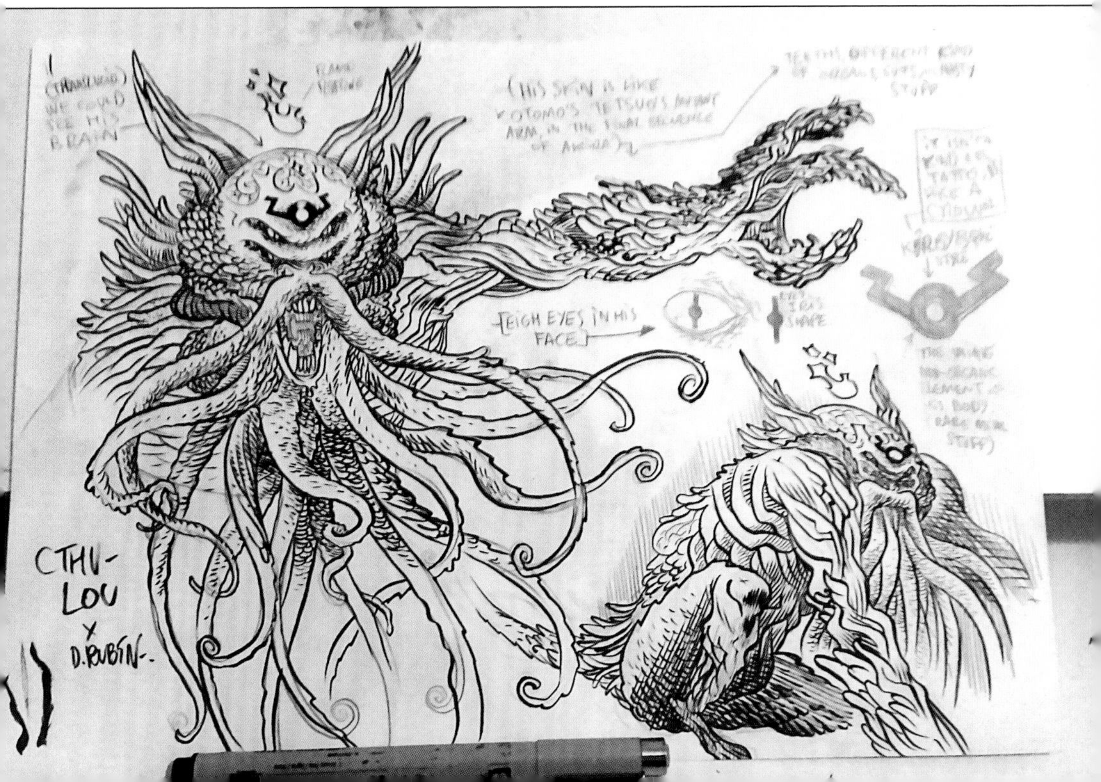
EIGH EYES IN HIS FACE
CTHU-LOU
X
D.RUBIN

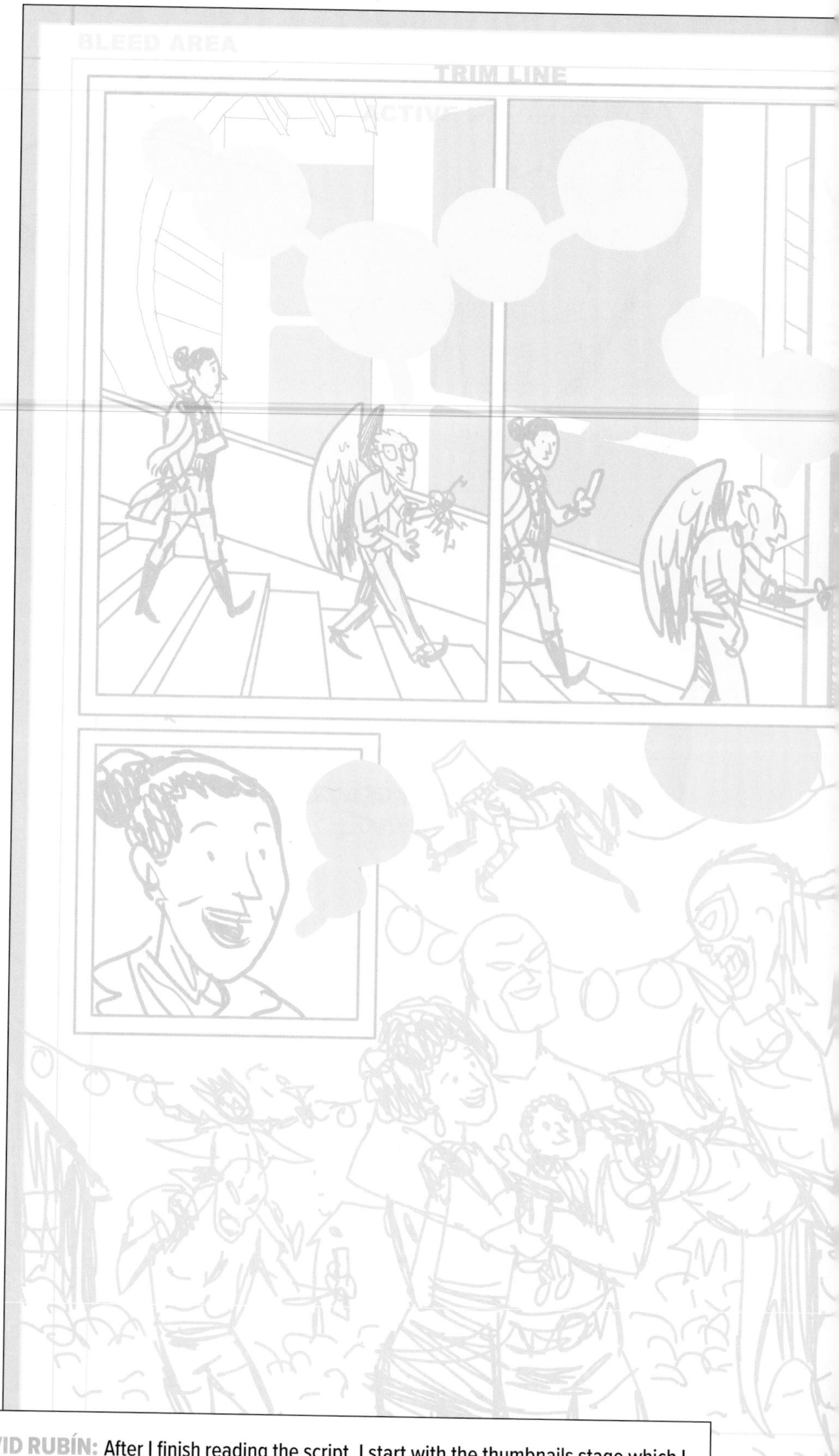
BLEED AREA
TRIM LINE

DAVID RUBÍN: After I finish reading the script, I start with the thumbnails stage which I do digitally. At this stage I don't care about the detail, all my attention is on the storytelling.

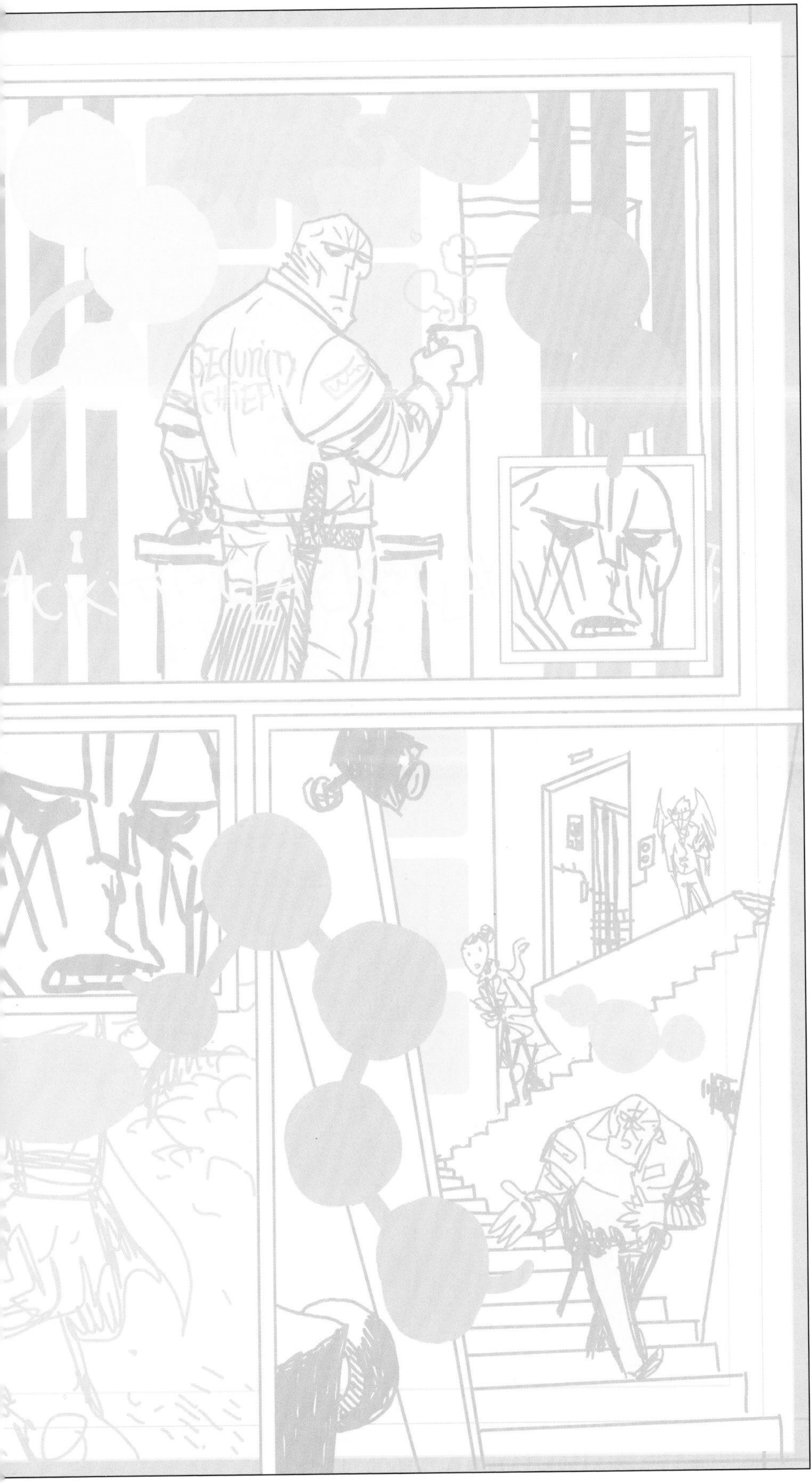
SECURITY CHIEF

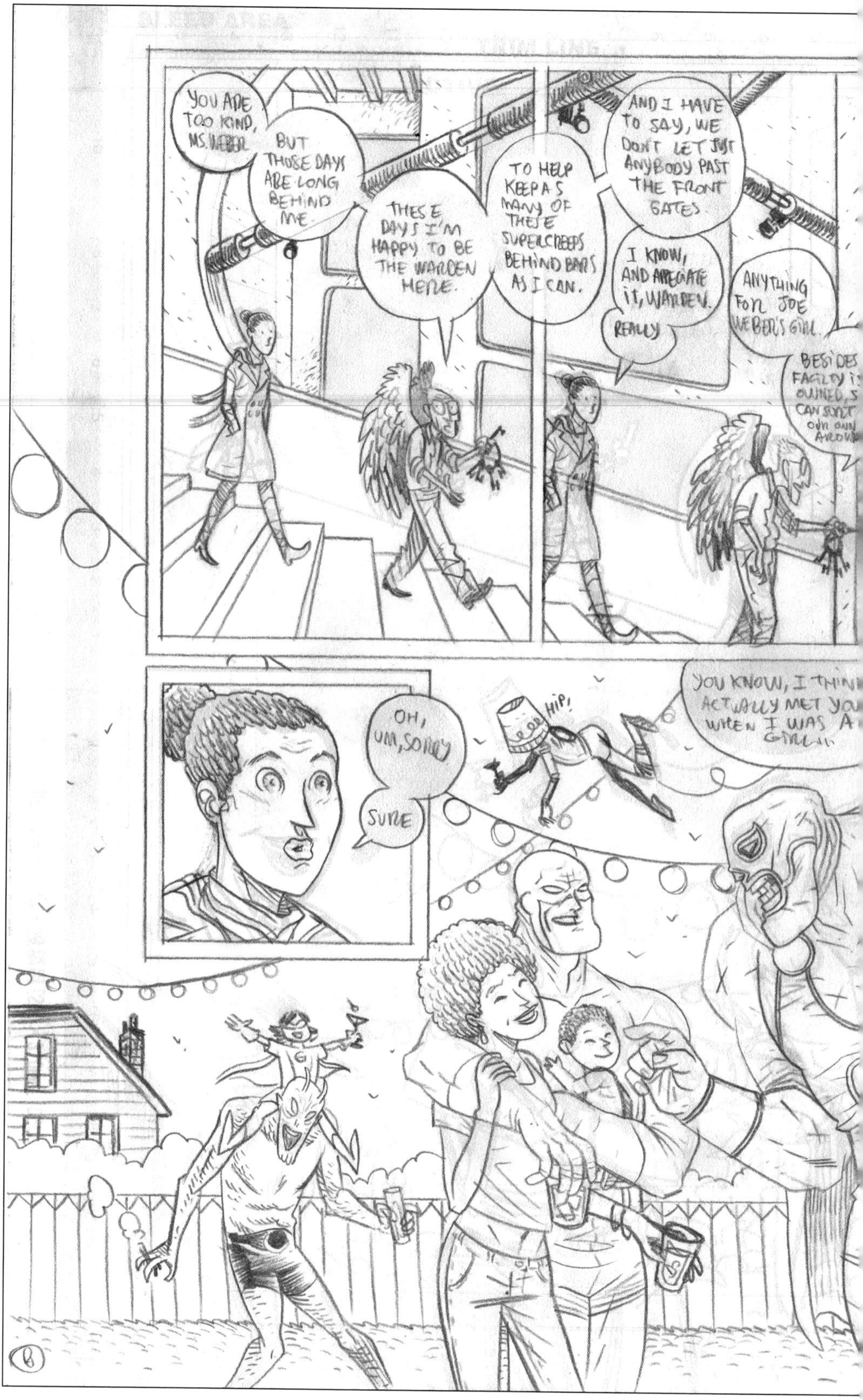
YOU ARE TOO KIND, MS. WEBER
BUT THOSE DAYS ARE LONG BEHIND ME
THESE DAYS I'M HAPPY TO BE THE WARDEN HERE.
TO HELP KEEP AS MANY OF THESE SUPERCREEPS BEHIND BARS AS I CAN.
AND I HAVE TO SAY, WE DON'T LET JUST ANYBODY PAST THE FRONT GATES.
I KNOW, AND APRECIATE IT, WARDEN.
REALLY
ANYTHING FOR JOE WEBER'S GIRL.
OH, UM, SORRY
SURE
HIP!
6

DR: Here's the same double page spread, but now with pencil art. This first issue was the last issue that I with traditional pencil art. The rest of issues of the miniseries are completely done with digital art, from rough layouts to the final colors. I hope that you *don't* see the difference.

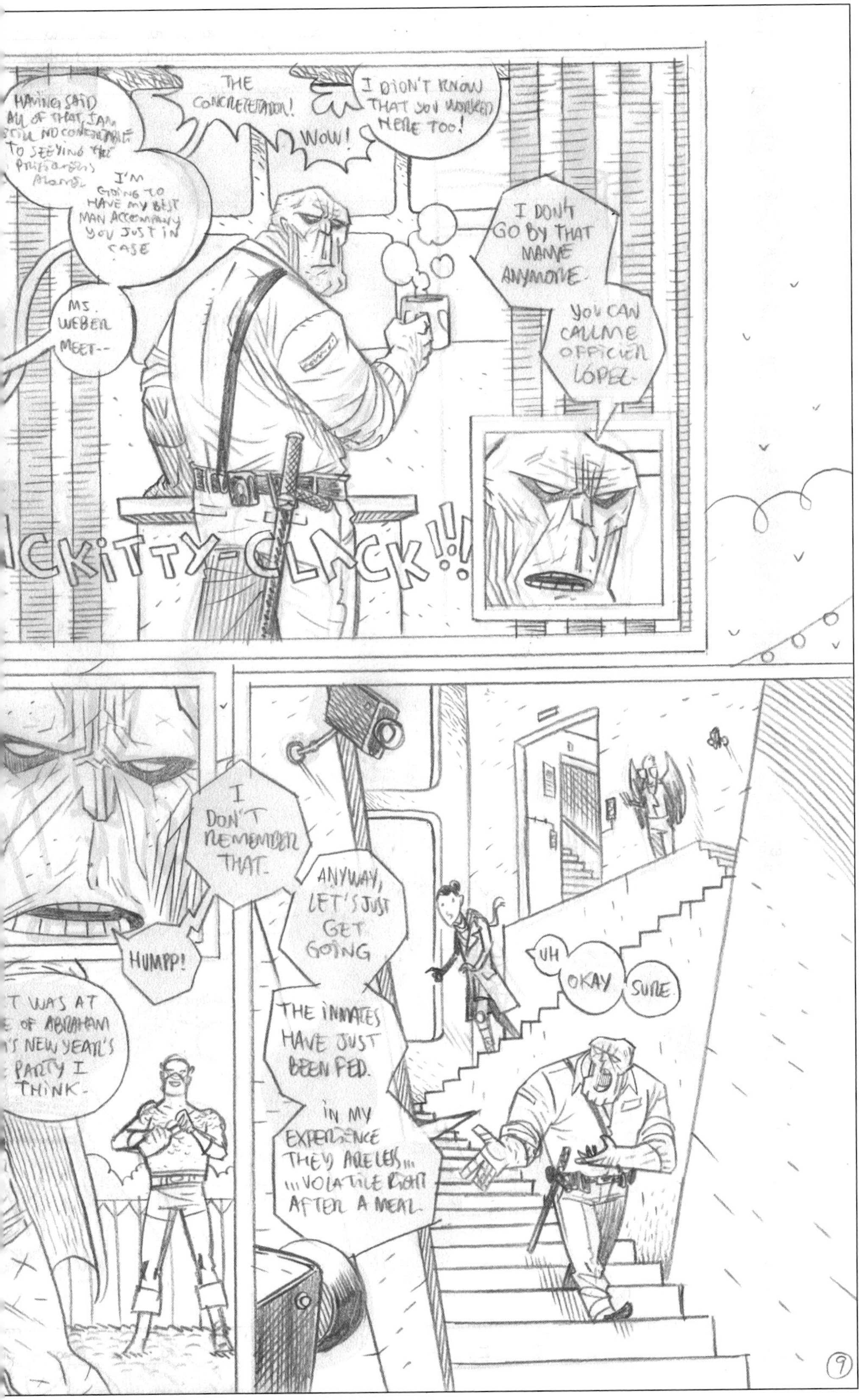
HAVING SAID ALL OF THAT, I AM
I'M GOING TO HAVE MY BEST MAN ACCOMPANY YOU JUST IN CASE
MS. WEBER MEET--
THE CONCRETETATOR!
WOW!
I DIDN'T KNOW THAT YOU WORKED HERE TOO!
I DON'T GO BY THAT NAME ANYMORE.
YOU CAN CALL ME OFFICER LÓPEZ.
...CKITTY-CLACK!!!
I DON'T REMEMBER THAT.
HUMPP!
T WAS AT
E OF ABRAHAM
'S NEW YEAR'S
PARTY I THINK.
ANYWAY, LET'S JUST GET GOING
THE INMATES HAVE JUST BEEN FED.
IN MY EXPERIENCE THEY ARE LESS... ...VOLATILE RIGHT AFTER A MEAL.
UH
OKAY
SURE.
9

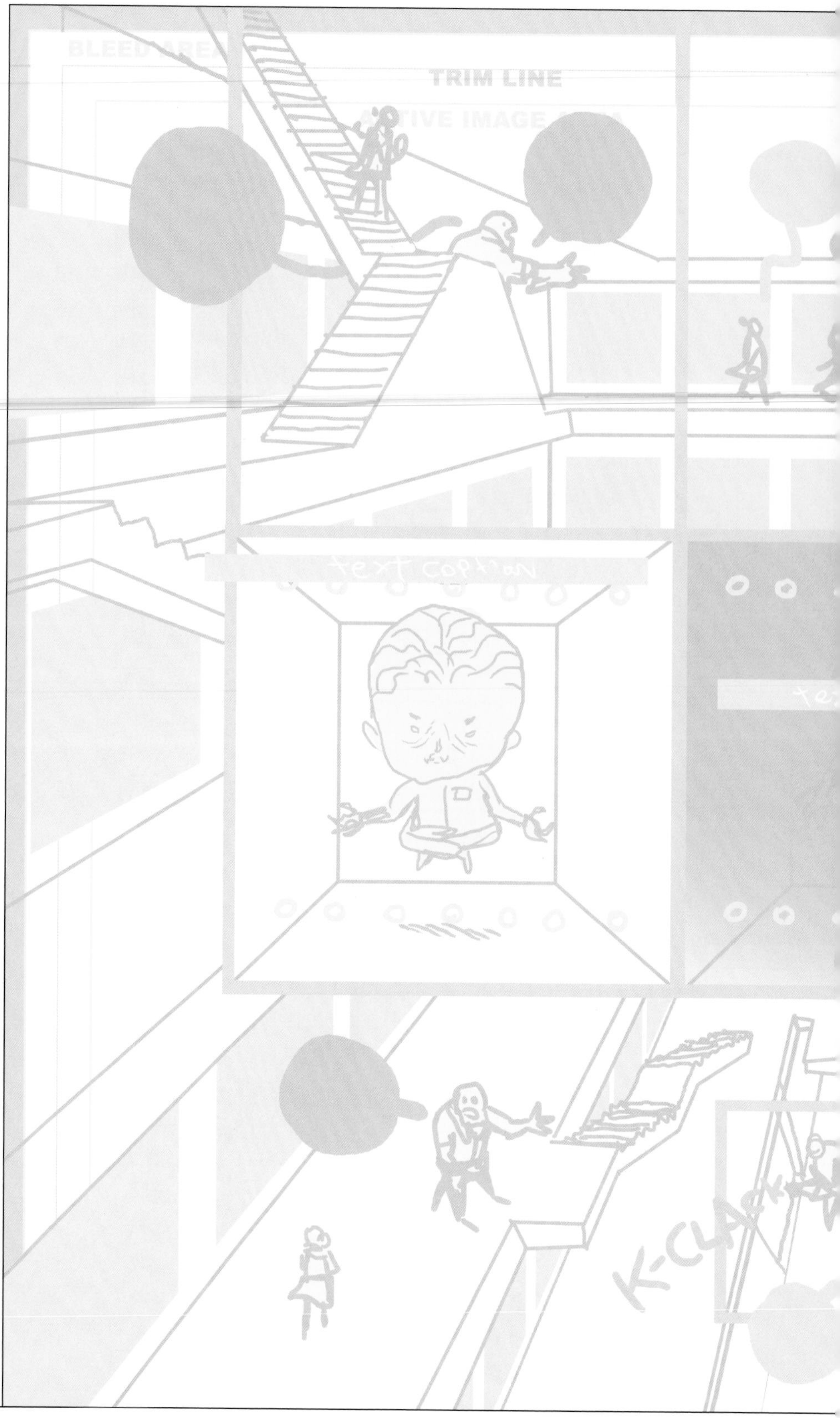
TRIM LINE
text caption

DR: This double page spread drove me nuts. I spent more time on this thumbnail than in the pencil stage. Here I attempted to move the reader's eyes in a spiral reading order as a metaphor for the madness in this mental sanitarium and also as a subtle nod to the name of the city where the action takes place: Spiral City.

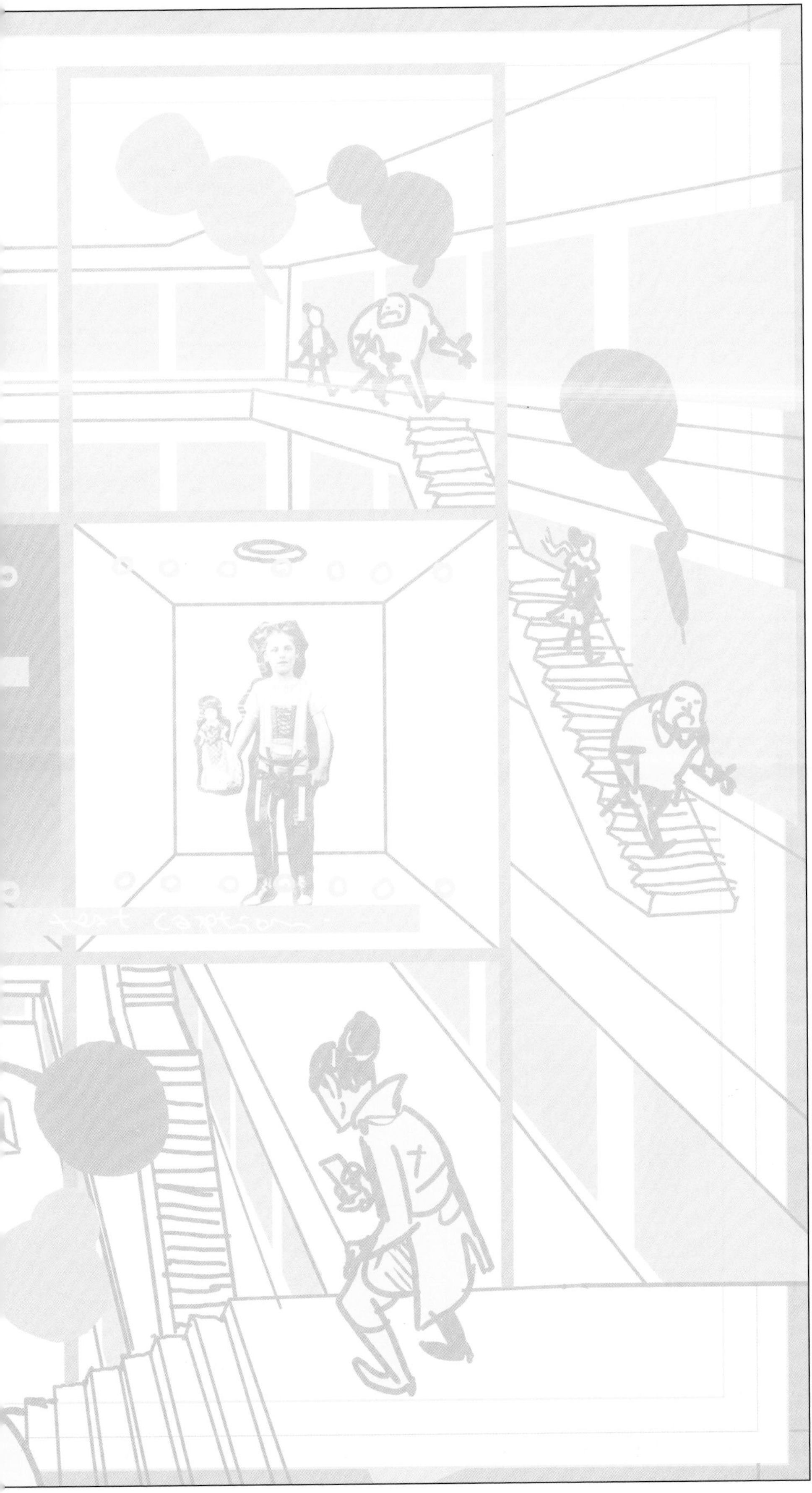
text caption

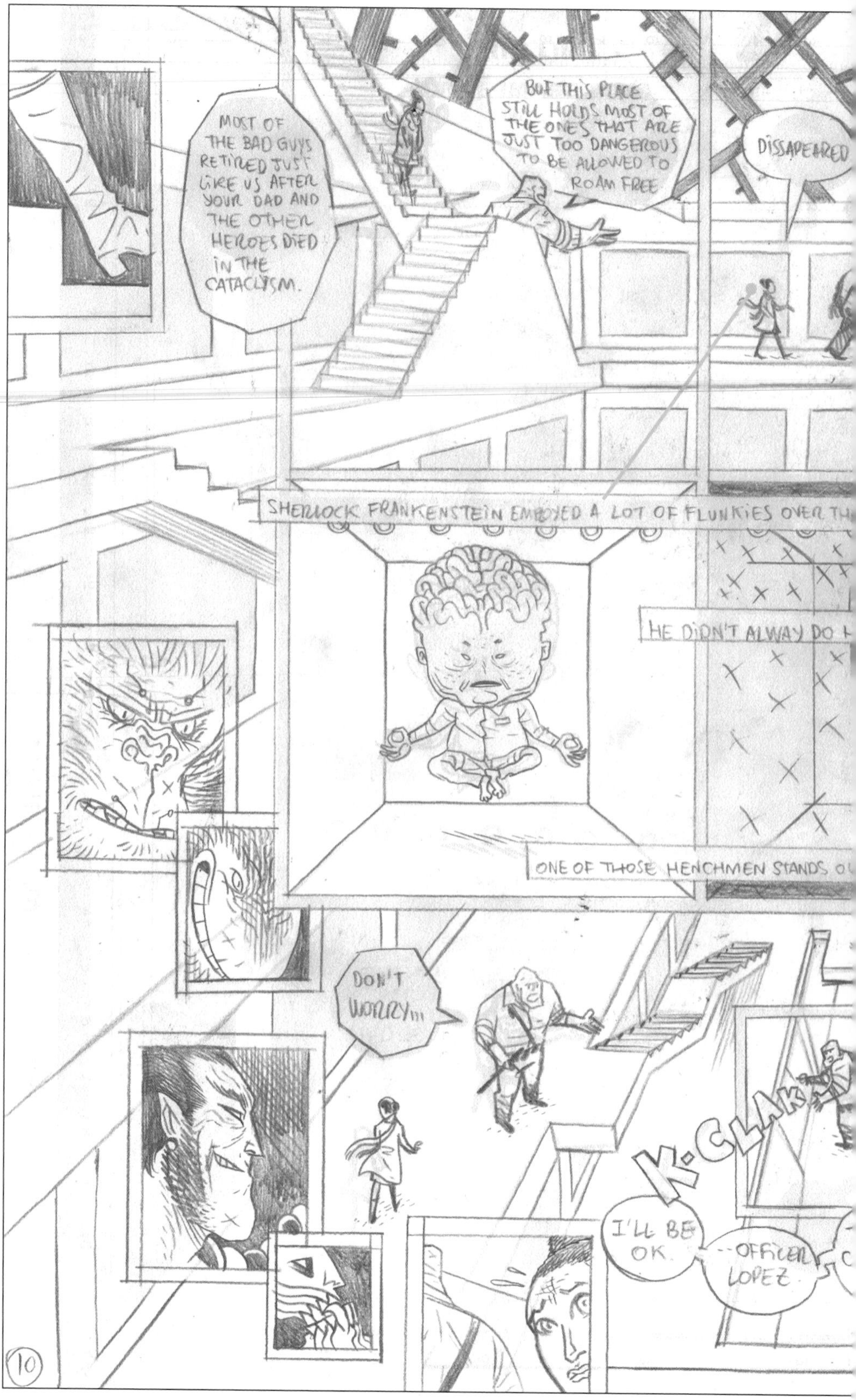

MOST OF THE BAD GUYS RETIRED JUST LIKE US AFTER YOUR DAD AND THE OTHER HEROES DIED IN THE CATACLYSM.
BUT THIS PLACE STILL HOLDS MOST OF THE ONES THAT ARE JUST TOO DANGEROUS TO BE ALLOWED TO ROAM FREE
DISSAPEARED
SHERLOCK FRANKENSTEIN EMPLOYED A LOT OF FLUNKIES OVER TH
HE DIDN'T ALWAY DO H
ONE OF THOSE HENCHMEN STANDS O
DON'T WORRY...
K-CLAK
I'LL BE OK.
OFFICER LOPEZ
10

DR: Here's the pencil art for the same spread as before. I added little insert panels that I thought helped find the way to move the reader in the spiral direction, and also showed some of the undesirable "tenan of the sanitarium.

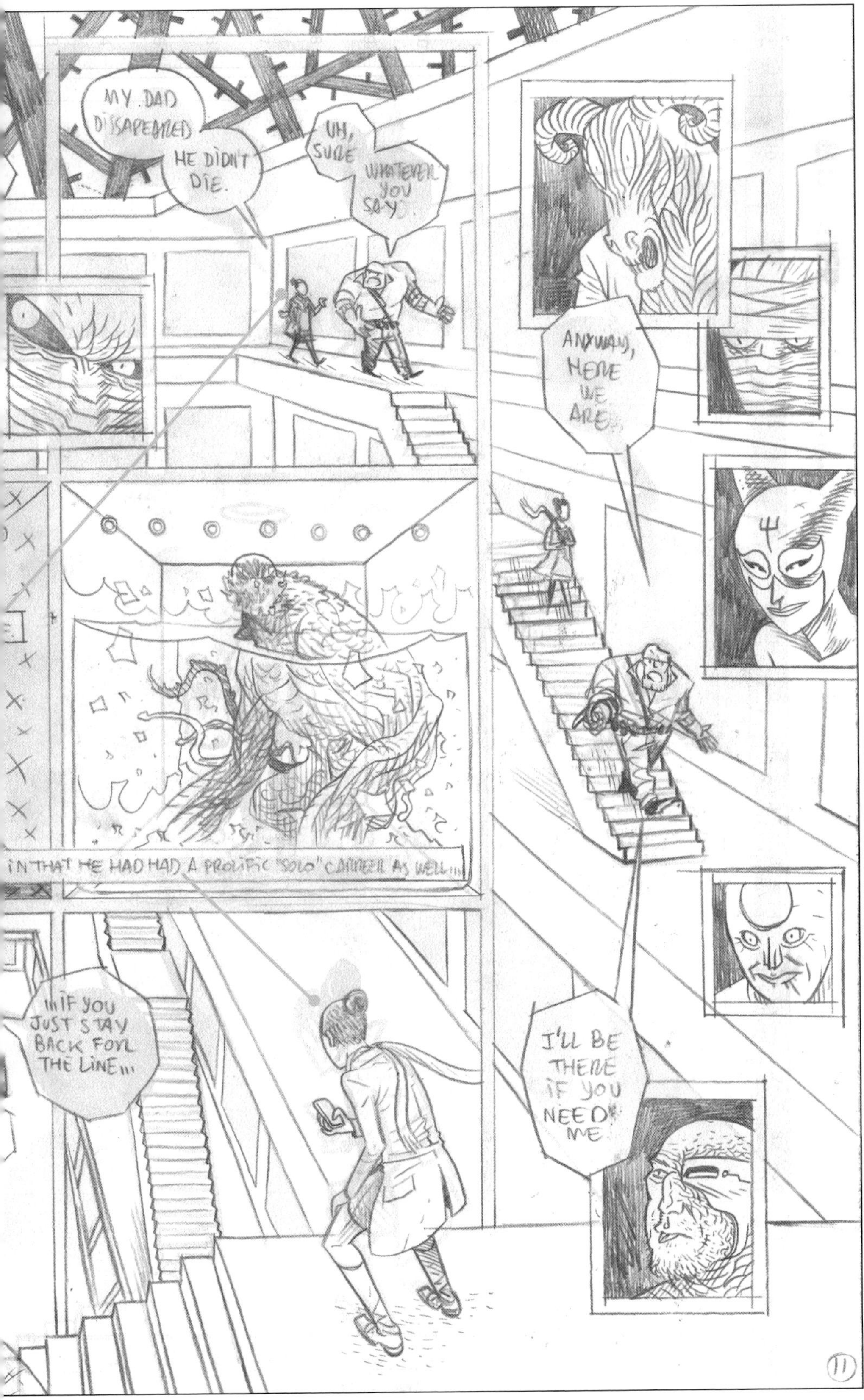
MY DAD DISAPEARED
HE DIDN'T DIE.
UH, SURE
WHATEVER YOU SAY
ANYWAY, HERE WE ARE.
IN THAT HE HAD HAD A PROLIFIC "SOLO" CAREER AS WELL...
...IF YOU JUST STAY BACK FOR THE LINE...
I'LL BE THERE IF YOU NEED ME
11

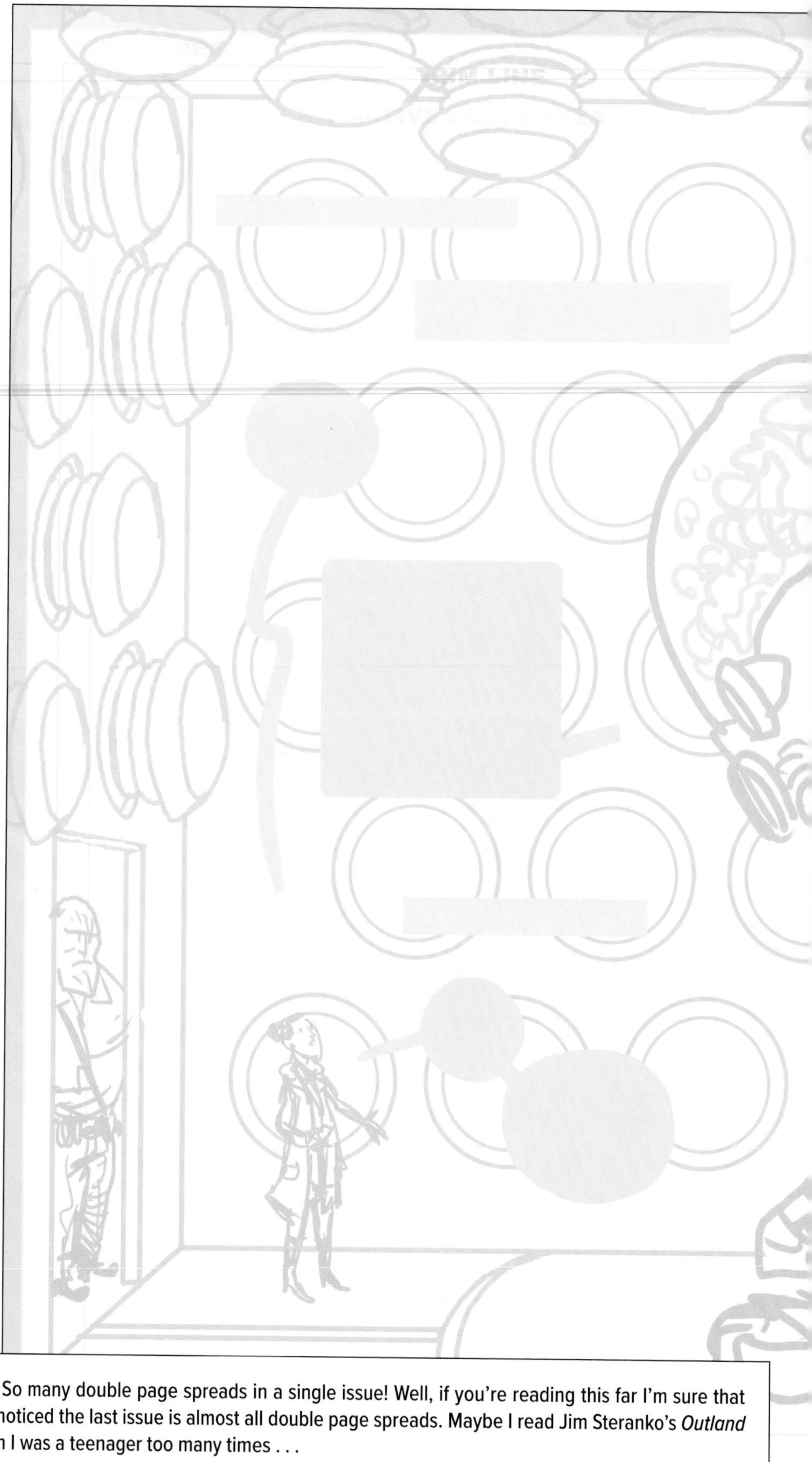

DR: So many double page spreads in a single issue! Well, if you're reading this far I'm sure that you noticed the last issue is almost all double page spreads. Maybe I read Jim Steranko's *Outland* when I was a teenager too many times . . .

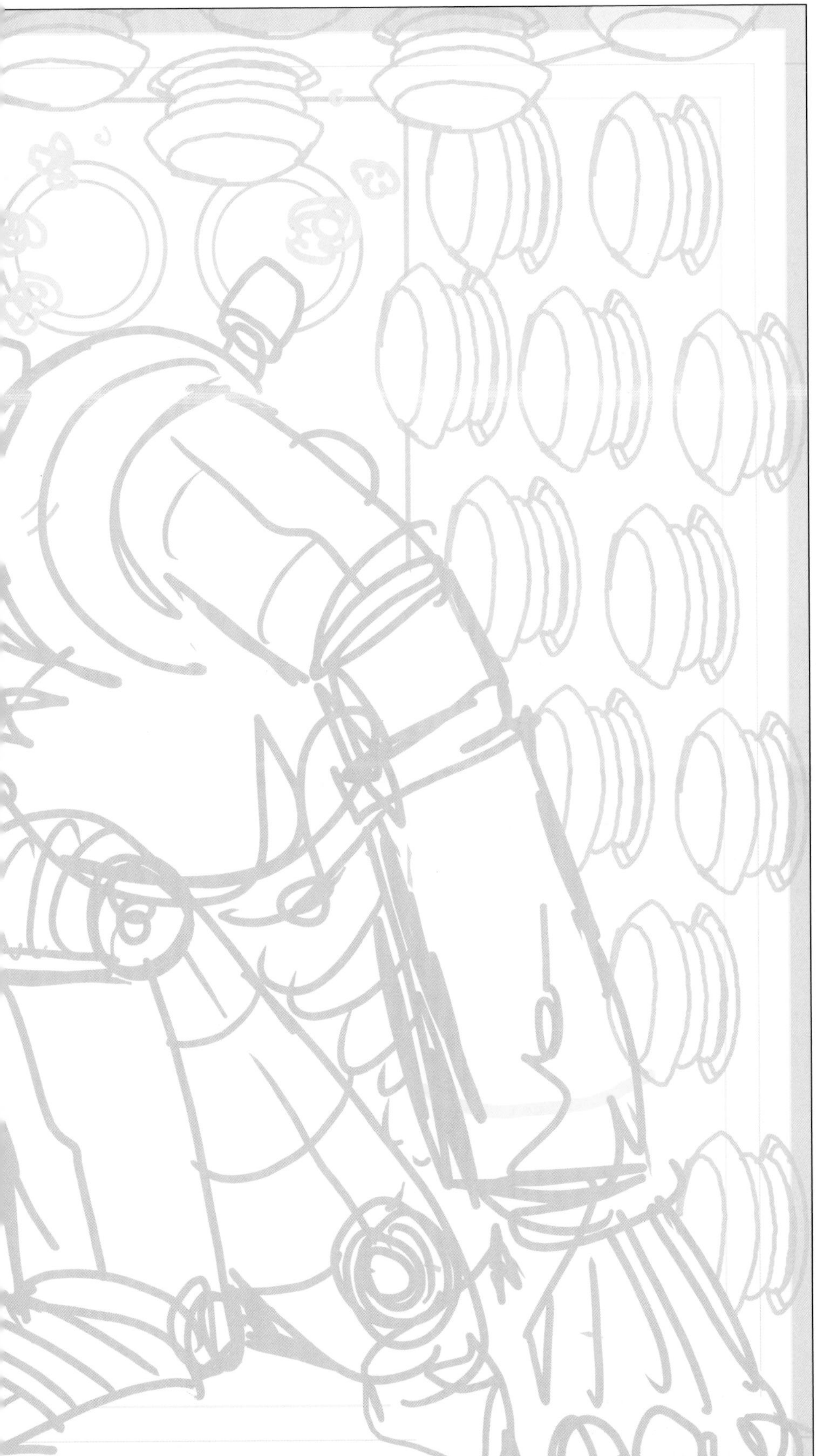

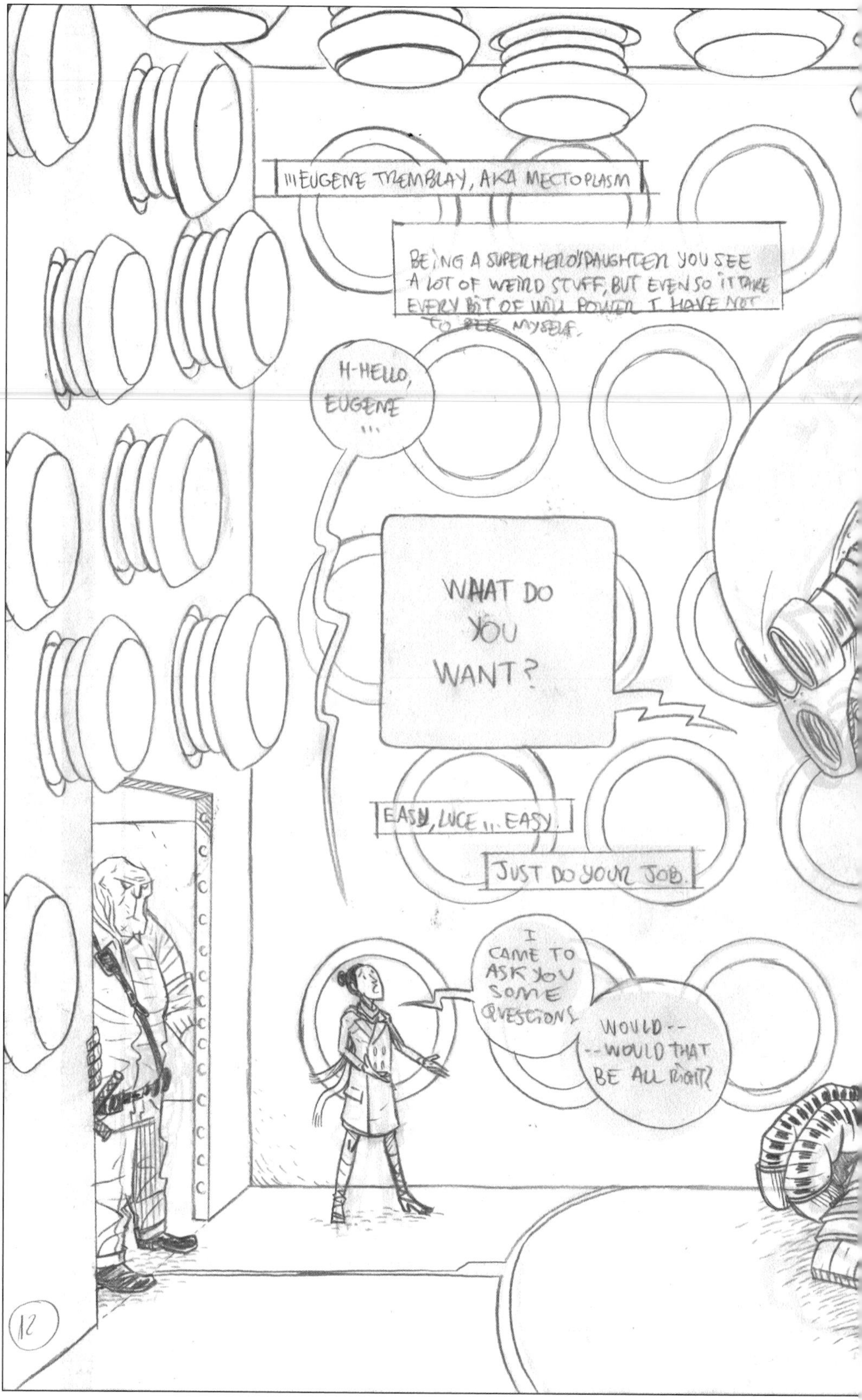
...EUGENE TREMBLAY, AKA MECTOPLASM
BEING A SUPERHERO'S DAUGHTER YOU SEE A LOT OF WEIRD STUFF, BUT EVEN SO IT TAKE EVERY BIT OF WILL POWER I HAVE NOT TO PEE MYSELF.
H-HELLO, EUGENE ...
WHAT DO YOU WANT?
EASY, LUCE ... EASY.
JUST DO YOUR JOB.
I CAME TO ASK YOU SOME QUESTIONS.
WOULD-- --WOULD THAT BE ALL RIGHT?
12

DR: After the previous double page spread, I thought we needed some air; a large image that would give reader a bit of eye rest, and serve to show the monstrous Mectoplasm.

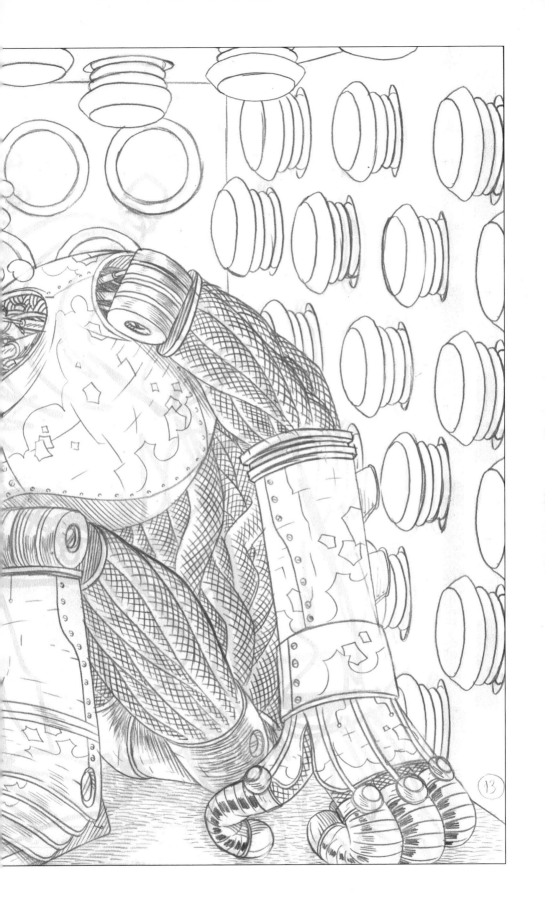

13

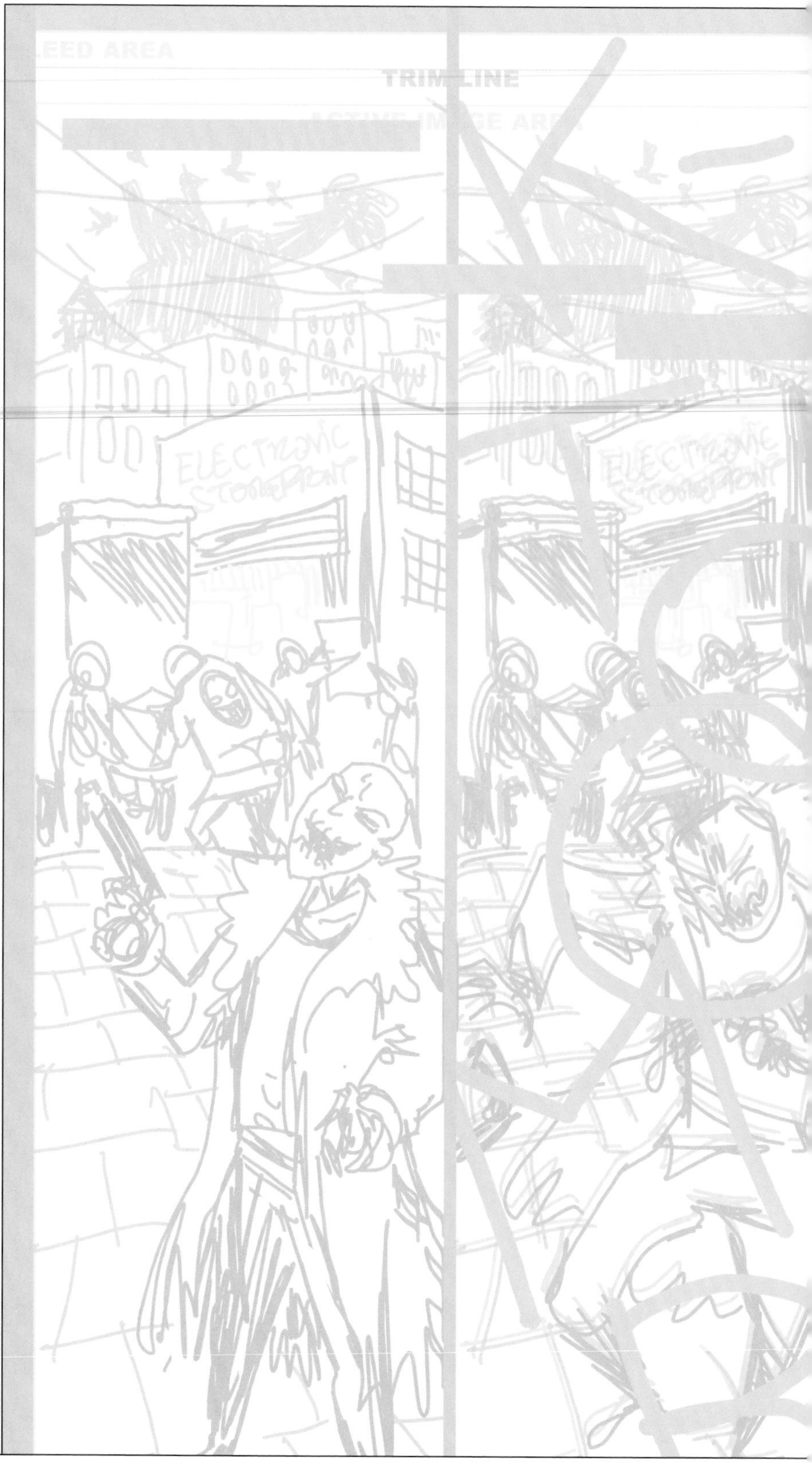
ELECTRONIC STOREFRONT

DR: This flashback sequence was so much fun to draw! The ideas that Jeff described in the script were so pulpy and gritty: slum warehouses, gangs robbing them, a criminally insane villain, and a super powerful GIANT ROBOT! The dream of every cartoonist! I deserved another double page for sure!

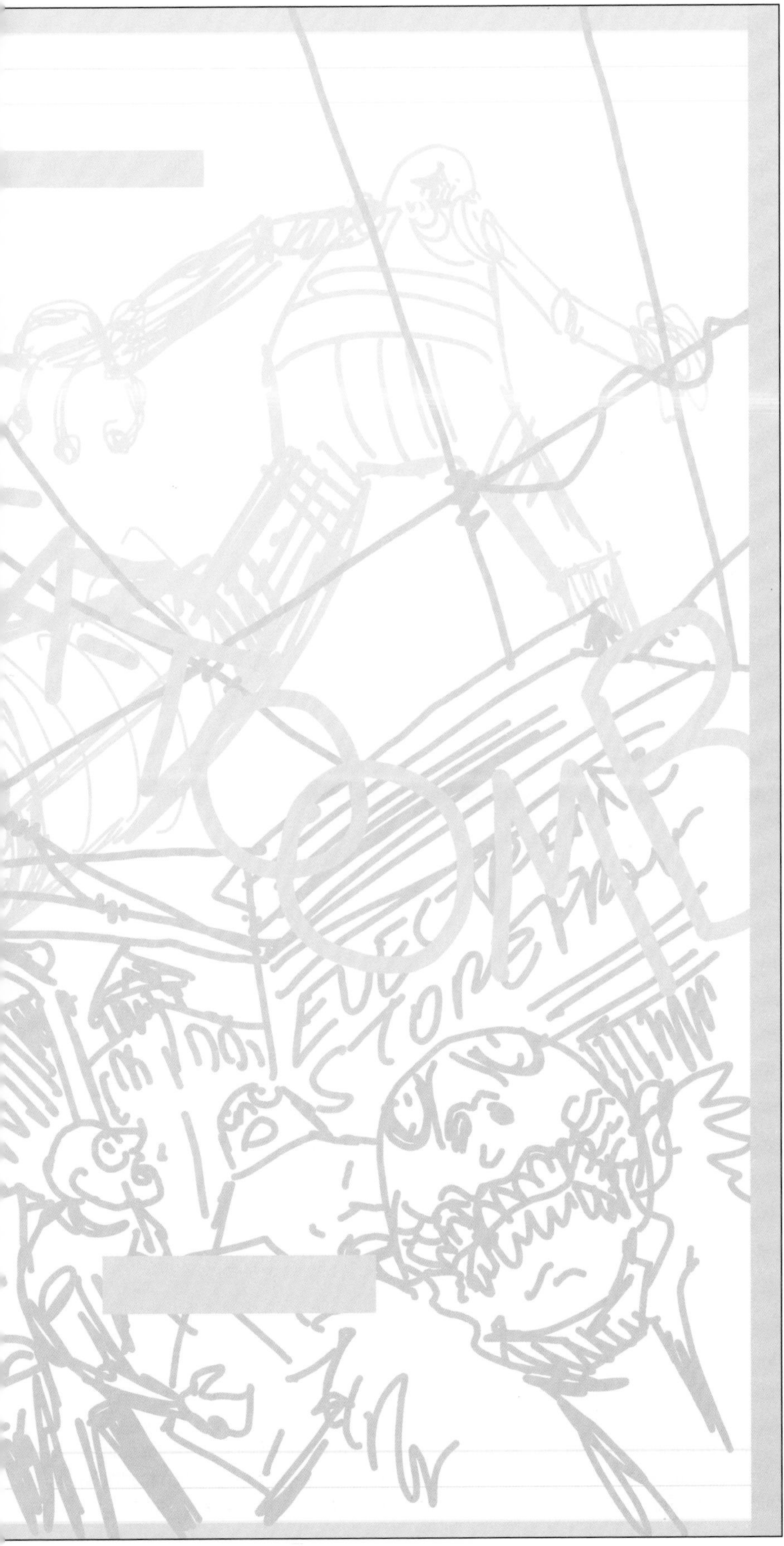

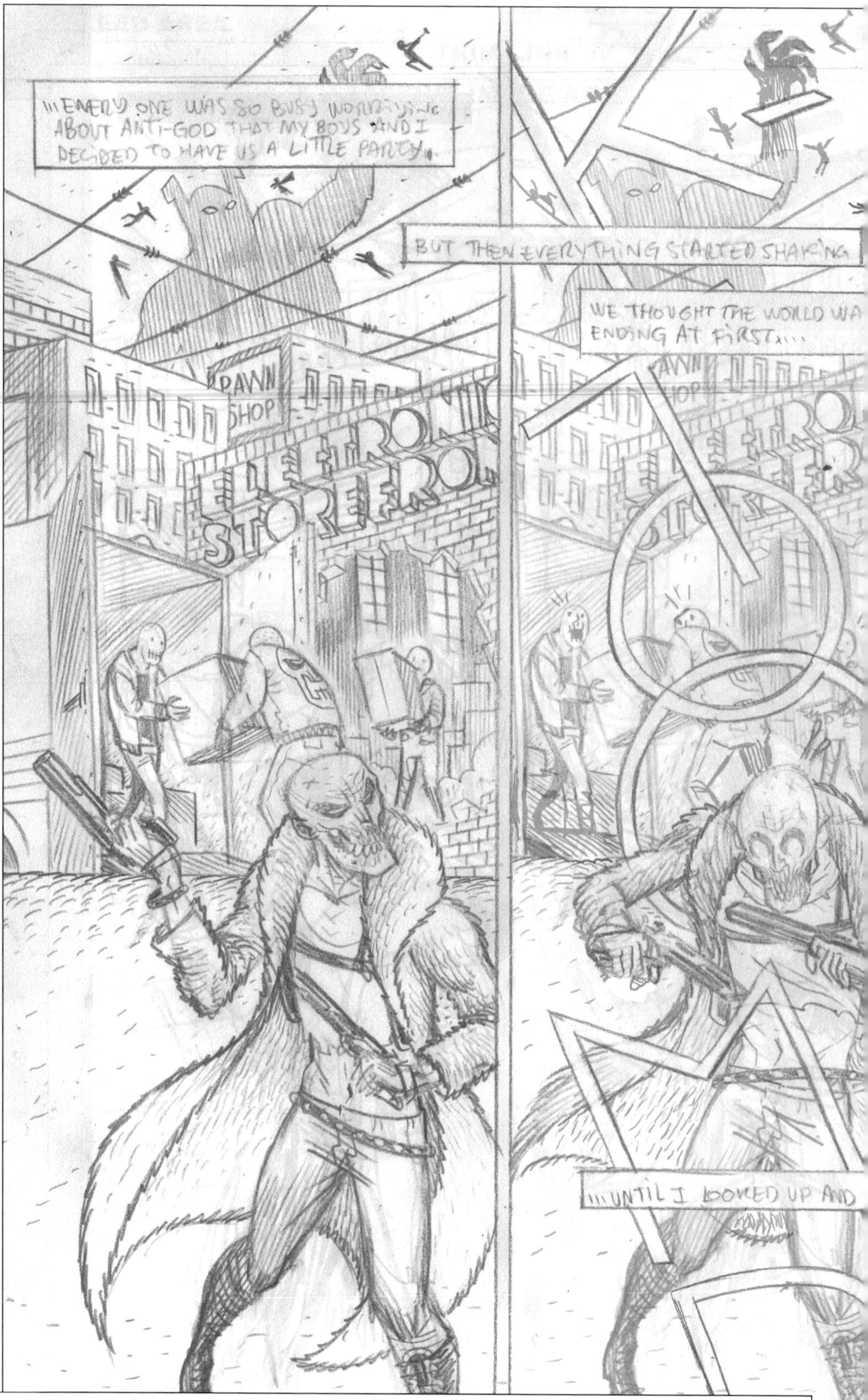

...EVERY ONE WAS SO BUSY WORRYING ABOUT ANTI-GOD THAT MY BOYS AND I DECIDED TO HAVE US A LITTLE PARTY...
PAWN SHOP
BUT THEN EVERYTHING STARTED SHAKING
WE THOUGHT THE WORLD WA
ENDING AT FIRST....
...UNTIL I LOOKED UP AND

DR: You can't see it in these pencil pages, because I introduce it in Photoshop in the color stage, but GrimJim wears a Britney Spears t-shirt. I think that it is the most powerful evidence that he's an evil and mad criminal mind, for sure! Apologies to Britney's fans!

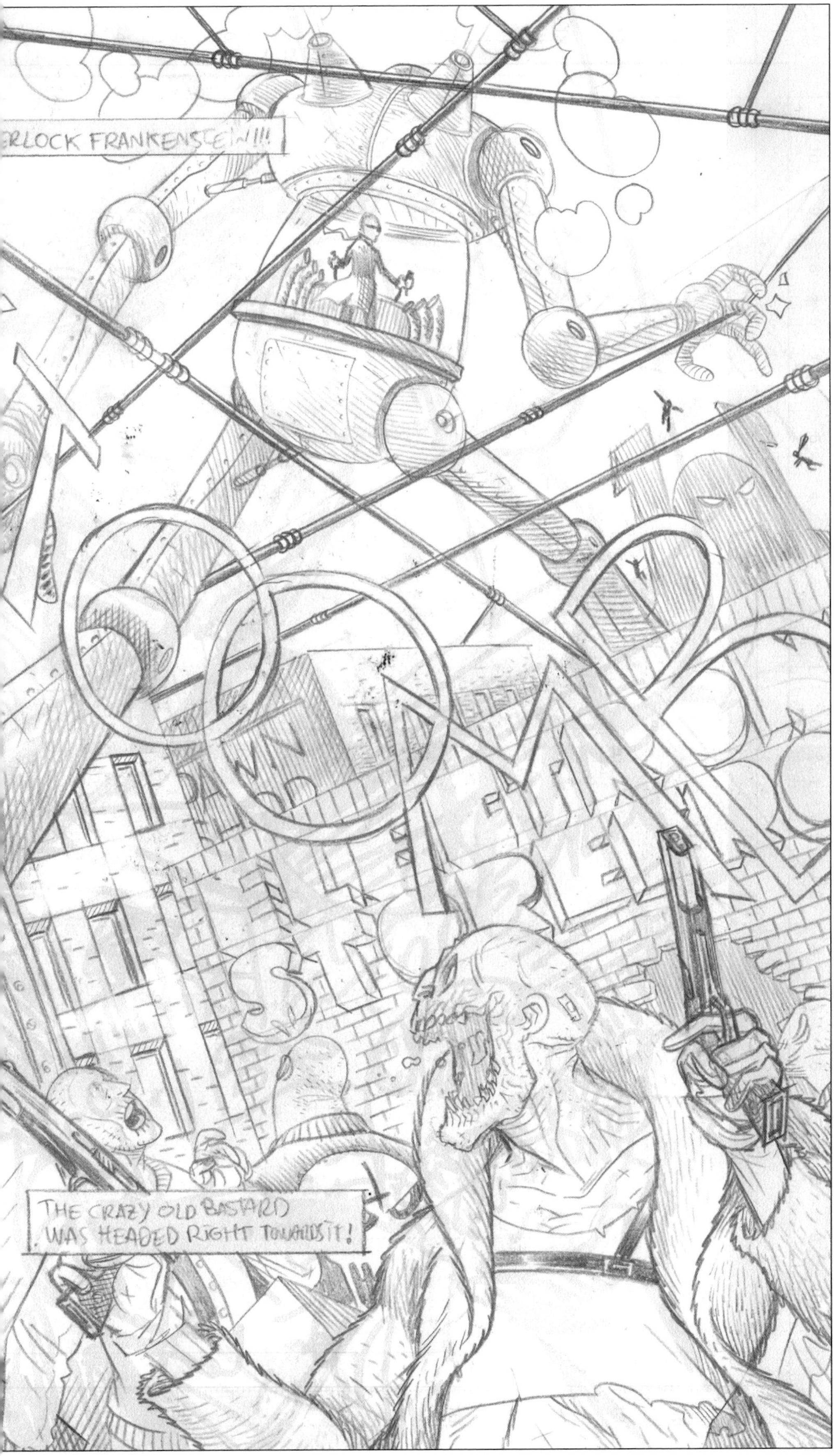

ERLOCK FRANKENSTEIN!!!
THE CRAZY OLD BASTARD WAS HEADED RIGHT TOWARDS IT!

DR: Here's the art process from roughs to inks for the cover for *Black Hammer* #12. That issue originally served as a prequel of the *Sherlock Frankenstein* miniseries and is the first chapter of this collection.

Also shown here are different Black Hammer suits I designed for the background of the cover. You can see the variety of the Black Hammer suits here for the Golden Age, the Silver Age and the 90s style.

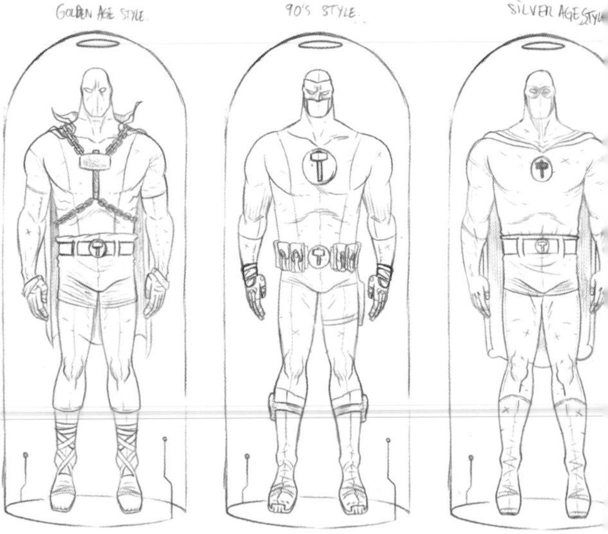
GOLDEN AGE STYLE
90'S STYLE

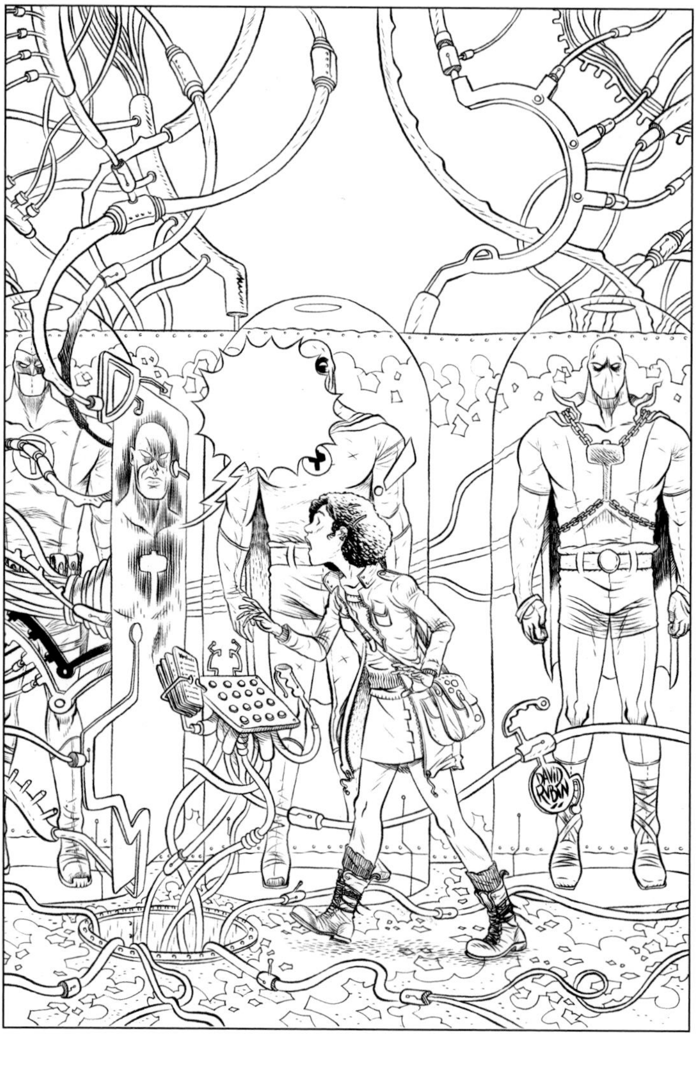
DAVID RUBIN

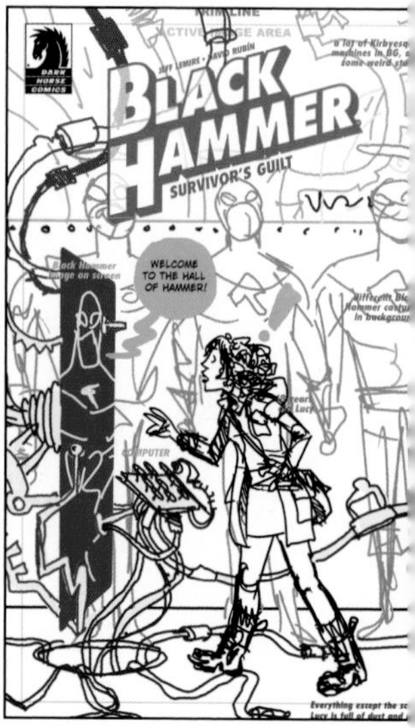
DARK HORSE COMICS
BLACK HAMMER
SURVIVOR'S GUILT
WELCOME TO THE HALL OF HAMMER!

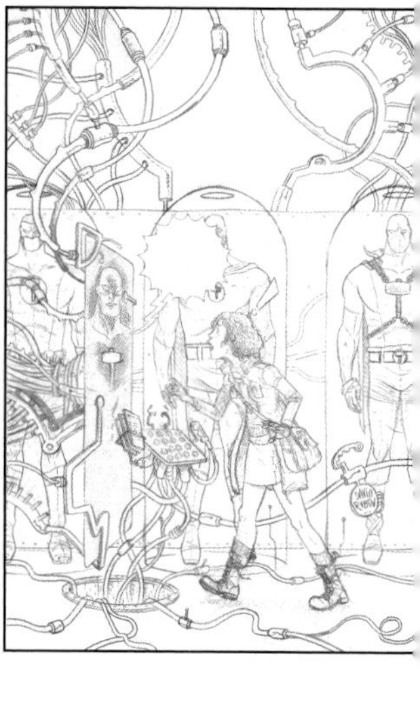

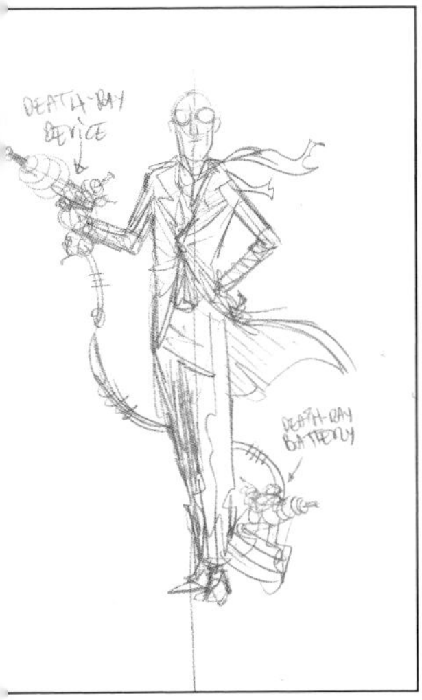
DEATH-RAY DEVICE
DEATH-RAY BATTERY

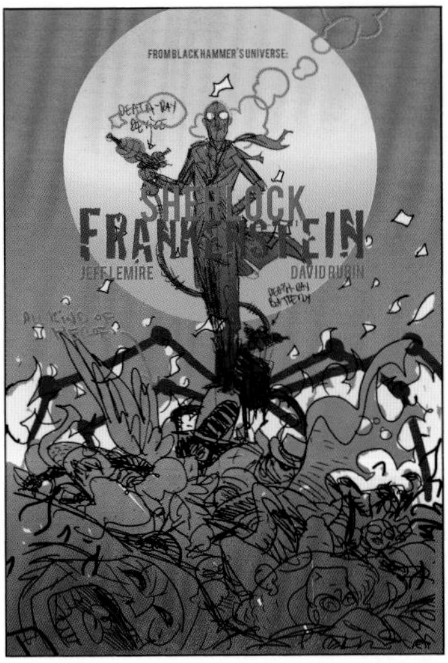
FROM BLACK HAMMER'S UNIVERSE:
DEATH-RAY DEVICE
SHERLOCK FRANKENSTEIN
JEFF LEMIRE
DAVID RUBIN
DEATH-RAY BATTERY

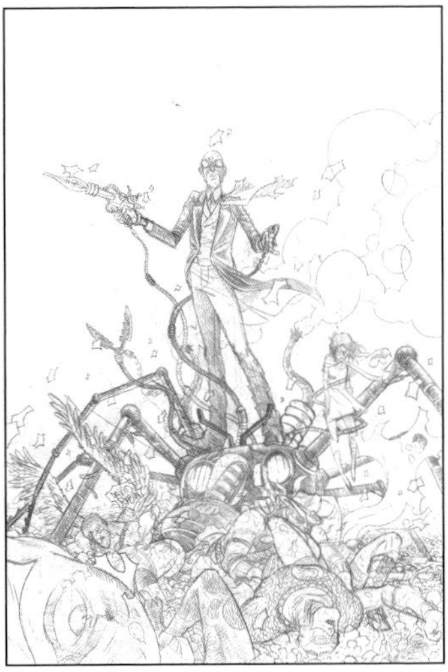

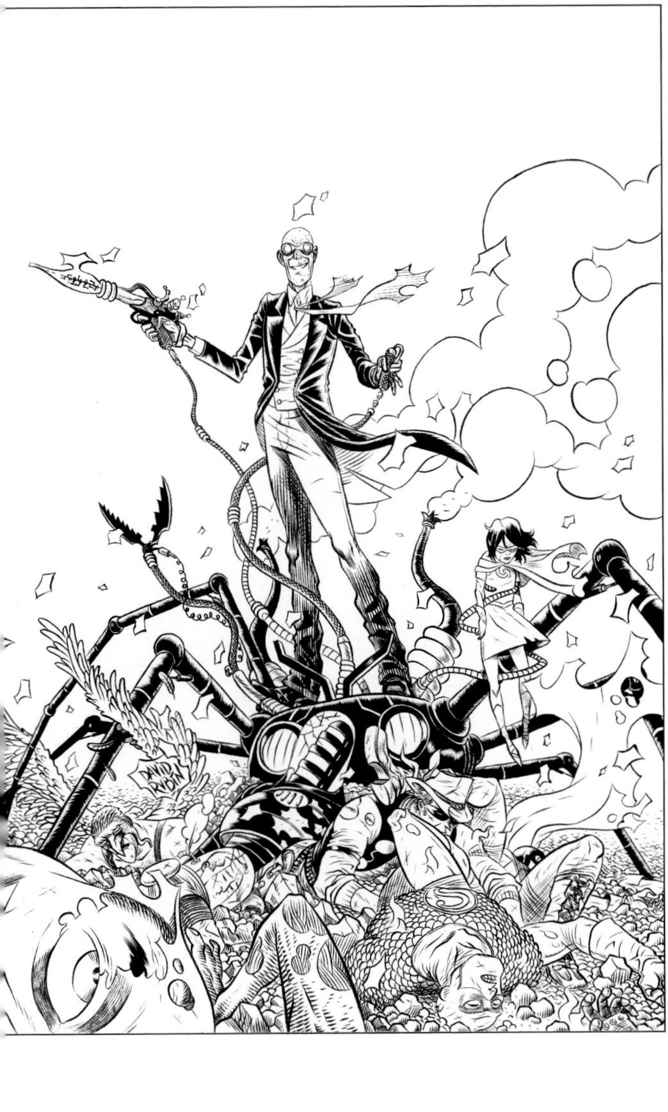
DAVID RUBIN

DR: Here's the cover process for issue one. This was the first time that I drew Sherlock Frankenstein, I think. The original design of that main character is by Dean Ormston. My idea with the first cover was create an image that showed the reader how dangerous and terrible Sherlock can be—and also make it a really kickass image for a kickass character.

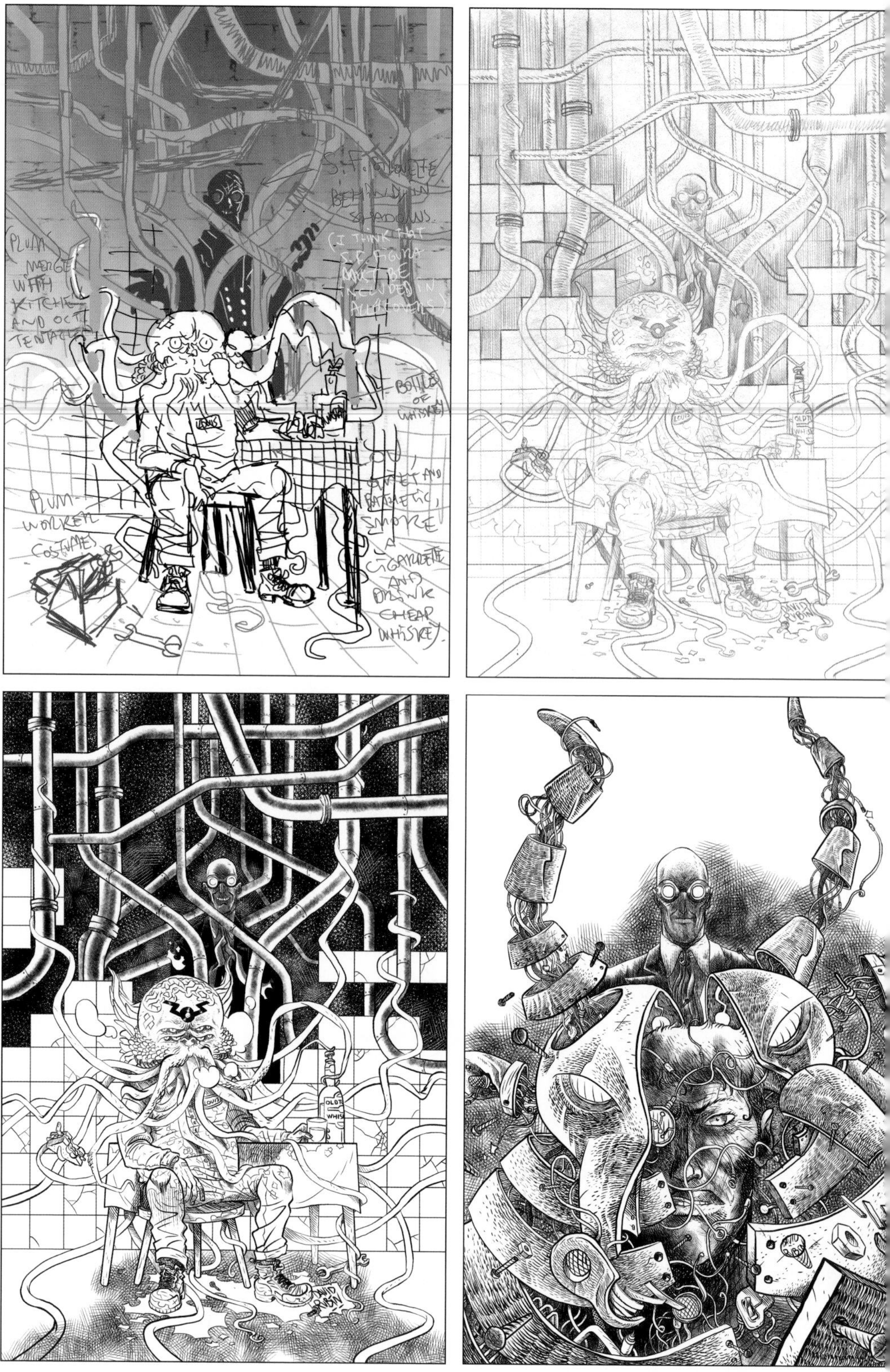
BOTTLE OF WHISKEY
(I THINK THAT S.F. FIGURA MUST BE INCLUDED IN ALL COVERS)
CHEAP WHISKEY
LOUIS

DR: On this page you can see the art process from roughs to inks of the issue #2 cover featuring the n
Cthu-Lou—my favorite villain of the miniseries. Also shown here and on the right are the inks for the issue
and #4 covers which were totally done in digital.

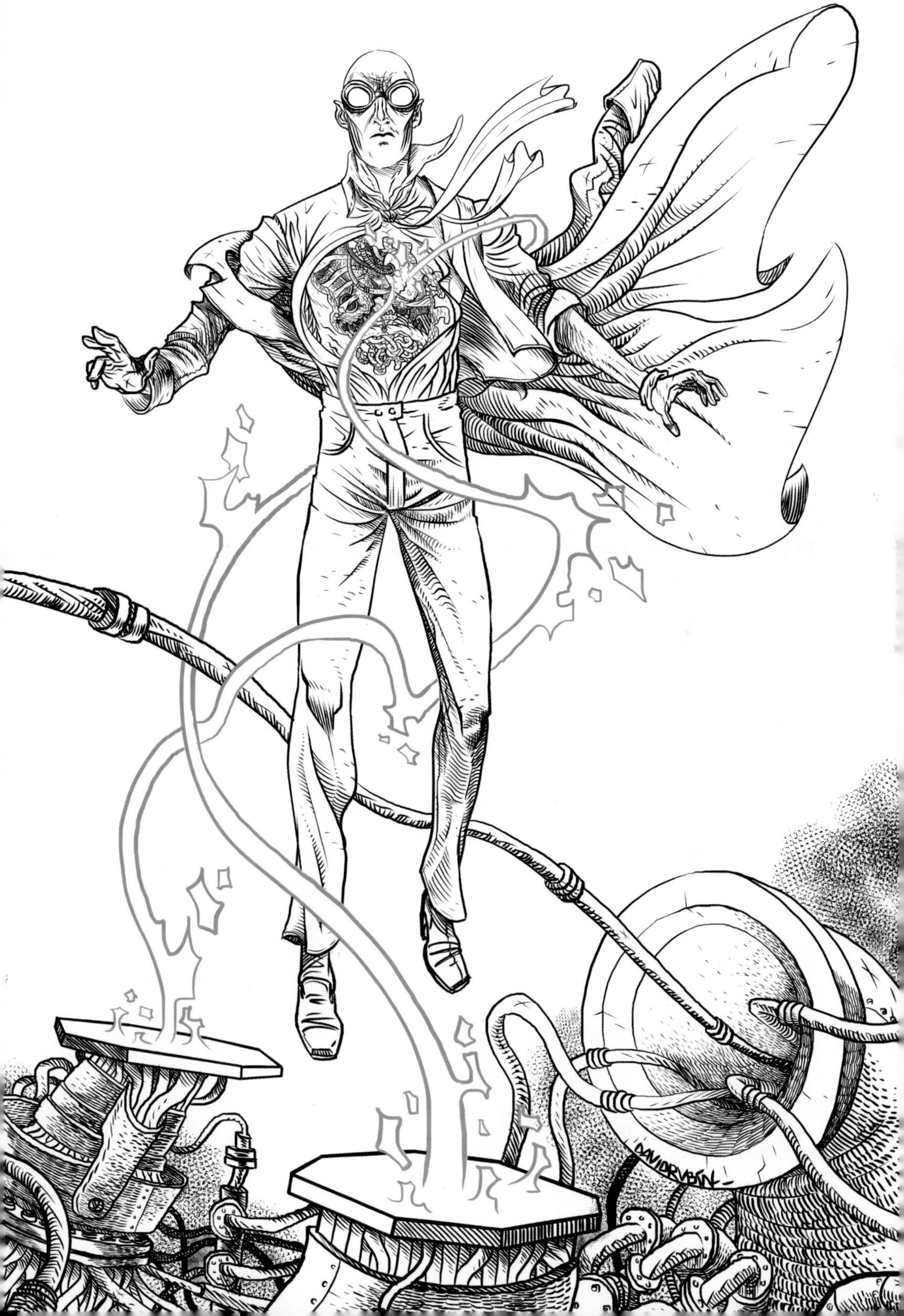

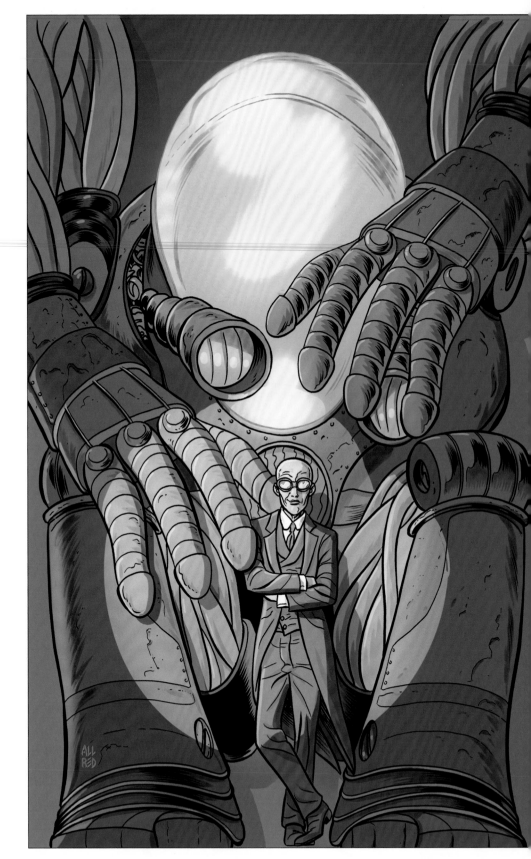

Cover by Michael and Laura Allred

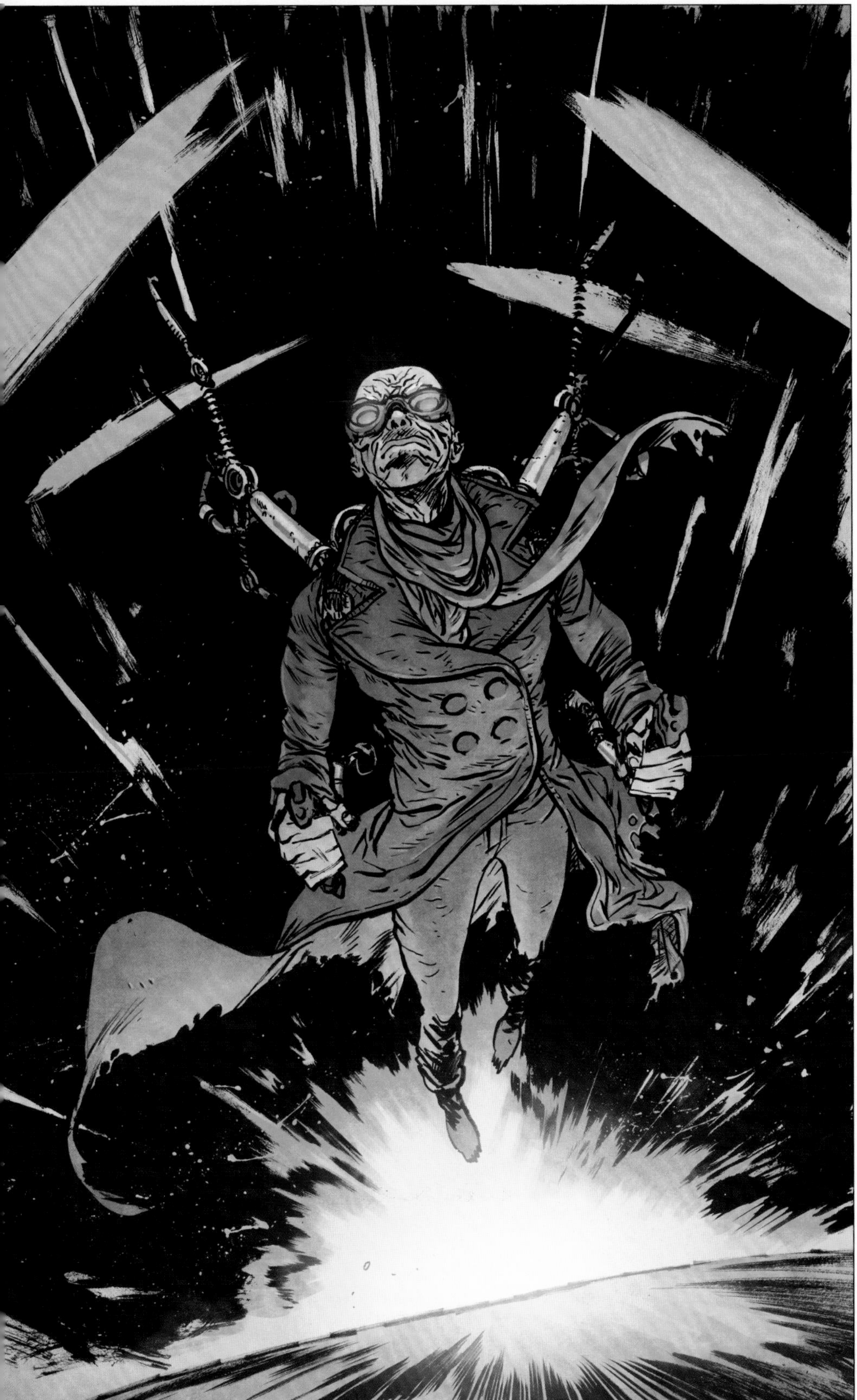

Cover by Daniel Warren Johnson and Mike Spicer

SUPER:POWERED BY CREATORS

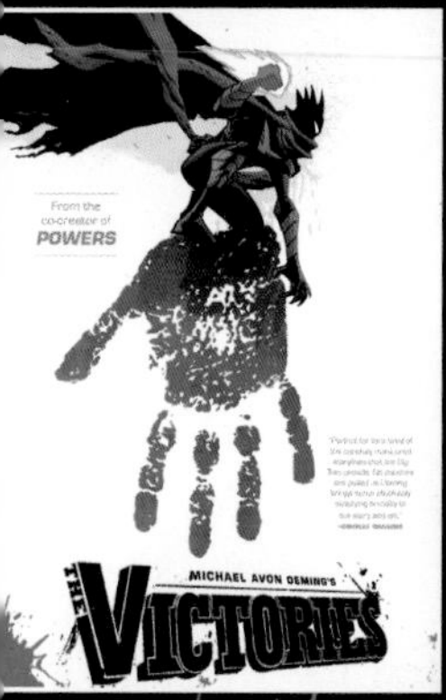
From the co-creator of POWERS
MICHAEL AVON OEMING'S
THE VICTORIES

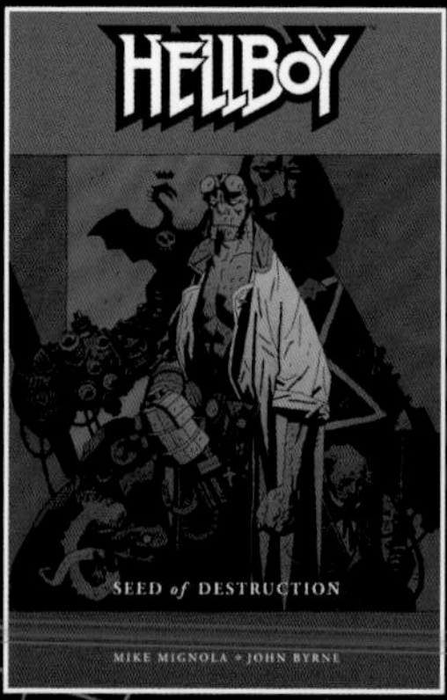
HELLBOY
SEED of DESTRUCTION
MIKE MIGNOLA • JOHN BYRNE

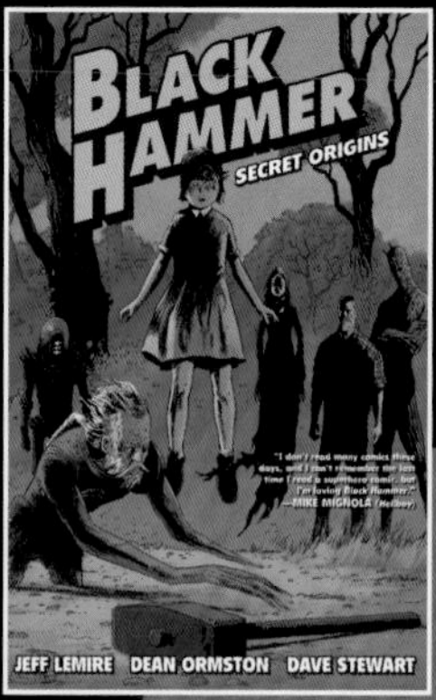
BLACK HAMMER
SECRET ORIGINS
JEFF LEMIRE DEAN ORMSTON DAVE STEWART

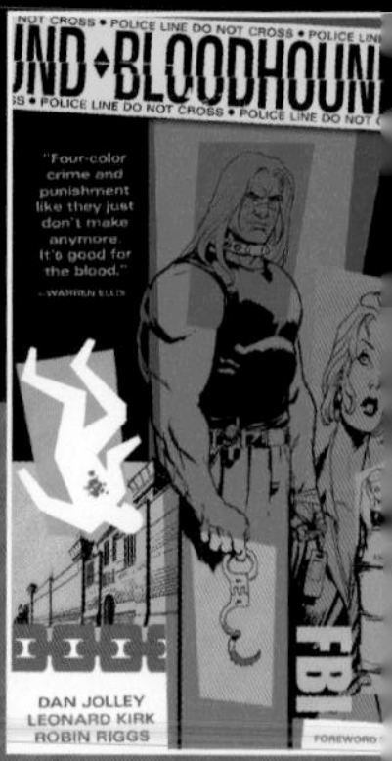
BLOODHOUND
"Four-color crime and punishment like they just don't make anymore. It's good for the blood."
DAN JOLLEY
LEONARD KIRK
ROBIN RIGGS

BLACK HAMMER
Jeff Lemire and Dean Ormston
VOLUME 1: SECRET ORIGINS
ISBN 978-1-61655-786-7 | $14.99

VOLUME 2: THE EVENT
ISBN 978-1-50670-198-1 | $19.99

DREAM THIEF
Jai Nitz and Greg Smallwood
VOLUME 1
ISBN 978-1-61655-283-1 | $17.99

VOLUME 2: ESCAPE
ISBN 978-1-61655-513-9 | $17.99

THE BLACK BEETLE
Francesco Francavilla
NO WAY OUT
ISBN 978-1-61655-202-2 | $19.99

KARA BOCEK
ISBN 978-1-50670-537-8 | $12.99

THE ANSWER!
Mike Norton and Dennis Hopeless
ISBN 978-1-61655-197-1 | $12.99

BLOODHOUND
Dan Jolley, Leonard Kirk, and Robin Riggs
VOLUME 1: BRASS KNUCKLE PSYCHOLOGY
ISBN 978-1-61655-125-4 | $19.99
VOLUME 2: CROWBAR MEDICINE
ISBN 978-1-61655-352-4 | $19.99

MICHAEL AVON OEMING'S THE VICTORIES
Michael Avon Oeming
VOLUME 1: TOUCHED
ISBN 978-1-61655-100-1 | $9.99
VOLUME 2: TRANSHUMAN
ISBN 978-1-61655-214-5 | $17.99

VOLUME 3: POSTHUMAN
ISBN 978-1-61655-445-3 | $17.99

VOLUME 4: METAHUMAN
ISBN 978-1-61655-517-7 | $17.99

HELLBOY: SEED OF DESTRUCTION
(third edition)
Mike Mignola
ISBN 978-1-59307-094-6 | $17.99

ORIGINAL VISIONS—THRILLING TALES!

"These superheroes ain't no boy scouts in spandex. They're a high-octane blend of the damaged, quixotic heroes of pulp detective fiction and the do-gooders in capes from the Golden and Silver Ages." —Duane Swierczynski

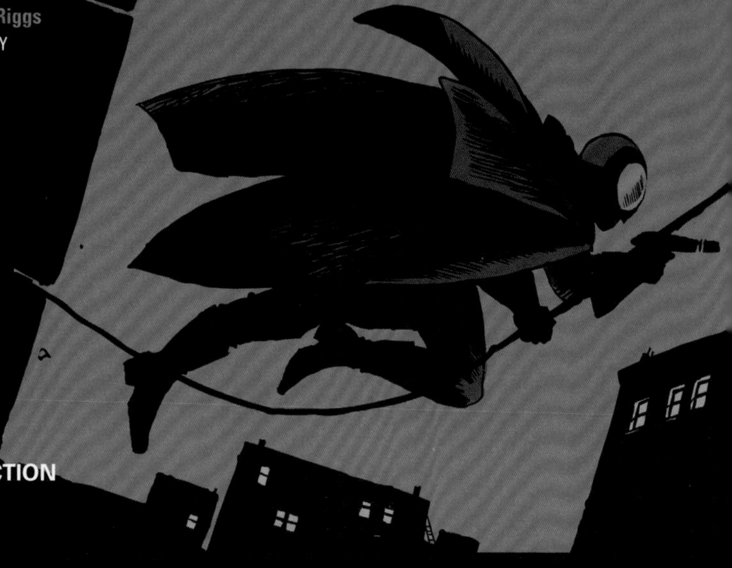

AVAILABLE AT YOUR LOCAL COMICS SHOP OR BOOKSTORE! • To find a comics shop in your area, visit comicshoplocator.com.
For more information or to order direct visit DarkHorse.com or call 1-800-862-0052 Mon.–Fri. 9 a.m. to 5 p.m. Pacific Time. Prices and availability subject to change without notice.